THE ROLE OF PROVIDENCE IN THE FOUNDING OF

AMERICA

*76 Important Events that Helped to Shape
the United States of America*

*And for the support of this Declaration, with a firm reliance on the
protection of divine Providence, we mutually pledge to each other our Lives,
our Fortunes, and our sacred Honor.* The last line in The Declaration of
Independence.

Bob Gingrich

Printed in the United States of America.

Library of Congress Control Number: 2022934296

ISBN   Paperback   978-1-68536-404-5
               eBook   978-1-68536-405-2

Westwood Books Publishing LLC
Atlanta Financial Center
3343 Peachtree Rd NE Ste 145-725
Atlanta, GA 30326

www.westwoodbookspublishing.com

CONTENTS

AUTHOR'S PREFACE

As students of the Bible, most of America's Founding Fathers believed that God superintended the events leading up to their war for independence and its successful conclusion – many of them referred to God's intervention as "the invisible hand." Few of the Founders were shy in stating their faith in God's on-going provision.

Their writings are loaded with examples of their commonly-held belief in Providence including a speech delivered by Benjamin Franklin, one of the more prominent of the Founders. He is on record as having said, "I have lived, Sir, a long time, and the longer I live, the more convincing proofs I see of this truth – that God governs in the affairs of men. And if a sparrow cannot fall to the ground without His notice, is it probable that an empire can rise without His aid? We have been assured in the Sacred Writings that except the Lord build the house, they labor in vain that build it. I firmly believe this. I also believe that, without His concurring aid, we shall succeed in this political building no better than the builders of Babel."

Franklin, who may have been a deist in his younger days, also had this to say later in life: "I have so much faith in the general government of the world by Providence that I can hardly conceive a transaction of such momentous importance [as the framing of the *Constitution*] should be suffered to pass without being in some degree influenced, guided, and governed by that omnipotent, omnipresent, and beneficent Ruler in whom all inferior spirits live and move and have their being." Those would be strange words coming from a deist.

While many historians question Franklin's beliefs regarding God, he made this clarifying statement that has mostly been overlooked or ignored: "I love Him [God] for His Goodness, and I adore Him for His Wisdom."

The purpose of this book is to remind today's American citizens of the value our ancestors placed on freedom and to fill the information gap created by a school system that has succumbed to "politically correct" teaching at the expense of truth. When reading many recently-written textbooks and other resources, it is good to keep in mind what Abraham Lincoln said on the subject: "History is not history unless it is the truth." Those who read this book will learn about many (but not all) of the important events and patriots who have been forgotten or ignored (sometimes willfully) by contemporary writers and re-writers of American history.

The considerable time I spent doing research for this book involved untold hours of reading, note-taking, compiling, and organizing information from hundreds of resources. It was rewarding because I learned so much about many important events and the exceptional men and women who were caught up in them as I delved deeply into our amazing history. Along with so many of those exceptional men and women, I believe more than ever that the one true God of the Judeo-Christian Bible superintended the discovery and development of the United States of America.

PROLEGOMENON

When read as entertainment, stories about the discovery of America, our miraculous founding as a nation, and our extraordinary development as the greatest nation in all recorded history, are more interesting and exciting than most fiction ever written. Those who choose not to delve into early American history are depriving themselves of the opportunity to vicariously experience the extraordinary series of events that produced such a nation.

Throughout the seventy-six chapters of this book, you will read about the nation-building events and the character of the people involved in them that generated the term "American Exceptionalism." It's important that all Americans understand how their country is different, why that is important, and how it happened. Understanding the chronology of the consequential milestones in our history provides us with valuable insight into what we must do to be informed and responsible citizens today. No one is properly equipped for citizenship who does not understand the biblical/moral foundation upon which the United States of America was built.

We owe it to those who defiantly risked their freedom, their lives, and all they owned to remember and understand the vision, courage, and character from which we all have benefited. Only then can we fully appreciate the inestimable value of the heritage they established for us and what we need to do to preserve it for future generations of Americans. John Quincy Adams, sixth President of the United States, put it this way: "Posterity – you will never know how much it cost my generation to preserve your freedom. I hope you will make much of it."

"If you don't know history," said author Michael Crichton, "you don't know anything. You're a leaf that doesn't know it's part of a tree." In a more serious reflection regarding the value of understanding history, author/philosopher/politician Edmund Burke put it this way: "When ancient opinions and rules of life are taken away, the loss cannot possibly be estimated. From that moment, we have no compass to govern us, nor can we know distinctly to what port we steer."

Soon after news of Christopher Columbus' famous 1492 discovery became known, a significant number of European leaders and adventurers realized something truly earth-shaking was happening on the other side of the Atlantic Ocean. And, of course, it wasn't long before monarchs and others understood that a whole "new world" with vast economic potential was possibly available to them. In 1513, Spanish explorer Ponce de Leon, in search of gold, landed on the east Florida coast in the vicinity of what is now Melbourne and claimed all the Atlantic seaboard for Spain. Other nations soon followed.

The Pilgrims who arrived on the shores of the "new world" in 1620 aboard the Mayflower were convinced there was a Providential element involved in what they were experiencing. We can know that because hundreds of those prominent men and women provided us with accounts of their experiences in letters, diaries, and other writings that make it possible for us to understand what motivated and encouraged them.

In a book entitled *The Rebirth of America* published by the Arthur S. DeMoss Foundation, there is an essay entitled "The Invisible Hand: God's Influence in America's History." It gives us this glimpse into the minds of the approximately two hundred men we recognize as Founding Fathers and others who were special contributors to American exceptionalism:

> *George Washington, John Adams, Benjamin Franklin and Abraham Lincoln, to name only a few figures in American history, seemed to see clearly the Providence of God behind the events of their day. The nation did not unfold by accident or happenstance, they insisted, but by divine design. The settlement of America, timed as it was in the wake of the Reformation, assured its Christian foundations.*
>
> *Nor could our Founding Fathers account for the victory over England, against such extreme odds, apart from the seeming intervention of God in key events during the Revolutionary War.*
>
> *In a major address before the Assembly of Connecticut in 1783, Ezra Stiles, then president of Yale, reviewed these events and suggested why near disasters time and time again suddenly turned to victories: "In our lowest and most dangerous state, in*

1776 and 1777, we sustained ourselves against the British army of sixty thousand troops, commanded by the ablest generals Britain could procure throughout Europe, with a naval force of twenty-two thousand seamen in above eighty British men-of-war."

"Who but a Washington inspired by Heaven," asked Stiles, "could have conceived the surprise move upon the enemy at Princeton – that Christmas eve when Washington and his army crossed the Delaware?"

"Who but the Ruler of the winds," he asked, "could have delayed British reinforcements by three months of contrary ocean winds at a critical point of the war?"

"Or what but a 'Providential miracle,'" he insisted, "at the last minute detected the treacherous scheme of traitor Benedict Arnold, which would have delivered the American army, including George Washington himself, into the hands of the enemy?"

On the French role in the Revolution, he added "It is God who so ordered the balancing interests of nations as to produce an irresistible motive in the European maritime powers to take our part."

This statement included in the Declaration of Independence made it clear to the world that Americans were convinced of God's involvement in their cause: "And for the support of this Declaration, with a firm reliance on the protection of divine Providence, we mutually pledge to each other our Lives, our Fortunes and our sacred Honor."

In one of his frequent references to God's superintending care, Washington said, "No people can be bound to acknowledge and adore the invisible hand which conducts the affairs of men more than the people of the United States. Every step, by which they have advanced to the character of an independent nation, seems to have been distinguished by some token of Providential agency."

In a letter written to General Thomas Nelson during the Revolutionary War, Washington wrote, "The hand of Providence has been so conspicuous in all this, that he must be worse than an infidel that lacks faith, and more than wicked, that has not gratitude enough to acknowledge his obligations, but, it will be time enough for me to turn preacher, when my present appointment ceases; and therefore, I shall add no more on the Doctrine of Providence."

Public and private libraries contain thousands of volumes containing the actual words written and spoken by men and women who left an accurate record to which we have easy access. The revisors of American history rely on the widespread ignorance of accurate and honest history made possible by an irresponsible, "politically correct" public school system.

Many untaught or mistaught Americans, I believe, would like to know much more about our origin as a nation, but the study of early American history can seem like an overwhelming task. That's why I selected a conversational, easy-to-read format for this book. It is made up of seventy-six short chapters each of which deals with a single important event in early American history. Each chapter is a short, stand-alone essay; the chapters are arranged chronologically to form a logical narrative but they don't have to be read in chronological order to be enjoyed by readers seeking important historical information.

The book begins with Columbus's incredible westward ocean voyage of 1492 and ends with the Spanish-American War of 1898, a war that confirmed the United States of America as a military and economic world power.

While not an exhaustive study on the subject, this book will help almost anyone curious about their heritage to have a deeper appreciation for what we were given by a remarkable collection of uncommonly insightful and courageous forefathers. Passing along the truth and nobility of our history is an excellent way of emphasizing to our younger generations the love of God and country that characterized those forefathers.

"I always consider the settlement of America with reverence and wonder," said John Adams, "as the opening of a grand scheme and design of Providence for the illumination of the ignorant and emancipation of the slavish part of mankind all over the earth."

Regarding the *Declaration of Independence*, Samuel Adams, known as the "Father of the American Revolution," said, "The people seem to recognize this resolution as though it were a decree promulgated from heaven."

1.

Columbus Makes Landfall in the New World

October 12, 1492

Christopher Columbus arrived on the shores of the "New World" in 1492.

When his expedition landed on what is now known as San Salvador, meaning "Holy Savior," he had his crew erect, as he did on each island upon which they landed, a large wooden cross. At the foot of the cross, he offered this prayer: "O Lord, Almighty and everlasting God, by Thy holy Word Thou has created the heaven, and the earth, and the sea; blessed and glorified be Thy Name, and praised be Thy Majesty, which hath deigned to use us, Thy humble servants, that Thy holy Name may be proclaimed in this second part of the earth."

There has been what seems like an orchestrated campaign by humanists in recent years to portray Columbus as one of history's villains. A view of Columbus as a hard-hearted exploiter is, to say the least, at odds with what those who knew him personally have written. Queen Isabella and others closely associated with Columbus strongly refute revisionists' attempts to portray him as a greedy tyrant and merciless killer of natives. Facts refute the revisionists' agenda but that doesn't keep them from trying. As a humorist once correctly observed, the living can make the dead do any tricks they think necessary to advance their political agenda.

According to Catherine Millard in *The Rewriting of America's History*, of the ten modern Columbus biographies she reviewed, "none makes mention of Christopher Columbus's faith in Christ and no mention of his motivation for the furtherance of the gospel. This phenomenon conforms to the style and content of the vast majority of [contemporary] history books, textbooks, dramatic presentations and exhibitions promoted throughout America on the life and adventures of Christopher Columbus."

That he was a devoted Christian is clear from many of his own journals. He was convinced God was calling him to an important task, a belief he made clear in his *Libro de las profecias* (Book of Prophecies) where he wrote:

> *At a very early age I began to sail upon the ocean. For more than forty years, I have sailed everywhere that people go. I prayed to the most merciful Lord about my heart's desire, and He gave me the spirit and the intelligence for the task: seafaring, astronomy, geometry, arithmetic, skill in drafting spherical maps and placing correctly the cities, rivers, mountains, and ports. I also studied cosmology, history, chronology and philosophy.*
>
> *It was the Lord who put into my mind (I could feel His hand upon me) the fact that it would be possible to sail from here to the Indies. All who heard of my project rejected it with laughter, ridiculing me. There is no question that the inspiration was from the Holy Spirit, because he comforted me with rays of marvelous illumination from the Holy Scriptures, a strong and clear testimony from the 39 books of the Old Testament, from the four Gospels, and from the 23 Epistles of the blessed Apostles, encouraging me continually to press forward, and without ceasing for a moment they now encourage to make haste.*

Later in the same document, Columbus wrote:

> *For the execution of the journey to the Indies I did not make use of intelligence, mathematics or maps. It is simply the fulfillment of what Isaiah had prophesied. All this is what I desire to write down for you in this book. No one should fear to undertake any task in the name of our Savior if it is just and if the intention is purely for His holy service. The working out of all things has been assigned to each person by our Lord, but it all happens according to His sovereign will even though He gives advice.*

*He lacks nothing that is in the power of men to give him.
Oh what a gracious Lord, who desires that people should perform
for Him those things for which He holds Himself responsible! Day
and night moment by moment, everyone should express to Him
their most devoted gratitude.*

*I said that some of the prophecies remained yet to be
fulfilled. These are great and wonderful things for the earth, and
the signs are that the Lord is hastening the end. The fact that the
gospel must still be preached in so many lands in such a short time,
this is what convinces me.*

Columbus's concern regarding the spiritual condition of the natives is obvious in his *Testament of Founding Hereditary Family Estate* dated February 22, 1498: "Also I order to said Don Diego, my son, or to him who will inherit said mayorazgo, that he shall help to maintain and sustain on the island Espanola four good teachers of the holy theology with the intention to convert to our holy religion all those people in the Indias, and when it pleases God that the income of the mayorazgo will increase, that then also be increased the number of such devoted persons who will help all these people to become Christians. And may he not worry about the money that it will be necessary to spend for the purpose."

Columbus wrote that his crew was under orders "to treat the people with care." The revisionists who try to sell the idea that he mistreated the natives willfully ignore this statement: "I know that they are a people who can be made free and converted to our Holy Faith more by love than by force."

It should be obvious that words spoken and written by historical figures provide a more reliable testimony to their true personalities and character than the statements of modern day writers motivated by their politically-inspired agenda. Samuel Butler made note of that unfortunate fact with this sly observation: "Though God cannot alter the past, historians can."

Born in Genoa, Italy, in 1451, Cristoforo (his Italian name) Columbus ended up in Spain in search of financing for his proposed explorations. With the help of a trusted advisor to King Ferdinand and Queen Isabella, Columbus was finally able to successfully argue his point that the risk was small compared to the potential monetary gains and other advantages his proposal could garner for whoever would underwrite his proposed expedition.

After making four trips to the New World, Columbus died in 1506 without realizing his original dream of finding a route to Asia by sailing westward from Europe. He was, however, successful in demonstrating the accessibility of a vast and rich new world and in increasing the wealth and power of his adopted country. Ferdinand and Isabella financially rewarded Columbus generously for his contribution to the Spanish treasury. They also honored his vision, courage, and seamanship skills with the title "Admiral of the Ocean Sea."

2.

Cape Henry Chosen as Site for a New Colony

<u>May 13, 1607</u>

A couple of weeks after landing at the mouth of the Chesapeake Bay in late April of 1607, the adventurers who had made the four-month-long ocean crossing aboard three small sailing vessels, set about doing what they had been commissioned to do – establish the first permanent English colony on the North American continent.

Upon coming ashore at Cape Henry, a name they chose for their initial landing site in honor of King James' son, Prince Henry of Wales, Reverend Robert Hunt, chaplain for the expedition, conducted a thanksgiving celebration. As part of the ceremony, the settlers planted a seven-foot cross they had carried with them aboard one of the ships for that specific purpose.

"Every plantation, which my Heavenly Father hath not planted, shall be rooted up," Hunt stated during the service giving voice to a belief he shared with the members of his flock. They were convinced *their* plantation would be permanently established and protected because God had decreed it. Hunt established daily morning and evening prayer services at a designated open-air chapel until a permanent church building could be erected in the center of what would soon become known as Jamestown.

Sponsored by The London Company, a joint stock enterprise made up of "Knights, Gentlemen, Merchants, and other Adventurers," the expedition operated under *The First Charter of Virginia* dated April 10, 1606. According to that charter, they were given "License to make Habitation, Plantation, and to deduce a colony of sundry of our People into that part of America commonly called VIRGINIA, and other parts and Territories in America, either appertaining unto us, or which are not now actually possessed by any Christian Prince or People." Many of the non-Christian natives, while friendly at first, soon added to the problems facing the more civilized settlers.

The charter went on to say, "We, greatly commending, and graciously accepting of, their Desires for the Furtherance of so noble a Work, which may, by the Providence of Almighty God, hereafter tend to the Glory of his Divine Majesty, in propagating of Christian Religion to such People, as yet live in Darkness and miserable Ignorance of the true Knowledge and Worship of God, and may in time bring the Infidels and Savages, living in those parts, to human Civility, and to a settled and quiet Government."

After waiting a few days at Cape Henry, the *Constant*, the *Godspeed*, and the *Discovery*, under the command of Captain John Smith, sailed approximately forty miles up a river they named the *James* where council president Edward Wingfield selected an inland site he felt met the company's criteria – a site upon which they could build a fort that would offer protection from the possibility of attack by French or Spanish expeditions also looking for potential settlement locations in the area.

They soon realized the threat of attack by other European nations was not their only concern. Because of the swampy nature of the area on which they located their upstart colony, malaria-bearing mosquitoes became a serious hazard and they soon discovered the locale was not well suited to hunting or raising crops. If that weren't enough, occasional Indian attacks on the fort and on their foraging parties soon led to increasingly serious grumbling.

In a growing atmosphere of discontent, stability was temporarily achieved with the election of Captain Smith as Council President in September of 1608. Believing a major source of the discontent had to do with laziness on the part of the gentry and the resentments it generated, Smith established a military form of discipline and ordered *everyone* to work. "He that will not work shall not eat, except by sickness he be disabled," Smith said.

Improvements resulting from Smith's leadership were short-lived when he was injured in a fire a year later and returned to England. Things continued to go badly for the colony in 1609-1610 (sometimes referred to as "the starving time") and, after suffering on-going hunger, disease, and Indian attacks, most of the survivors were ready to give up and return to England.

Then, on June 10, 1610, Thomas West, who possessed the aristocratic title of Baron De La Warr, arrived on a ship appropriately named the *Deliverance* with 150 men and desperately-needed supplies. West conducted a series of successful attacks against the Indians which helped to persuade the discouraged settlers to hang on a bit longer.

John Rolfe also arrived in 1610 and introduced tobacco farming into the colony, an event with Providential implications for the area as was Rolfe's marriage to Pocahontas, daughter of local chieftain Powhatan, in 1614. That marriage helped to maintain peace between the colonists and the Indians. The introduction of tobacco farming and privately-owned farmland brought about a period of prosperity and stability that generally prevailed even though interrupted periodically by problems between Indians and tobacco farmers after the death of Pocahontas in 1617.

The word "Providence" was frequently used by explorers of the "New World" in describing their experiences. Most of the early settlers had been motivated to take on the daunting tasks associated with resettling in a potentially hostile environment because they understood that they were part of something much larger than themselves; they believed they would be the beneficiaries of *divine guidance and care,* a concept that is central to the Calvinist doctrine that had been gaining acceptance in Europe. According to Calvin "Providence means not that by which God idly observes from heaven what takes place on earth, but that by which, as keeper of the keys, He governs all events."

"When the world appears to be aimlessly tumbled about," Calvin said, "the Lord is everywhere at work."

There is much evidence in the way events unfolded over time in the Jamestown settlement that seems to justify the original settlers' belief in the superintending hand of a Divine Governor. At the many low points, something always happened at the right time to provide the faithful with the encouragement and provisions they needed to endure.

Jamestown was the capital of Virginia until 1699 when the capital was moved to Williamsburg. The area is now a tourist attraction that includes replicas of the original ships, a recreated fort, and an Indian village.

3.

Mayflower Sets Sail for the New World

September 6, 1620

"Hope springs eternal in the human breast," wrote Alexander Pope. His words, written in the eighteenth century, well describe the motivation of a marginalized minority that left England around the end of the sixteenth century and moved about Europe for several years in search of religious freedom. They were determined to find a place somewhere in the world in which they could practice their religion and raise their families according their firmly-held beliefs without government intrusion.

Ronald Reagan may have had this band of early visitors to these shores in mind when he said, "I've often thought that God put this land of ours where He did to be found by a special kind of people – those who love liberty enough and have courage enough to make any sacrifice, even to leave home, to secure it; those who dare to live the motto, 'Where liberty dwells, there is my country.'"

Reagan's observation aptly described the Protestant Puritans, later called Pilgrims, that had lived for years on the hope of someday finding a place they could live without interference by a hostile, state-controlled church. Their hope and determination combined with faith eventually resulted in one of the most famous ocean voyages of all time.

Since the late 1500s, many Separatists, as they were pejoratively labeled, had begun breaking away from the heavy-handed Church of England. In 1608, an organized group of Separatists/Puritans left their homes in Scrooby, England to resettle in Leyden, Holland, where they believed a more laissez faire attitude towards religion would allow them to establish a religiously-liberated community based on Biblical morality, self-discipline, and devotion to God's commandments. While they were accepted and treated well in Leyden, they eventually became particularly concerned about the effect exposure to the much more liberal Dutch society was having on their children.

Under the leadership of William Bradford and John Carver, and with the backing of a group of London investors, the Leyden Puritans secured a charter in 1620 for the establishment of a colony in Virginia; English leaders were happy to get rid of them. When Carver was able to charter a ship, a group of thirty-five Puritans along with sixty-five adventure-seekers set sail from Plymouth, England on September 6 enroute to an eagerly-anticipated new life in the "New World." That ship's name was the *Mayflower*.

As a result of storms encountered as they crossed the Atlantic Ocean, the Mayflower arrived off the coast of Massachusetts in November nearly 500 miles north of their original destination in an area for which they had no charter. Strong winds then blew them into what is now Provincetown Harbor, an event many believe to have been Providential. Alexis de Tocqueville described the arrival of the Puritans as "the scattering of the seed of a great people which God with his own hands planted on a predestined shore."

In his *History of Plymouth Plantation*, Bradford provided us with this description of the Pilgrims' frame of mind at the end of their perilous ocean voyage: "Being thus arrived in a good harbor, and brought safe to land, they fell upon their knees and blessed the God of Heaven who had brought them over the fast and furious ocean, and delivered them from all the perils and miseries thereof, again to set their feet on the firm and stable earth, their proper element."

Because they had no charter from the King to establish a colony in what is now New England, many of the Pilgrims were concerned that their doing so could be considered an act of defiance. They dropped anchor on Cape Cod to take some time in deciding what they should do. As part of the decision-making process, they conducted a search to ascertain whether or not it was a suitable area in which to locate a colony. As it turned out, the Cape Cod area was a much more favorable location for the establishment of a colony than the part of Virginia for which their charter had been granted.

Once the decision was made to locate in what is now Plymouth, Massachusetts, the Puritan leaders, led by Carver and Bradford, made the wise decision to produce a carefully-worded document to both provide a basis for the government of their colony and to assure the King that they were, indeed, loyal subjects of the Crown.

On November 11, the adult Pilgrim males signed the document known as the *Mayflower Compact*. In its original form, it says:

> *In the Name of God, Amen. We, whose names are underwritten, the loyal subjects of our dread sovereign Lord King James, by the grace of God, of Great Britain, France and Ireland King, defender of the faith, etc., having undertaken for the glory of God, and advancement of the Christian faith, and honor of our kind and country, a voyage to plant the first colony in the northern parts of Virginia, do, by these presents, solemnly and mutually, in the presence of God and one of another, covenant and combine ourselves together into a civil body politic, for our better ordering and preservation, and furtherance of the ends aforesaid; and by virtue hereof to enact, constitute and frame such just and equal laws, ordinances, acts, constitutions, and offices, from time to time, as shall be thought most meet and convenient for the general good of the colony; unto which we promise all due submission and obedience. In witness whereof we have hereunder subscribed our names at Cape Cod the 11 of November, in the year of the reign of our sovereign lord, King James of England, France, and Ireland and the eighteenth, and of Scotland the fifty-forth, Anno Domini 1620.*

More than two centuries later, John Adams called the *Mayflower Compact* "the foundation of the U.S. Constitution."

Speaking of those English Puritans known as Pilgrims, President Calvin Coolidge said, "Measured by the standards of men of their time, they were the humble of the earth. Measured by later accomplishments, they were the mighty. In appearance weak and persecuted they came – rejected, despised – an insignificant band; in reality strong and independent, a mighty host of whom the world was not worthy, destined to free mankind.

11

Many historians have labeled the *Mayflower Compact* America's birth certificate and consider it an antecedent of constitutional law in America.

4.

Fundamental Orders of Connecticut Adopted

January 14, 1639

Of the many documents said to have influenced the content of the *Constitution of the United States*, one clearly stands out. Known as the *Fundamental Orders of Connecticut*, it is recognized by most historians as the first written constitution in America.

It was produced in 1639 (some accounts say 1638 due to differences between the British and Gregorian calendars) by leading citizens of three Connecticut towns –Windsor, Hartford, and Wethersfield. That historic document established the authority for a unified state government and provided a self-rule model that eventually guided the writers of most other state constitutions.

A precedent-setting provision incorporated into the *Fundamental Orders* was the idea that citizens of the new Colony owed their allegiance to Connecticut, not to Great Britain. Also, all authority was to be based on the consent of the governed, a revolutionary concept in the theory of government for its time and one of the most important tenets embodied in the US Constitution.

Many of the Puritans who settled in the area had arrived in America on the *Mayflower* in 1620; the *Mayflower Compact* is often credited with influencing concepts included in *The Fundamental Orders*. Based on their strict obedience to Biblical precepts, the Puritan leaders set high standards regarding moral behavior, individual responsibility, the education of their children, and the general principles upon which they were convinced effective self-government must rest.

The three major contributors to the composition of the *Fundamental Orders* were Roger Ludlow, John Haynes, and Thomas Hooker. Haynes became the first governor of the new colony in 1639, a position he held until he died in 1654. Ludlow was an attorney and Hooker was a prominent Puritan preacher. Later, Hooker would play a role in planning the *New England Confederation* that united the predominantly Puritan colonies, then known separately as Massachusetts, Plymouth, Connecticut, and New Haven.

Hooker was the driving force in generating the *Fundamental Orders*. As a Puritan preacher and civic leader, he emphasized the tangible benefits realized by societies and governments that based their laws on God's laws as revealed in the Judeo-Christian Bible. He taught that the Bible was to be revered above all other books and that it provided the only completely reliable guide for righteous living with its emphasis on honesty and ethical dealings.

In his role as pastor, Hooker also emphasized the strongly-held Puritan belief in personal accountability to God. He preached that ungodly living was an affront to God and could result in a nullifying of the colonists' special relationship with Him. He also preached that God superintends all human activities. Those Puritan tenets were reflected in the *Fundamental Orders* and most of the state constitutions that soon followed.

The Preamble to *The Fundamental Orders* begins as follows:

> *For as much as it hath pleased Almighty God by the Wise disposition of his divine providence so to order and dispose of things that we the Inhabitants and Residents of Windsor, Hartford and Wethersfield are now cohabiting and dwelling in and upon the River of Connectecotte and the lands thereunto adjoining; and well knowing where a people are gathered together the word of God requires that to maintain the peace and union of such a people there should be an orderly and decent Government established according to God, to order and dispose of the affairs of the people at all seasons.*

Appearing below the preamble were eleven orders that provided for the election of an executive, a legislature, and the democratic principles under which the state government would be required to operate. In accordance with order number one, the elected leaders "which being chosen and sworn according to an Oath recorded for that purpose, shall have the power to administer justice according to the Laws here established, and for want thereof, according to the Rule of the Word of God."

Did the Puritans who contributed so much to the founding documents believe in the *separation of church and state?* Yes, in that they were adamantly opposed to any kind of state-controlled, state-sanctioned church; that's why they left England. But, they just as adamantly expected the church and the state to support each other.

Founders involved in producing the First Amendment to the U.S Constiutution, clearly intended for the government to be *completely* neutral and uninvolved where religious issues were concerned. Evidence is incontrovertible that originators of the *Fundamental Orders*, never imagined a time when the church would NOT be looked to for moral and ethical leadership.

In 1959, Connecticut paid tribute to their Puritan founders by adopting *The Constitution State* as its official nickname and to commemorate the contribution to the *U.S. Constitution* provided by the *Fundamental Orders of Connecticut.*

5.

Massachusetts Adopts *Old Deluder Satan Act*

September 1, 1647

Before Massachusetts was a separate state, the governing body of the Massachusetts Bay Colony recognized the value of providing their citizenry with at least a basic education. Americans may be surprised today when informed of their motivation.

To the Puritans who founded Massachusetts, Satan was always a factor to be dealt with in everyday life. Being steeped in Scripture, they were aware of this warning by the Apostle Paul: "…in order that no advantage be taken of us by Satan; for we are not ignorant of his schemes" (2 Corinthians 2:11). They believed one of Satan's most insidious schemes was to keep people from reading and believing the teachings of the Bible. Puritans recognized the Bible as God's instruction manual and they believed that Biblically literate people were much less likely to be deceived by the *Old Deluder*, as they referred to Satan. Bible knowledge, they were convinced, was the only effective protection against the wiles of the "Evil One."

A law that laid the groundwork for what was labeled the *Old Deluder Satan Act* was passed in 1642 and is recognized today as the first law enacted in the colonies that provided for some form of public education. As early as 1635, a few special purpose or "Latin" schools were operating in and around Boston but their mission was primarily to prepare boys for the ministry rather than to educate the general public.

Motivation behind passage of the 1642 law came from a belief that all citizens needed to know how to read and write in order to be law-abiding members of society. That law did not establish a public school system; it only required that all citizens teach those under their supervision, including their children and young apprentices, to read so that they could understand the laws under which they were to live. Failure to meet all requirements of the law could result in the removal of young people from negligent homes.

In 1647, the second, and most famous of three laws known collectively as *The Massachusetts School Laws*, was passed. That law became known as the *Old Deluder Satan Act* and it emphasized maintaining and improving public morality through familiarity with Scripture. To the original 1642 law, the 1647 law added the requirement that townships, upon reaching a minimum population level, must provide teachers who should be adequately paid for their services. It further required that towns provide rudimentary "grammar" schools when they grew to other specified population levels. The second law was short and to the point:

> *It being one chief project of that old deluder, Satan, to keep men from the knowledge of the Scriptures, as in former times by keeping them in an unknown tongue, so in these latter times by persuading from the use of tongues, so that at least the true sense and meaning of the original might be clouded and corrupted with false glosses of saint-seeming deceivers; and to the end that learning may not be buried in the grave of our forefathers, in church and commonwealth, the Lord assisting our endeavors.*
>
> *It is therefore ordered that every township in this jurisdiction, after the Lord hath increased them to fifty households, shall forthwith appoint one within their town to teach all such children as shall resort to him to write and read, whose wages shall be paid either by the parents or masters of such children, or by the inhabitants in general, by way of supply, as the major part of those that order the prudentials of the town shall appoint; provided those that send their children be not oppressed by paying much more than they can have them taught for in other towns.*
>
> *And it is further ordered, that when any town shall increase to the number of one hundred families or householders, they shall set up a grammar school, the master thereof being able to instruct youth so far as they may be fitted for the university, provided that if any town neglect the performance hereof above one year that*

every such town shall pay 5 pounds to the next school till they shall perform this order.

In 1648 a third law became part of *The Massachusetts School Laws* which, in addition to the provisions of the earlier acts, required that children and apprentices receive training for "some honest lawful calling, labour or employment." That training was also to be guided by Puritan principles.

Soon thereafter, other New England colonies began passing similar laws. Little by little, the education movement spread to the central and, finally, the southern colonies.

The New England Puritans had originally migrated to America to escape religious persecution directed toward them as dissenters who believed the Church of England was corrupt and incorrigible. As products of the Reformation led by Martin Luther, they frequently had found themselves in direct opposition to the authority of the church and the King. In looking for a place where they could control their own destinies and that of their children, they were drawn to the "New World" that seemed to offer a unique opportunity for religious freedom and control over the education of their children.

Upon their arrival in America, the Puritans organized their churches as well as their early attempts at government in accordance with Biblical precepts reflecting their strongly held belief that the Bible was the source of all truth, knowledge and wisdom. They believed the tenets of education, commerce, government, law, and everything else should be based on precepts contained in the Judeo-Christian Bible. The men who generated the *Declaration of Independence* and the *Constitution*, many of whom were of Puritan stock, shared a reverence for the Bible with the New England Puritans who preceded them.

In a letter to his cousin and fellow Founding Father John Adams, Samuel Adams, sometimes called "the last Puritan," expressed this opinion regarding the importance of basing education on Biblical precepts: "Let divines and philosophers, statesmen and patriots, unite their endeavors to renovate the age, by impressing the minds of men with the importance of educating their little boys and girls, of inculcating in the minds of youth the fear and love of the Deity and universal philanthropy, and, in subordination to these great principles, the love of their country; of instructing them in the art of self-government without which they never can act a wise part in the government of societies, great or small; in short, of leading them in the study and practice of the exalted virtues of the Christian system."

The fact that Puritans helped in a major way to create the pattern upon which the foundation of American society was built is undeniable by those who are familiar with accurate early American history. Because early American history is so poorly and inaccurately taught in public schools today, too many Americans don't understand their own history. It appears that the *Old Deluder* himself is still at work in America today in public education and in academia in general.

6.

Jonathan Edwards Delivers Famous Sermon

<u>July 8, 1741</u>

Sinners in the Hands of an Angry God was the title of an attention-grabbing sermon that startled most sinners and many saints more than two-and-a half centuries ago. Delivered by Jonathan Edwards on July 8, 1741, in Enfield, Connecticut, it was a landmark event during what we now know as the *First Great Awakening,* usually said to have been at its zenith from 1735 to 1743.

Still read today, Edwards' jolting exhortation is often referred to as the most famous sermon ever preached in America. Many believe Edwards' intense style of preaching established a pattern that became typical of the revivals experienced from time to time in America.

Grandson of Solomon Stoddard, one of the best known Puritan leaders of colonial America, Edwards is considered by Christian historians to have been one of the most effective of the many preachers who generated the *Awakening* that quickly spread among the colonies. In addition to saving souls, the revival preachers created feelings of unity, purpose, and strength that many historians believe were necessary ingredients for a successful American Revolution.

As a result of the *Great Awakening,* belief in the Providential nature of the establishment of the American colonies was also revived throughout the land and channeled into the independence movement. A reinvigoration of the colonists' Christian faith gave America's future rebels, especially those we recognize as Founding Fathers, the confidence to declare their independence and go to war against the most powerful nation on earth.

The *Great Awakening* was a reaction by Puritan leaders to the humanist movement we now know as *The Enlightenment* that had begun in the late 1600s in Europe before spreading to the colonies. It was an amalgamation of the teachings of philosophers including Montesquieu, Hobbes, Spinoza, Locke, Hume, and others. Johann Friedrich Zoellner called *The Enlightenment* "a movement which devoted itself to undermining the basics of morality, to denying the value of religion and turning hearts away from God."

While most of the Founders generally agreed with Zoellner's characterization of the movement as anti-Christian, they did cherry-pick a few of the philosophers' ideas, especially Locke's belief that sovereignty resides with the people, not the state, and that the state was responsible for protecting the people's natural rights including the right to own property.

As Puritan influence in the colonies had weakened over the years, imported *Enlightenment* attitudes had increasingly created an atmosphere in the colonies that was beginning to fit Zoellner's description; liberal theology had noticeably undermined many traditional Christian beliefs and moral values. Christian leaders, led by Edwards who had conducted his own local revival of 1733-35 in the Boston area, realized they needed to meet this challenge head on in order to lead their fellow colonists back to the orthodox Christianity that had previously served the colonists so well in providing a pattern upon which they had been able to build successful communities.

Edwards' often terrifying sermons, based on the sometimes wrathful side of the First Person of the Trinity, were effective in getting the attention of his audiences so that he could then explain the saving grace available to sinners through the loving and forgiving nature of Jesus, the Second Person of the Trinity.

In his most-famous sermon, Edwards got his audience's rapt attention by citing reminders of the precarious position of unsaved sinners with statements such as: "The bow of God's wrath is bent, and the arrow made ready on the string, and justice bends the arrow at your heart, and strains the bow, and it is nothing but the mere pleasure of God, and that of an angry God, without any promise or obligation at all, that keeps the arrow one moment from being made drunk with your blood. Thus all you that never passed under a great change of heart, by the mighty power of the Spirit of God upon your souls; all you that were never born again, and made new creatures, and raised from being dead in sin, to a state of new, and before altogether unexperienced light and life, are in the hands of an angry God."

Later in the sermon, he gave them the good news: "And now you have an extraordinary opportunity, a day wherein Christ has thrown the door of mercy wide open, and stands calling and crying with a loud voice to poor sinners; a day wherein many are flocking to him, and pressing into the kingdom of God. Many are daily coming from the east, west, north and south; many that were very lately in the same miserable condition are now in a happy state, with their hearts filled with love to him who has loved them, and washed them from their sins in his own blood, and rejoicing in hope of the glory of God. How awful is it to be left behind at such a day!"

Although Edwards was preeminent, he wasn't alone as an effective deliverer of powerful messages explaining man's inability to save his own soul. Audiences were frequently moved to tears and repentance by well-known traveling evangelists including George Whitefield, George Tennent, John Wesley, and Charles Wesley. Along with many other lesser known but highly effective itinerant preachers, they convincingly awakened large numbers of the backslidden while bringing the good news of the Gospel to the uninformed.

Whitefield, an English preacher/orator and friend of the Wesley's, is said to have been closely associated with Edwards in organizing the traveling evangelistic campaign. While Edwards is primarily known for his revivalist efforts at his church in Northampton, Massachusetts, Whitefield is best known for his outdoor preaching and his tour of all thirteen colonies. Both men were known for highly theatrical preaching styles. Whitefield is recognized for his unique teaching method of acting out Biblical stories in which he played the part of important Bible characters, including Satan, which often left his audiences shaken.

Whitefield's evangelical preaching tour, perhaps Providentially, caught the attention of Benjamin Franklin who became an admirer of the gifted preacher and the ability he had to effectively communicate his revival message. In the *Pennsylvania Gazette*, Franklin devoted the front page of forty-five issues to Whitefield's sermons which helped to build the itinerant preacher's personal fame while spreading the message of the *Great Awakening.*

In his autobiography, Franklin paid this tribute to Whitefield: "It was wonderful to see the change soon made in the manners of our inhabitants. From being thoughtless or indifferent about religion, it seems as if all the world were growing religious, so that one could not walk through the town in an evening without hearing psalms sung in different families of every street."

Both Whitefield and Edwards always ended their hard hitting sermons with the encouraging message of salvation through God's grace. Edwards concluded his *Sinners in the Hands of An Angry God* with this admonition: "Therefore, let every one that is out of Christ, now awake and fly from the wrath to come. The wrath of Almighty God is now undoubtedly hanging over a great part of this congregation: Let every one fly out of Sodom: Haste and escape for your lives, look not behind you, escape to the mountain, lest you be consumed."

The great evangelical revivalists who were active during the *Great Awakening* are little known today because of the success of an organized campaign to marginalize Christians and Christianity conducted by humanist (anti-Christian) organizations supported by the newsmedia, the entertainment industry, academia, and activist judges.

John Witherspoon, a signer of the Declaration of Independence and President of Princeton College, would have had humanists in mind when he said, "Whoever is an avowed enemy of God, I scruple not [do not hesitate] to call him an enemy of his country."

7.

French and Indian War Ends; Amerca Wins

February 10, 1763

More than twelve years before the "shot heard 'round the world" was fired during the battle of Lexington, another long war, partially fought on American soil, finally ended. That war laid much of the groundwork for the American Revolution although few colonists were thinking about a break with the mother country at that time.

Known as the *French and Indian War* in the colonies, it was part of what historian Paul Johnson labeled "the first world war in human history." It was part of a world conflict fought on three continents – North America, Europe, and Asia – and involved England, France, Spain, Prussia, Austria, Sweden, Russia and the American colonies. As loyal subjects to the King, the American colonists fought on the side of England.

Armed conflicts between the British and French had been on-going at various locations on the North American continent since 1689 as each country maneuvered for dominance. Spain usually allied itself with France.

The *French and Indian War* began in 1753. In the American theater, it was England and her American colonies versus France and a powerful confederation of Indian tribes. In the years leading up to the war, most Indian tribes had maintained a neutral position between the European powers, trading with all comers. Eventually the powerful

Indian confederacy turned away from the French to support the British. The evolving alliance forged among the Indians, the colonists, and the British proved to be too much for the French and their remaining allies.

An escalation of the *French and Indian War* in America led first to the *Seven Years War* in Europe, then to the *Third Carnatic War* in Asia. Hostilities in Europe and Asia began in 1756 as a declared war. The "world war" finally ended February 10, 1763, with the signing of the first *Treaty of Paris*.

Many favorable circumstances, often attributed to Providence, accrued to the benefit of the American colonies as a result of this series of interconnected wars, circumstances many historians believe put the colonies in a much better position from which to pursue their freedom even though independence wouldn't be an issue for some time.

The immediate winner was England who took control of French Canada and all French territory east of the Mississippi River including Florida. Also, the French gave title to their land west of the Mississippi, known at that time as Louisiana, to Spain. In 1800, Napoleon won Louisiana back from Spain which, as a result of occurrences that now seem Providential, led to the Louisiana Purchase, an 800,000 square mile land area that became part of the United States in 1803.

Those who believe in the Providential nature of the *French and Indian War* point to the fact that England, with whom the colonies had the strongest ties, emerged as the overwhelmingly dominant European power in North America freeing the colonies from threat of domination by other European countries. Engaging in a prolonged "world war" drained the English treasury which led Parliament to initiate a series of taxes and restrictions that created growing animosity between them and their American colonies. Also, the French, smarting from their series of defeats at the hand of England, became inclined to support the colonies when their war for independence began a few years later, a decided benefit to the colonies.

Because of the colonies' involvement in the war, a number of future colonial military leaders gained experience that would be invaluable when the *Revolutionary War* broke out. George Washington was among those Americans whose introduction to military life began when he served as a young British Army Officer.

Many historians believe the first shot fired in the *French and Indian War* was fired by Washington, then the 21-year-old commander of a group of Virginians sent to confront the French who had defied an earlier order to leave an area considered by the British to be their territory. Washington's shot is believed to have killed the French commanding officer. Later, Washington, then a Colonel, served under British General Edward Braddock in the battle in which Braddock was killed in an ambush by the French and their Indian allies. In that battle, 900 of Braddock's men were killed or wounded. Washington, who led the survivors to safety, believed he was Providentially spared on that and other occasions during the war. He also believed in a predestined victory for the colonies in their war for independence.

"The man must be bad indeed," said Washington, "who can look upon the events of the American Revolution without feeling the warmest gratitude towards the great Author of the Universe whose divine interposition was so frequently manifested in our behalf."

History revisionists claim Washington was a deist rather than a theologically conservative, Bible-believing Christian, but there is nothing about Washington's life to support that supposition. Deists believe that God created the world and its natural laws but takes no part in its functioning. Prayer would be a waste of time to a deist because, according to their beliefs, God is merely a disinterested spectator who would not respond to prayer; a deist couldn't, by definition, believe in Providence which is defined as "the care or benevolent guidance of God."

To the contrary, there is much historical evidence that effectively refutes revisionists' claims including Washington's well-documented study of Scripture, his often mentioned devotion to prayer, and his frequent references to God's involvement in America's struggle for freedom.

8.

Sugar Act Provides the Spark of Rebellion

April 5, 1764

Seeking ways to generate revenue and to increase control over the colonies, Britain's Parliament began in 1764 to pass a series of acts that raised the ire of their American subjects. The *Sugar Act*, also known as *The American Revenue Act*, was the first of those disagreeable and belittling measures to be imposed upon the colonists. Parliament's stated goal in passing the Sugar Act was to raise 100,000 pounds annually from the colonies to prop up the British economy.

As a result of the *French and Indian War*, other military actions against both France and Spain, and the substantial cost of maintaining a 10,000-man army in the colonies, the Exchequer found itself in debt and badly in need of additional sources of income. Since the purpose of the troops stationed in the colonies was supposedly to protect the frontier from Indian attacks, King George III felt it proper that the colonies contribute financially to their situation. Parliament agreed but the colonists thought otherwise and they let their displeasure be known.

Colonial leaders did not accept the idea that Parliament had the right to force *any* taxes upon them especially since they would have no say regarding how they were to be taxed, how much they were to be taxed, nor how the money generated by such taxes would actually be used. Typical of the public reaction to any tax imposed on the colonies by Parliament was a comment recorded at a Boston Town Meeting: "If taxes are laid upon us in any shape without ever having a legal representation where they are laid, are we not reduced from the character of free subjects to the miserable state of tributary slaves?"

"No taxation without representation" quickly became an effective mobilizing slogan among the colonists.

The colonists had developed their own systems of taxation through local assemblies. Suddenly becoming subjected to taxes imposed by ruling elites living on the other side of an ocean added to a slowly-growing recognition that independence might be something to seriously consider. Even though most historians agree the *Sugar Act* itself did not lead directly to revolutionary fervor, its passage did create a hostile environment into which the *Stamp Act* that followed in 1765 was introduced. Because the seeds of rebellion sewn by the *Sugar* Act had begun to sprout, the *Stamp Act* provided a powerful application of fertilizer.

The colonists also saw the *Sugar Act* as a threat to their developing economy in which the exportation of rum was an important factor; sugar and molasses were major ingredients in its production. At about the same time, controls were placed on the exportation of lumber which, because wood was plentiful in America, was a major contributor to the economy. According to provisions of the act, many American products could only be shipped to British ports which had the effect of reducing the number of markets available to American merchants. Many other imported household items including coffee, wine, textiles, and miscellaneous products used in daily life were subject to the tax.

Adding insult to injury were the new revenue collectors who, according to Benjamin Franklin, were "the low-born and needy people – anyone better would not take them." Franklin went on to say, "Their necessities make them rapacious, their offices make them proud and insolent, their insolence and rapacity make them odious, and being conscious they are hated they become malicious; their malice urges them to a continual abuse of the inhabitants in their letters of administration, presenting them as disaffected and rebellious, and (to encourage the use of severity) as weak, divided, timid and cowardly...I think one may clearly see, in the system of customs now being exacted in America by Act of Parliament, the seeds sown of a total disunion of the two countries."

Another even more alarming provision of the act allowed the British to send colonists accused of sugar and rum smuggling in violation of the act to Nova Scotia where they would be tried by a vice-admiralty court.

In those courts, such trials were often heard by judges more interested in securing convictions than they were in seeing justice done since judges were customarily awarded a percentage of the value of confiscated cargoes.

The vice admiralty courts also put the burden of proof on the accused, a reversal of British judicial philosophy. The idea that Americans could be tried by judges without juries of their peers in locations far from where the alleged violations took place was unacceptable to the colonists. Soon after the act was disseminated, the Massachusetts Legislature sent a petition to the British House of Commons in which they pointed out the obvious fact that such a change in judicial procedure "deprived the colonies of one of the most valuable of English liberties, trial by jury."

What began with passage of the *Sugar Act* led, through a series of provocative events by both sides, including the Boston Tea Party, to passage of an additional series of acts by Parliament that colonial leaders labeled the *Intolerable Acts*. With their passage, the point of no return was rapidly approaching.

Ironically, the *French and Indian War* had militarily strengthened the colonies while economically weakening England to the point that the colonies were able to resist the ill-advised provocations of Parliament. Conditions for a successful rebellion had, little by little, been supernaturally arranged, a belief shared by most of the Founding Fathers.

Several years after the war for independence was successfully concluded, President George Washington again stated his belief in God's superintending hand in the colonists' quest for freedom: "May the same wonder-working Deity, who long since delivering the Hebrews from the Egyptian Oppressors planted them in the promised land – whose Providential agency has lately been conspicuous in establishing these United States as an independent Nation – still continue to water them with the dews of Heaven and make the inhabitants of every denomination participate in the temporal and spiritual blessings of the people whose god is Jehovah."

9.

Stamp Act Adds Fuel to the Fire

March 22, 1765

When news arrived in the colonies regarding passage of the *Stamp Act* by the British Parliament, angry and determined opposition quickly developed taking various forms including boycotts and riots by large numbers of colonists. "The *Stamp Act*," said John Adams, "has raised and spread through the whole continent a spirit that will be recorded to our honor with all future generations."

Colonial resistance soon turned the controversy into a full-blown crisis. Most colonial leaders, including Samuel Adams, saw it as much more than a revenue-generating tax. "The *Stamp Act* itself was contrived with a design only to inure the people to the habit of contemplating themselves as slaves of men; and the transition from thence to a subjection to Satan is mighty easy."

Sam Adams was one of the leaders of an organization known as the *Sons of Liberty* which began to expand rapidly as an effective organizer of opposition to the British revenue-grabbing initiatives. Coming on the heels of the *Sugar Act*, the *Stamp Act* was vehemently opposed because it taxed paper on which nearly everything was printed including newspapers, legal documents, pamphlets, and even playing cards. It was considered a major threat to the economy of the colonies as well as to their freedom.

Acting quickly, a committee of the whole of the Virginia House of Burgesses met and, under the leadership of Patrick Henry, produced the *Virginia Stamp Act Resolutions* dated May 30, 1765. Four of the five resolves were strong reminders that colonists were entitled to "all the liberties, privileges, franchises, and immunities that have at any time been held, enjoyed, and possessed by the people of Great Britain."

They also restated the principle that taxes should be imposed only by the people "affected by every tax." That was a British tradition, they said, and it had never "been forfeited or yielded up." A fifth resolve was rescinded before the *Resolves* were published after Henry had departed the meeting because most members thought it would be viewed as treasonous. "If this be treason," an unintimidated Henry later said, "make the most of it."

At a town meeting held in Braintree, Massachusetts, September 24, John Adams drafted an official protest of the *Stamp Act* that succinctly included all the reasons the colonists felt the Act violated their rights. The *Braintree Instructions*, as the document became known, said:

> *We further apprehend this Tax to be unconstitutional. By the great Charter no American shall be assessed but by the oath of Honest & Lawful men of the land. And by the same Charter no Freeman shall be taken or imprisoned or be dispossessed of his Freedom or Liberties, nor condemned but by Lawful Judgment of his Peers. And we have always understood it to be a grand & fundamental principal of the British Constitution that no Freeman should be subjected to any Tax to which he has not given his own consent in person or by proxy. And the maxims of the Law are to the same effect. That no Freeman can be separated from his property but by his own act or Fault. We take it clearly therefore to be inconsistent with the spirit of the Common Law & of the essential Fundamental principles of the British Constitution that we should be subjected to any Tax imposed by the British Parliament because we are not Represented in that assembly in any sense unless it be by a Fiction of Law."*

Published in newspapers throughout the Commonwealth, the *Braintree Instructions* were endorsed by over forty cities and towns in petitions to the General Court of Boston. Those *Instructions* were instrumental in setting the stage for the *Stamp Act Congress* that convened in New York October 7, 1765.

By October 19, the delegates had agreed upon a fourteen-point declaration to be sent to Parliament delineating the reasons why the *Stamp Act* should be repealed. The *Declaration of Rights and Grievances* emphasized these strongly-held convictions of the colonists: The Colonies were only subject to taxes imposed by their own assemblies; the Admiralty Courts illegally took away the colonists' right to trial by juries of their peers; the colonists had always been loyal British subjects and were, therefore, entitled to all the rights of Englishmen as provided in the *Magna Carta* and the *English Bill of Rights*; and, because colonists did not vote in Parliamentary elections, Parliament, could not impose taxes on the colonies.

A boycott of British goods by New York merchants went into effect October 19. Because British business owners believed the boycott would spread and could adversely affect the British economy, a movement to repeal the *Stamp Act* rapidly gained strength in London. On March 18, 1766, Parliament repealed the *Stamp Act* while at the same time passing the *Declaratory Act* that reaffirmed the on-going rights of Parliament to make laws for the colonies. In an attempt to smooth ruffled feathers, colonial leaders formally thanked King George and Parliament for repealing what they sincerely considered to be an unjust legislative act.

The colonists had won a battle, but a campaign of oppression by the British was just getting started.

10.

The *Loyal Nine* Launch *Sons of Liberty*

August 13, 1765

Although the exact date of origin of the *Loyal Nine* is not known, it is a fact that all members of that patriotic group met the evening of August 13, 1765, to talk about their opposition to the *Stamp Act* scheduled to go into effect November 1. The next day, all hell broke loose, or so Andrew Oliver, who had been appointed Distributor of Stamps for Massachusetts, must have thought.

When the sun rose Thursday, August 14, Oliver's effigy was hanging from one of Deacon Elliott's elm trees, a spectacle that quickly drew a crowd. It was a market day and market days always attracted large numbers of farmers with fresh produce to sell to city dwellers. The gathering that particular morning originally took on a festive air as people were amused to see an effigy labeled A.O. dangling from a tree. As the day wore on, the initial joviality was replaced by more serious grumbling about the hated tax.

By evening, the crowd's mood had changed into one of anger. They cut down the effigy, placed it in a coffin, and carried it to the governor's mansion, then to the Old State House, and finally to a building Oliver had recently constructed to use as his Stamp Office. A proclamation issued by the Boston Council Chamber and printed in the *Boston News-Letter* described what happened next:

> *Whereas yesterday, towards evening, a great number of people unlawfully and riotously asembled themselves together, in the town of Boston, armed with clubs, staves, etc. and with great Noise and Tumult, pulled down a newly erected building belonging to the Secretary of the Province and having done so surrounded his Dwelling House, pulled down part of his fences, Broke his window and at length with Force and Violence entered the House and damaged and destroyed his Furniture, and continued thus unlawfully assembled until Midnight, and committed diverse Other Outrages and Enormities to the great Terror of his Majesty's liege subjects.*

The proclamation went on to require all civil authorities to find those responsible for the damage and it included the offer of a reward of 100 pounds for information leading to the conviction of the perpetrators. Oliver, though, had had enough; he resigned the following morning. With encouragement from the *Sons of* Liberty, a group whose roots were connected to the *Loyal Nine*, many more tax collectors would also soon resign.

Although Samuel Adams was not one of the original Boston merchants known as the *Loyal Nine,* he was on friendly terms with each of them. That little-known group was made up of John Avery, Henry Bass, Thomas Chase, Stephen Cleverly, Benjamin Edes, Joseph Field, John Gill, John Smith, and George Trott.

Other prominent Founding Fathers whose names are commonly associated with that group of patriots were John Adams, Paul Revere, Joseph Warren, Patrick Henry, John Hancock, James Otis, John Dickinson, and Silas Downer. But it was Sam Adams who became the prime mover in establishing and expanding the *Sons of Liberty*, a name Isaac Barre, a Member of Parliament, once applied to all American rebels when addressing his fellow members. Barre, one of the few friends of America in the British government, had vigorously opposed passage of the *Stamp Act.*

Within six months, the *Sons of Liberty* had established chapters in New York, Connecticut, Rhode Island, New Hampshire, New Jersey, Maryland, Virginia, North Carolina, South Carolina, and Georgia. By the end of the year, under increasing pressure brought to bear by members of the new rebel group, most of the Stamp distributors had resigned.

The rapidly-growing patriot organization soon became more influential among the colonists than the Royal government; many of the governors went into hiding to avoid the "Oliver treatment."

Although British loyalists often referred to them pejoratively as "Sons of Violence," the *Sons of Liberty* originally considered themselves to be loyal to the King because they believed Parliament would soon get the message and repeal the hated *Stamp Act*, which they actually did in May of 1766.

Emboldened by the group's success in getting rid of the *Stamp Act*, even larger numbers of colonists were drawn to the *Sons of Liberty*, an entity through which they were able to communicate and organize effective resistance to future edicts that would come from Parliament.

Publishers Benjamin Edes and John Gill, key members of the *Loyal Nine*, were the first newspaper owners to put the power of the emerging American press to work for the patriot cause. Gill's *Boston Gazette and Country Journal* became an important publication prior to and during the war for independence. Soon, nearly every newspaper in the colonies carried editorials and news stories regarding the anti-tax activities of the *Sons of Liberty*. Newspapers, of course, had a vested interest in helping the *Sons of Liberty* succeed in rallying opposition to the paper tax because their everyday operations would be especially impacted by it.

Many patriots including Hancock, Warren, Otis, and both Sam and John Adams regularly contributed articles to *The Gazette* in which they effectively attacked the *Stamp Act*. British authorities called Edes and Gill trumpeters of sedition and recommended that they be arrested and tried for libel. The Massachusetts governor called *The* Gazette "an infamous weekly paper which has swarmed with Libells of the most atrocious kind."

Edes' office became an unofficial gathering place for members of the *Sons of Liberty*, a fact known to the British. Most historians also believe that participants in the *Boston Tea Party* changed into their Indian disguises in *The Gazette* offices prior to launching the famous raid on British ships and their cargoes of tea in Boston Harbor.

Most knowledgeable historians name the *Loyal Nine* as the original source of effective political organization in the colonies. By providing inspiration and intellectual support for the formation and rapid expansion of the *Sons of Liberty*, who were then instrumental in expanding the concept of *Committees of Correspondence* and other vitally important organizational concepts, nine little-remembered but exceptional patriots may well have contributed more to the independence movement than any other group of people whose names are probably much more familiar to students of American history.

Providentially, the patriots who made up the *Loyal Nine* were the right men at the right place at the right time. They provided a spark that helped to ignite the flame of freedom.

11.

Boston Massacre Adds to Revolutionary Sentiments

March 5, 1770

An event labeled a "massacre" that occurred in Boston the evening of March 5, 1770, hardly matches the dictionary definition (*to kill indiscriminately and mercilessly and in large numbers*) for such events. The body count was five, three of whom died at the scene and two who died later of their wounds. But the event soon heralded as the *Boston Massacre* was enough to move the colonies one giant step closer to their war for independence.

A tense situation had existed between colonists and the "lobsterbacks," as the British troops were sneeringly called by the patriots, since the troops had arrived in the city on October 1, 1768. General Thomas Gage had sent them to Boston to protect British interests due to the hostility that had been growing since Parliament's passage of a series of acts considered punitive by the colonists. Many Boston patriots were spoiling for a fight.

An evening that began with what might have ended as a routine encounter between a few taunting patriots and fewer British soldiers ended with a mob of 400 angry colonists surrounding the soldiers in a manner considered to be life-threatening by British Captain Thomas Preston. As the crowd increased in size and as the possibility of violence became more likely, Preston first ordered his men to fix their bayonets, then, as the scene became more threatening, he told them to load their muskets.

When knocked to the ground by something thrown by a colonist, a British soldier fired his musket, perhaps accidentally or maybe as a warning shot. After a short pause as both sides tried to figure out what had happened, some of the soldiers fired into the crowd, ostensibly to protect themselves, and the mob quickly dispersed. When something resembling order had been restored, it was determined that eleven colonists had been either killed or wounded.

The colonists who died as a result of that brief but intense encounter are considered by some historians to have been the first fatalities of the American Revolution even though organized fighting between opposing forces wouldn't begin until five years later at Lexington and Concord.

Captain Preston and eight soldiers were arrested and put on trial for murder. To defuse the situation, British officials moved troops stationed in Boston to an island in Boston Harbor.

Inflammatory anti-British propaganda soon began to appear including a pamphlet entitled *The Horrid Massacre in Boston Perpetrated in the Evening of the Fifth Day of March, 1770, by Soldiers of the Twenty-Ninth Regiment Which With the Fourteenth Regiment Were Then Quartered There; With Some Observations of the State of Things Prior to that Catastrophe.* It was a bill of particulars that reminded readers in Boston and beyond of all the perceived wrongs committed against the colonists.

Excerpts from several depositions were included in the pamphlet offering eye-witness accounts stating the attack by the soldiers was unprovoked. To the colonists, it appeared to be an open and shut case. Finding a local attorney to represent the British soldiers proved to be a difficult task since most Boston attorneys assumed their careers would be harmed if not destroyed by defending the British soldiers in court.

In response to a personal plea by Preston, John Adams agreed to defend them because he believed it was important to all parties that a fair trial be held. Adams was of the opinion that British authorities who placed the soldiers in Boston were the real culprits. By the end of the trial, he was able to convince the jury that six of the soldiers acted in self defense and they were acquitted. Because the other two soldiers had fired directly into the crowd, they were convicted of murder. Those charges were later reduced to manslaughter.

In his diary, Adams said this about the trial: "The Part I took in Defence of Cptn. Preston and the Soldiers, procured me Anxiety, and Obloquy enough. It was, however, one of the most gallant, generous, manly and disinterested Actions of my whole Life, and one of the best Pieces of Service I ever rendered my Country. Judgment of Death against those Soldiers would have been as foul a Stain upon this Country as the Executions of the Quakers of Witches, anciently. As the Evidence was, the Verdict of the Jury was exactly right."

The writings of John Adams attest to his patriotism as well as his devotion to principle, integrity, and self control. Weakness of character was anathema to him and he placed great demands on himself to conform to his own high ideals. "May I blush," said Adams, "whenever I suffer one hour to pass unimproved."

Evidence of John Adams' strong belief in the importance of the Christian religion and Biblical principles as the foundation upon which the United States of America rests appears over and over again in his writings. In one of his many letters to his wife, Adams expressed his belief in God's protective care for America: "I have had many opportunities in the course of this journey to observe how deeply rooted our righteous cause is in the minds of the people . . . One evening as I sat in one room, I overheard a company of the common sort of people in another [room] conversing upon serious subjects . . . At length I heard these words: 'It appears to me the eternal Son of God is operating powerfully against the British nation for their treating lightly serious things.'"

Reflecting his concurrence with that commonly-held belief, Adams wrote in his diary, "America was designed by Providence for the theatre, on which man was to make his true figure, on which science, virtue, liberty, happiness, and glory were to exist in peace."

The incident known as the *Boston Massacre* provided a foreshadowing of the violence soon to be visited upon the land. In terms of size and strength of combatants, America's war for independence was a David and Goliath matchup. That the outcome was a Providential victory for the colonies was the only logical conclusion as far as the Founding Fathers were concerned.

George Washington spoke often of the role Providence played in the establishment of a free and independent United States of America: "No people can be bound to acknowledge and adore the invisible hand which conducts the affairs of men more than the people of the United States. Every step, by which they have advanced to the character of an independent nation, seems to have been distinguished by some token of Providential agency."

12.

HMS *Gaspee* Burned by Patriots

June 10, 1772

During the early months of 1772, *HMS Gaspee*, a schooner under the command of British Royal Navy Lieutenant William Dudingston, had become a thorn in the side of American smugglers and rum runners, many of whom were prominent citizens of Rhode Island. Although little remembered today, the *Gaspee* affair generated events that had important long term ramifications in favor of the American independence movement.

It was Dudingston's duty to enforce unpopular customs collections which usually involved inspection of cargo transported in boats operating in Narragansett Bay. Because he was uncommonly diligent in carrying out his duties, Dudingston and the *Gaspee* soon became unpopular among Rhode Islanders who were not used to such diligence by British authorities. Rhode Island governor Joseph Wanton had labeled Dudingston's tactics illegal and referred to him as a British pirate.

When an opportunity to strike back at the zealous young British Navy officer presented itself the evening of June 9, many colonists were only too happy to seize it. On that fateful occasion, the *Gaspee* attempted to stop and search the *Hannah*, a packet (mail) boat owned by John Brown, a county sheriff who also happened to be the son of a Providence businessman and shipping magnate. By this time, Brown had several scores to settle with Dudingston.

Ignoring the *Gaspee's* demand to drop their sail, the *Hannah* made a run for it across a submerged sandbar which the shallow-drafted *Hannah* easily cleared. The *Gaspee*, with more hull below the waterline, got hung up on the sandy shoal where they became helpless to prevent the *Hannah's* escape. Dudingston had no choice but to patiently await the incoming tide that would provide enough lift to get the *Gaspee* underway again.

Upon being informed by the *Hannah's* skipper of the plight of his adversary, Brown assembled a raiding party of sixty-seven men, most of whom were members of the *Sons of Liberty*. Quickly embarking in eight longboats, the raiding party shoved off and rowed the seven miles to where the *Gaspee* lay immobilized and approached her from an angle that prevented the crew from aiming the schooner's swivel guns in their direction. Because of the low-slung profile of the *Gaspee*, the attackers easily boarded the vessel and overpowered the crew of nineteen British sailors.

During the ensuing melee, Dudingston managed to get off one shot from his pistol before being seriously wounded by a musket ball. With their skipper incapacitated, the crew quickly surrendered. The raiders then removed the skipper and his crew, ransacked the schooner, and set it afire, completely destroying the *Gaspee*. The raiding party returned to their longboats and rode the incoming tide back to Providence.

Dudingston survived his wounds but was later convicted by a local court of conducting illegal searches of vessels in Narragansett Bay. The prosecutors successfully argued that Dudingston was only authorized to conduct searches of vessels "on the high seas." Because he was in London at the time of his trial in Providence, Dudingston was unaffected by the outcome. Eventually, he reached the rank of Admiral in the British Navy.

An official inquiry into the *Gaspee* attack lasted nearly two years and finally fizzled out. Assuming that anyone indicted for the attack would be sent to Britain for trial, the colonists did a masterful job of stonewalling the investigators while appearing to cooperate.

Even though the *Gaspee* affair rates only a brief mention in most American history books, the event led to a chain of events that were important ones in the colonies' march toward independence. The most important of those developments was Sam Adams' success in exploiting it as another reason to form a *Committee of Correspondence* in Boston. Adams' Boston *Committee* subsequently provided the impetus and the know-how for the formation of similar *Committees* throughout Massachusetts. Within months, permanent *Committees*, always closely associated with the *Sons of Liberty*, were formed in Virginia, Rhode Island, Connecticut,

New Hampshire, and South Carolina. Adams' instructed the *Committees* to define and disseminate information regarding the colonists' rights "as men, as Christians, and as subjects" throughout the colonies and the world beyond America's shores.

In addition to providing a means of inter-colonial communication, the *Committees of Correspondence* proved to be highly effective in creating a sense of unity among the colonies and an American identity, factors that were instrumental in the process of organizing and publicizing the First Continental Congress convened in1774 in Philadelphia. Led by Payton Randolph, that Congress became, for all practical purposes, the colonial revolutionary government. Prominent among the delegates were George Washington, Thomas Jefferson, Benjamin Franklin, and John Adams. Among other items of business conducted, they produced the *Declaration of Rights and Grievances* sent to King George III and set the stage for the Second Continental Congress in 1775.

During the official inquiry into the *Gaspee* affair, John Allen, pastor of the Second Baptist Church in Boston, published a pamphlet entitled *An Oration Upon the Beauties of Liberty, Or the Essential Rights of Americans*, in which he insisted the colonies were only acting in self defense in opposing British provocations. His pamphlet, which is said to be one of the most effective of all those published during the period leading up to the beginning of hostilities, was based on a sermon he delivered six months after the destruction of the *Gaspee*. Allen's point that America was judicially independent struck a chord with colonists who soon made his *Oration* a best seller.

Often referred to as "the forgotten men of the revolution," Allen and many of his fellow New England pastors speaking from their pulpits frequently used their influence to justify and advance the cause of freedom. When the fighting started a few years later at Lexington and Concord, several colonial pastors laid aside their Bibles and picked up their muskets to join the fight for freedom.

13.

Samuel Adams Throws a Tea Party in Boston

December 16, 1773

Samuel Adams relished the role he assumed as a pain in the neck of King George III who knew him well as one of the most effective of the American rebels in building support for independence and in generating effective opposition to the King's every political or military provocation.

Adams' name was forever linked with opposition to the *Tea Act*, passed by Parliament in May of 1773 when Adams and a few of his friends figured out how to dramatically demonstrate the colonists' displeasure with this particularly blatant and clumsy attempt to shake them down. Tea, because it had to be boiled, was a household staple among the colonists due to the often unsafe condition of drinking water; the tax directly affected a large majority of Americans.

Under cover of darkness the evening of December 16, a large group of agitated citizens, many of whom had disguised themselves as Mohawk Indians, boarded three British ships docked in Boston and dumped an estimated 350 chests of tea into the harbor. The *Boston Tea Party*, as it quickly became known, is an event closely associated in peoples' minds with the American independence movement.

Parliament soon reacted by passing the *Boston Port Act* along with several other pieces of legislation aimed at bringing the rapidly spreading attitude of rebellion under control. But, they were only successful in stirring up a hornet's nest with their "Intolerable Acts" as Parliaments actions were formally labeled by the colonists. Samuel Adams was one of the more vexatious hornets.

Whether or not there could have been such a bold and audacious challenge to British authority at that time without the determined leadership of Sam Adams can be debated, but there can be no doubt about his courage and influence in creating momentum for the independence movement. Openly building support for revolution earned Adams titles such as "Father of the American Revolution" and "the Spirit of the Independence Movement," designations he sometimes shared with friend and fellow Founder Patrick Henry.

The dynamic role he played in organizing resistance to a series of provocations was understood by British leaders to the point that General Thomas Gage, in an effort to end hostilities with the colonists before they began, offered pardons to all rebels except Adams and John Hancock. Gage described their offenses as being "of too flagitious nature to admit of any other consideration than that of condign punishment."

Adams extensive writings also helped to make him one of the best known of the persistent promoters of the call to revolution. Most of his writings appeared originally in *The Boston Gazette*, a large circulation New England newspaper. In *A Statement of the Rights of the Colonists*, first circulated in 1772, he expressed this tenet of the revolution: "The right to freedom being the gift of the Almighty...may be best understood by reading and carefully studying the institution of The Great Law Giver and Head of the Christian Church, which are to be found clearly written and promulgated in the New Testament."

"The natural liberty of man," said Adams, "is to be free from any superior power on earth, and not to be under the will or legislative authority of man, but only to have the law of nature for his rule."

While many Christian denominations with differing doctrines were represented among the delegates to the First Continental Congress, Adams proposed that each days' business be opened with a prayer. "It was unseemly," Adams said, "for Christian men, who had come together for solemn deliberation in the hour of their extremity, to say there was so wide a difference in their religious belief that they could not, as one man, bow the knee in prayer to the Almighty, whose advice and assistance they hoped to obtain."

To many of his contemporaries, Adams was known as one of the last Puritans. That he was a man of character, steadfast in his Christian faith, is clear from the life he lived and many of the memorable words he spoke, especially on the importance of public morality. "A general dissolution of principles and manners," Adams said, "will more surely overthrow the liberties of America than the whole force of the common enemy. While the people are virtuous they cannot be subdued; but when once they lose their virtue they will be ready to surrender their liberties to the first external or internal invader. If virtue and knowledge are diffused among the people, they will never be enslaved. This will be their great security."

History's rewriters have, for the most part, not contested Samuel Adams' Christianity, as they have so many of the Founding Fathers. It would be difficult to twist these words that were included in his will: "Principally, and first of all, I resign my soul to the Almighty Being who gave it, and my body I commit to the dust, relying on the merits of Jesus Christ for the pardon of my sins."

14.

First of *Intolerable Acts* Passed by Parliament

<u>March 30, 1774</u>

In response to the *Boston Tea Party*, Parliament, with encouragement from King George III, passed four punitive acts primarily directed at Boston, the heart of resistance to British provocations and home of the some of the most notorious colonial agitators. The ill-advised acts became known collectively as the *Intolerable Acts* to some and as the *Coercive Acts* to others.

By whatever name, they proved to be a major blunder by the British King and his Parliament. King George thought he could bring the colonies into line by making an example of Massachusetts in general and Boston in particular. He should have thought again.

To a growing majority of colonists, the hated *Acts* had provided further proof that war was becoming inevitable. Because some colonists were highly reluctant to admit that inevitability, last-ditch efforts, such as the so-called *Olive Branch Petition* of July 5, 1775, had occasionally been initiated as attempts to defuse the state of affairs that had exploded at Lexington and Concord three months earlier. As a practical matter, few clear thinkers on either side had actually believed peace and tranquility could be successfully restored after those punitive measures had been imposed by Parliament in 1774.

The four provocative measures – the *Boston Port Act*, the *Massachusetts Government Act*, the *Impartial Administration of Justice Act*, and the *Quartering Act* – did not have the intended, or hoped for, effect. They had, in fact, stiffened the resolve of Bostonians and rallied support for armed resistance throughout Massachusetts and beyond. Farmers soon began arming themselves and forming units for military training in order to be ready at a "minute's notice" for potential confrontation with British troops. Thus was born the *Minutemen,* an organized militia supported by the Massachusetts Provincial Congress. They were to be ready to fight wherever and whenever called upon.

The first of the decrees to be enacted was the *Boston Port Act.* By closing one of the colonies' most important ports to international trade, the British goal was to exert economic pressure with the hope of causing economic damage that would turn the general population against the rebels. When it was announced that British troops would be sent to Boston to enforce a naval blockade and other provisions of the *Port Act,* citizens of the colony did what colonists usually did when faced with adversity; they scheduled a day of fasting and prayer on the date the act was to officially go into effect. To thwart the British blockade of Boston, colonists from many New England towns began sending needed food and supplies over land to their distressed compatriots.

Equally alarming to the colonists was the *Massachusetts Governing Act* that, for all practical purposes, would completely change the system of government in Massachusetts. According to that act, members of the Massachusetts Council would be appointed by the British Governor or the King. Elections would no longer be held and Town Meetings could only be held with permission of the Governor. The Governor or King would appoint *all* local officials including members of the judiciary and they would also decide who could serve on juries.

The *Administration of Justice Act* removed British officials from the jurisdiction of Massachusetts courts for crimes committed in the line of duty, a provision George Washington labeled the "Murder Act." Washington felt it could be used to protect British officials from prosecution for *any* crimes committed against colonists.

Although irritating to colonists, the *Quartering Act* didn't generate as much opposition as the others since it was just a new version of an earlier act of Parliament that had required the colonies to provide billets for British soldiers. Citizens of Massachusetts didn't like it, but it at least applied to all colonies.

A fifth bill passed by Parliament three weeks later wasn't aimed exclusively at Massachusetts, but the colonists lumped it in their minds with the *Intolerable Acts*. The *Quebec Act* extended the boundary of Quebec southward which the colonists believed gave the British a military advantage in the event of war. Because the prospect of armed conflict was growing with each passing month, both sides were weary of any strategic changes.

As usual, response to the *Intolerable Acts* was led by Samuel Adams along with other members of the *Sons of Liberty*. They effectively used the recently expanded *Committees of Correspondence* to generate opposition in Massachusetts and throughout the colonies.

Adams shared the label "spirit of the independence movement" with his friend and fellow Founding Father Patrick Henry. Both men made frequent references to their belief that independence was God-ordained and that He would give them victory over a much stronger opponent. "I should advise persisting in our struggle for liberty," said Adams, "though it were revealed from Heaven that nine hundred and ninety-nine were to perish, and only one of a thousand were to survive and retain his liberty! One such freeman must posses more virtue, and enjoy more happiness, than a thousand slaves; and let him propagate his like, and transmit to them what he hath so nobly preserved."

A few months later, Patrick Henry hammered that point home in his immortal "Give me liberty or give me death" speech before the Virginia Convention.

British attempts to enforce the *Intolerable Acts* led to formation of the First Continental Congress that convened on September 5, 1774. The primary purpose of the new Congress was to generate a series of united responses to the increasing British provocations. One accepted plan was to put in place a boycott of British goods, a measure that had proved effective in the past.

Members of Congress also made a few attempts at diplomacy to satisfy those who were still not convinced that war was inevitable, but the die had been cast. A year after Parliament's passage of the *Intolerable Acts*, the exchange of messages written on paper progressed into an exchange of bullets and bombs.

15.

First Continental Congress Convenes

September 5, 1774

A series of provocations against the British colonies in America that began shortly after the *French and Indian War had* ended climaxed with Parliament's passage of a collection of measures considered by the colonists to be intolerable in 1774.

The fateful agenda pushed by King George III began in 1764 when Parliament, at his behest, passed the Sugar Act. That tax and others levied after it eventually led to America's *Declaration of Independence*. With every revenue-grabbing and/or punitive act passed by Parliament during that ten-year period, a gulf between the two countries widened as resistance to England's attempts at over-reaching control became more widespread throughout the colonies. Relations steadily regressed from cordial to confrontational to irreparable.

Each side was incontrovertibly convinced of the righteousness of its position. King George III and Parliament firmly believed the colonies, as part of the British Empire, should agree to be taxed to help support it, especially the costs associated with maintaining a military establishment adequate to protect the Empire's interests. The colonists were just as firmly convinced that, since they had no representation in Parliament, they were not obligated to pay taxes imposed by a legislative body located on another continent. The colonists took the position that they might very well decide to financially aid the English treasury but any such decision would have to be made by colonial assemblies, not Parliament.

By 1774, colonial leaders had reached the only logical conclusion available to a freedom-loving people. They understood that provocations contained in the *Intolerable Acts* against Massachusetts, the colony most affected by many of the punitive acts, were in fact provocations against all colonies; it finally became obvious to patriots in each colony they could more effectively resist British outrages as one united body rather than as thirteen separate entities. Each colony valued its status as an independent state, but the necessity for unity in the face of such a powerful enemy forced them to focus on the bigger picture.

In May of 1774, the *Committee of Fifty-One*, a New York based offshoot of the militant *Sons of Liberty*, met for the specific purpose of generating support for the Massachusetts patriots who were "suffering for the defense of the rights of America." As a result of that meeting, they called for the establishment of a *Continental Congress*.

Following on the heels of the New York meeting, a group of Virginians led by George Washington met in Fairfax County to draft a statement intended to define the rights of the colonies under the British Constitution. On July 18, 1774, the Virginians approved a document that became known as *The Fairfax Resolves*, written by Washington and George Mason, which stated those rights. Among the twenty-four listed *Resolves* was one recommending that a general congress be established.

Item number sixteen of the *Resolves* called for a compact among the colonies, that stated "...it is the opinion of this meeting, that the merchants and venders of goods and merchandize within this colony shou'd take an oath, not to sell or dispose of any goods or merchandize whatsoever, which may be shipped from Great Britain {or Ireland} after the first day of September next...." That resolution later became the basis of a trade boycott agreement called the *Continental Association*, another of the major achievements of the First Continental Congress.

With influential leaders from Massachusetts, New York, Virginia, Maryland, and North Carolina in agreement that the establishment of a Continental Congress was in the colonies' best interest, *Committees of Correspondence* were given the assignment of formulating a plan for such a unified legislative body to be organized and to meet as soon as practicable. As a result, the first meeting was scheduled for September 5, 1774. Their stated purpose was to generate and approve an agreement as to the extent and form of their resistance to the mother country; drafting a declaration of war was not a part of the agenda. However, when war did come later, the *Continental* Congress became, for all practical purposes, the de facto government of the colonies.

Fifty-five delegates from the twelve participating colonies (Georgia sent no delegates) were in attendance on that momentous September day in Philadelphia when they began deliberations that produced two important documents. The first was known as the *Articles of Association*, which included provisions of the *Continental Association's* nonimportation agreement. The second document was the *Declarations and Resolves of the First Continental Congress*, also known as the *Declaration of Rights and Grievances*, which firmly defined the redress expected by the colonists.

The delegates also called for a Second Continental Congress to be convened May 10, 1775, if Parliament refused to repeal the *Intolerable Acts*. Rather than acceding to the colonist's threats and pleas, the British responded by passing other acts intended to put more stringent economic restrictions on them. British intransigence soon triggered the convening of the Second Continental Congress.

Authorship of the final version of the 1774 *Declarations and Resolves* has generally been attributed to John Adams who was elected as a delegate to the Continental Congress in recognition of his leadership role in opposing British oppression. For years, he had also worked diligently behind the scenes in generating support for the establishment of a general congress.

Renowned for the power of his intellect and the quality of his writing, Adams has been labeled by some as "the mind" of the Revolution. Summing up the important role Adams played in the formation of the republic, Bradley Thompson, author of "America's Revolutionary Mind," wrote, "Adams witnessed the American Revolution from beginning to end: In 1761 he assisted James Otis in defending Boston merchants against enforcement of Britain's Sugar and Molasses Act. Gradually, Adams became a key leader of the radical political movement in Boston and one of the earliest and most principled voices for independence at the *Continental Congress*. Likewise, as a public intellectual, he wrote some of the most important and influential essays, constitutions, and treatises of the Revolutionary period movement."

Adams spoke often of his personal belief that a free and independent America was God-ordained. As evidence of that belief, he said "America was designed by Providence for the theatre, on which man was to make his true figure, on which science, virtue, liberty, happiness, and glory were to exist in peace."

Twenty members of the First Continental Congress were among the fifty-six patriots who signed the *Declaration of Independence.* Each of them was affiliated with a mainline Christian Church.

16.

Patrick Henry Delivers Famous Speech

March 23, 1775

On March 23, 1775, Patrick Henry delivered one of the most famous speeches in all of early American history. It is still echoing in the memories of all who have become familiar with his impassioned and defiant exhortation to his fellow patriots to do what clearly had to be done for the long range benefit of their beloved country. That speech ended with these powerful words:

> *It is in vain, sire, to extenuate the matter. Gentlemen may cry peace, peace – but there is no peace. The war is actually begun! The next gale that sweeps from the North will bring to our ears the clash of resounding arms! Our brethren are already in the field! Why stand we here idle? What is it that gentlemen wish? What would they have? Is life so dear, or peace so sweet, as to be purchased at the price of chains and slavery? Forbid it, Almighty God! I know not what course others may take; but as for me, give me liberty or give me death!*

Most of those in attendance at the Virginia Convention when Henry delivered his immortal words, including Thomas Jefferson, were powerfully moved to the point that many began shouting "To arms! To arms!"

In his autobiography, Jefferson said "I attended the debate at the door of the lobby of the House of Burgesses, and heard the splendid display of Mr. Henry's talents as a popular orator. They were great indeed; such as I have never heard from any other man. He appeared to speak as Homer wrote."

Much had been written and spoken in favor of independence during the years of growing resentment directed at the mother country, but Henry's passionate oration, in which he drove home the point that the colonies must now choose between freedom and slavery, has been recognized by historians as a speech so powerful that it galvanized the final spark of revolution.

A spirit that eventually demanded freedom whatever the cost existed among all the men known as the Founding Fathers but Patrick Henry and Samuel Adams received special recognition; they have both been honored with the label "spirit of the independence movement." Henry and Adams were also frequently referred to as radicals but that label was applied more often to Henry.

In a tribute to Henry, William R. Drinkard wrote: "The cries of [Henry's] suffering countrymen pierced his heart, and he nobly resolved to hazard all in their defence. Prostrating himself before the altar of his country, he placed upon it the rich oblation of an honest heart… We might enquire, if the meekness of the Christian, and the fire of the patriot had not been so happily blended in him what might have been the result of the union of vice with the untamed majesty of his spirit-stirring eloquence? Such is the beauty and the force of virtue."

Henry was first elected to the Virginia House of Burgesses in 1765, the same year Parliament imposed the hated *Stamp Act* on the colonies. In response, Henry introduced several *Stamp Act* resolutions that many loyalist members of the House considered to be radical and even accused him of committing treason. His defiant response was vintage Henry: "If this be treason, make the most of it."

Henry, Jefferson and Richard Henry Lee were the driving force that resulted in the formation of a *Committee of Correspondence* in Virginia in 1773. In conjunction with other colonial *Committees*, they played an important role in the establishment of the First Continental Congress. In 1774, Henry was elected as a delegate to that Congress where he pushed hard for a strong united response to the *Intolerable Acts*. He was selected as a delegate to the *Second Continental Congress* that convened May 10, 1775.

Henry was an outspoken Christians who was motivated by the Scriptural Principle that says "Where the Spirit of the Lord is, there is liberty." Along with most of the other prominent Founding Fathers, he made frequent references to his belief that independence was God-ordained and that He would give the American colonies victory over a much stronger enemy.

In a less quoted portion of his most famous speech, Henry clearly stated that strongly held belief: "Sir, we are not weak, if we make a proper use of the means which the God of nature hath placed in our power. Three millions of people, armed in the Holy cause of Liberty, and in such a country as that which we possess, are invincible by any force which our enemy can send against us. Besides, sir, we shall not fight our battles alone. There is a just God who presides over the destinies of nations; and who will raise up friends to fight our battles for us. The battle, sir, is not to the strong alone; it is to the vigilant, the active, the brave."

Henry has been labeled a deist by some history revisionists who have tried to impugn the reputations of prominent heroes of the revolution. Their false assertions have been used recently by those whose desire it is to separate uninformed and misinformed modern Americans from an understanding of their Christian roots. Here, in his own words, is his response to that charge: "...I hear it is said by the deists that I am one of their number; and indeed that some good people think I am no Christian. This thought gives me much more pain than the appellation of Tory, because I think religion of infinitely higher importance than politics...Being a Christian...is a character which I prize far above all this world has or can boast."

To those who say the United States of America was never a Christian nation, Founder Patrick Henry's own words take issue: "It cannot be emphasized too strongly or too often that this great nation was founded, not by religionists, but by Christians; not on religions, but on the Gospel of Jesus Christ. For this very reason people of other faiths have been afforded asylum, prosperity, and freedom of worship here."

Henry's words leave no room for doubt that the current humanist campaign to marginalize Christianity would have been anathema to him. "It is when a people forget God," Henry said, "that tyrants forge their chains. A vitiated state of morals, a corrupted public conscience, is incompatible with freedom. No free government, or the blessings of liberty, can be preserved to any people but by a firm adherence to justice, moderation, temperance, frugality, and virtue; and by a frequent recurrence to fundamental principles."

The fundamental principles to which he referred are those whose basis is found in the Judeo-Christian Bible. "The Bible," he said, "is a book worth more than all the other books that were ever printed."

17.

First Abolition Society Founded in America

April 14, 1775

One of the charges most often leveled against the Founding Fathers by secular humanists is that, had they truly been Christians, they would have outlawed slavery in the *United States Constitution*.

Most of the two hundred men recognized as Founding Fathers would have done exactly that except for one important fact: They could not have succeeded in getting an acceptable national constitution written and ratified had such a provision been included during the emotionally charged *Constitutional Convention* of 1787. As the *Civil War* and events leading up to it later made clear, the issue of slavery was an impossibly divisive one between northern and southern colonies.

History revisionists ignore the evidence found in the words of many of the Founders who clearly indicated it was their desire that slavery be eliminated as soon as politically possible. The Founders understood they had to secure the Union as their first order of business. To secure the union, they also understood that they had to produce a constitution acceptable to nine of the thirteen colonies, the number required for ratification. Without a new *U.S. Constitution*, there could have been no effective federal government, no functioning United States of America. Because the southern states were unflinchingly convinced that slavery was vital to their economic survival, the issue had to wait.

Benjamin Rush was one of many Founders who spoke out emphatically against the practice of owning slaves. He was speaking for most of his fellow Founders when he said, "Domestic slavery is repugnant to the principles of Christianity. It is rebellion against the authority of a common Father. It is a practical denial of the extent and efficacy of the death of a common Savior. It is an usurpation of the prerogatives of the great Sovereign of the universe who has solemnly claimed an exclusive property in the souls of men."

George Washington, who was known to be opposed to the very idea of slavery, probably had that issue in mind when he said, "I wish the *Constitution* which is offered had been made more perfect, but I sincerely believe it is the best that could be obtained at this time. And, as a constitutional door is opened for amendment hereafter, the adoption of it, under the present circumstances of the Union, is in my opinion desirable." After the *Constitution* was ratified, Washington freed his slaves.

Rush's native state of Pennsylvania had passed an anti-slavery law in 1773 which was vetoed, along with similar laws in other northern states, by King George III. Writing in *The Role of Pastors & Christians in Civil Government*, historian and author David Barton points out facts little known to today's history students: "The King was pro-slavery; the British Empire practiced slavery; and as long as America was part of the British Empire, it too would practice slavery...Since the only way for America to end slavery was to separate from Great Britain, many Founders believed that separation would be an appropriate course of action...Ending slavery was so important to so many of the Founders that when America did separate from Great Britain in 1776, several states began abolishing slavery, including Pennsylvania, Massachusetts, Connecticut, Rhode Island, Vermont, New Hampshire, and New York."

The Atlantic slave trade, the business of transporting black Africans to various areas of the New World – primarily to Spanish and Portuguese colonies in South America – began in the 1500s; it was not invented in North America as some history revisionists would lead the uninformed to believe. Slavery was an important factor in the economy of the British Empire long before the American colonies declared their independence. Slavery in some form still has not been totally eliminated in many parts of the world.

All of the aforesaid began to change on April 14, 1775, when Rush and his friend Benjamin Franklin joined forces to advance the *Pennsylvania Society for Promoting the Abolition of Slavery and the Relief of Free Negroes Unlawfully Held in Bondage.* The organization was a reconstituted version of a small anti-slavery society founded originally in Philadelphia by Anthony Benezet, a French Huguenot, who had immigrated to Philadelphia from Europe to escape religious persecution in 1731. After arriving in Philadelphia, he became a member of *the Religious Society of Friends*, also know as *Quakers*, who had a history of opposing slavery.

Rush had gone on record in 1774 with a powerfully worded pamphlet entitled *On Slavekeeping*. In it, he wrote: "Ye men of sense and virtue – Ye advocates for American liberty, rouse up and espouse the cause of humanity and general liberty. Bear a testimony against a vice which degrades human nature, and dissolves that universal tie of benevolence which should connect all the children of men together in one great family.

The plant of liberty is of so tender a nature, that it cannot thrive long in the neighbourhood of slavery. Remember the eyes of all Europe are fixed upon you, to preserve an asylum for freedom in this country, after the last pillars of it are fallen in every other quarter of the globe."

Abolishing the slave trade in the United States took longer than the Founders intended, but that issue, as a study of unrevised early American history reveals, wasn't theirs to decide at that time. When that contentious issue threatened to derail the *Convention*, a special committee of delegates worked out an agreement known as the *Commerce & Slave Trade Compromise* by which the Southern states would be allowed to continue trading slaves until 1808. Most delegates from northern states believed the practice would die-out on its own during the intervening twenty years.

On March 2, 1807, the United States Congress, in accordance with Article I, Section 9 of the *U.S. Constitution*, banned the importation of African slaves, a ban that took effect January 1, 1808.

18.

Battles of Lexington and Concord

April 19, 1775

When it became clear to King George that Parliament's *Intolerable Acts* had not achieved their intended purpose of bringing the American colonies to heel, he decided a show of military strength was his next best option.

Believing the colonists were no match for his army and knowing they had no navy, the King issued marching orders to General Thomas Gage, Commander in Chief of his North American forces. The decision to flex British military muscle was based on the King's assumption that "once those rebels have felt a smart blow they will submit."

King George had reason to be confident of victory with four thousand experienced troops and a fleet of twenty-four combat ships already stationed in and around Boston. Gage's troops were ordered to capture a stockpile of weapons and ammunition known to have been assembled in Concord. And while they were at it, they were instructed to capture Samuel Adams and John Hancock who were reportedly in the area. The King was confident his orders could quickly and easily be carried out.

When the smoke cleared the evening of April 19, 1775, the King had reason to rethink his ill-conceived remark and his inaccurate assessment of colonial resolve. While the Boston-based British troops had suffered nearly three hundred casualties on that fateful day, the American Minutemen had suffered fewer than one hundred during the battles that raged at both Lexington and Concord. No one knows who fired the first shot, but it was immortalized by Ralph Waldo Emerson in his *Concord Hymn:*

> *By the rude bridge that arched the flood,*
> *Their flag to April's breeze unfurled,*
> *Here once the embattled farmers stood,*
> *And fired the shot heard round the world.*

The first military action of the day, and of the war, began at Lexington where approximately seventy Minutemen under the command of Captain John Parker stood in the way of an estimated 700 British troops advancing toward Concord. Parker's famous statement to his troops served notice to the world that the colonists were not intimidated by the powerful British military: "Stand your ground; don't fire unless fired upon, but if they mean to have a war, let it begin here."

Having been warned of the impending attack by a group of patriots including Paul Revere, Adams and Hancock were able to escape capture and make their way to Philadelphia where they became active in organizing the Second Continental Congress that convened in Philadelphia only three weeks later. Hancock served as its President.

A few months before Patriot militiamen would engage British regulars at Lexington and Concord, two extralegal bodies of colonists had been convened, one in Suffolk County (Boston) and one in Concord. At each gathering, the need to have organized and trained fighting men available upon short notice was addressed. The *Suffolk Resolves*, signed September 4, 1774, called on each colony to create a trained militia of its own. Written by Ross Weiman and Dr. Joseph Warren, the *Resolves* were delivered to the First Continental Congress where they were adopted September 17.

Officials in each Massachusetts community were ordered to train one third of their militiamen as *Minutemen* who could be ready to respond "at a minute's notice." They also had mandated that a stockpile of arms and ammunition be gathered at Concord; that stocklpile was the target of Gage's attack on April 19.

In describing the militiamen who ran to the fight at Lexington and Concord, Dr. Warren, in a letter to Adams, made these laudatory remarks: "A sudden alarm brought them together, animated with the noblest spirit. They left their houses, their families with nothing but the clothes on their backs, without a day's provision, and many without a farthing in their pockets."

Warren had become noted for his rhetorical skills in a 1772 address on the subject of liberty. He had concluded those remarks with these inspiring and encouraging words calling attention to his belief in Providential involvement: "If you perform your part, you must have the strongest confidence that the same Almighty Being who protected your venerable and pious forefathers, who enabled them to turn a barren wilderness into a fruitful field, who so often made bare his arm for their salvation, will be still mindful of you, their offspring. May this Almighty Being graciously preside in all our councils. May he direct us to such measures as He Himself will approve and be pleased to bless. May we ever be a people favored of God."

Warren, who had given up his medical practice in 1765 after passage of the *Stamp Act*, was killed in combat June 17, 1775, during the battle of Bunker Hill. Emerson's *Concord Hymn* ends with these words of tribute that apply to Warren and all the patriots who died to give us our freedom:

The foe long since in silence slept,
Alike the conqueror silent sleeps.
And Time the ruined bridge has swept
Down the dark stream which seaward creeps.
On this green bank, by this soft stream,
We set to-day a votive stone;
That memory may their deed redeem,
When, like our sires, our sons are gone.
Spirit that made those heroes dare
To die, and leave their children free,
Bid Time and Nature gently spare
The shaft we raise to them and thee.

19.

Second Continental Congress Convenes

May 10, 1775

While some colonists still clung to the hope of avoiding war and remaining part of the British Empire, most had become convinced that independence was their best and perhaps only acceptable option. When the Second Continental Congress convened three weeks after the battles of Lexington and Concord, the specter of war was reflected in the deliberations of the delegates.

They tried to focus on steps necessary to preserve the unity of the thirteen colonies and to generate a constitution of sorts to guide the potentially independent country through a future for which they were poorly prepared. It was in that kind of foreboding atmosphere that committees were established to develop plans for increasing international trade, to formulate fiscal policies, and to look for ways to secure military and financial assistance from overseas.

Their most important decision was a near unanimous one: Virginia delegate George Washington was commissioned to organize and command a Continental Army. It was John Adams who proposed creation of the Continental Army and it was also Adams who nominated Washington as Commander in Chief. The fact that Washington was from Virginia was considered an advantage by the Massachusetts delegate because it would help to convince the British that the colonies were united in their determined campaign for independence.

Simultaneously with the development of war plans, a long-shot attempt to avoid all out war was approved on July 5. Entitled the *Olive*

Branch Petition, it was authored primarily by John Dickinson who headed up a faction that still hoped a peaceful solution to differences between the two countries could be found. That turned out to be a waste of time and energy; it was haughtily rejected upon receipt by King George who said he considered the colonies to be "in open and avowed rebellion" against Britain.

On July 6, a document entitled the *Declaration of Causes and Necessity of Taking up Arms* was also approved by the American Congress. The purpose of the *Declaration* was to present to the world reasons Congress felt justified in taking up arms against the mother country. It also included an offer to stop the fighting if Parliament would repeal the hated tax acts and trade regulations, an offer also rejected by the King. From that point on, Samuel Adams, John Hancock, and those who agreed with them that a war for independence was the only available option were firmly in control of the Continental Congress which then became the revolutionary government of the colonies.

On the same day Congress convened in Philadelphia, an important military victory for the colonies was achieved in upper New York when Fort Ticonderoga was captured from the British. The Green Mountain Boys, commanded by Ethan Allen with an assist from Benedict Arnold, had launched an early morning attack on the surprised British soldiers; the militiamen took the Fort with no casualties. Allen accepted their surrender "in the Name of the Great Jehovah and the Continental Congress."

That victory was an especially important one because of the Fort's strategic location on Lake Champlain and because of the arms and ammunition, including approximately one hundred artillery pieces, that were captured by the patriots. Possession of the cannons soon made it possible for the American army to pressure General Gage into evacuating Boston during the spring of 1776. The presence of enemy artillery in the Dorchester Heights area was a threat to British ships in Boston Bay and became a deciding factor in Gage's decision to remove his troops.

As future events would prove, Congress' selection of George Washington as Commander in Chief of the Continental Army was a fortuitous one. With an ill-equipped, thrown-together army of civilians, Washington is credited with winning a highly unlikely and hard-fought victory over one of the world's dominant military powers, a victory Washington consistently attributed to "the providence of Almighty God."

Washington's first task was to organize and train the collection of militiamen from which he was to create a national military force. He placed great importance and emphasis upon Godly behavior among those under his command and established what was to become the Chaplain Corps and made attendance at regular worship services mandatory. Washington's first general order read: "The General most earnestly requires and expects a due observance of those articles of war [passed by Congress June 30, 1775] established for the government of the army, which forbid profane cursing, swearing, and drunkenness. And in like manner he requires and expects of all officers and soldiers, not engaged in actual duty, a punctual attendance on Divine service, to implore the blessing of Heaven upon the means used for our safety and defense."

Prior to the Continental Army's initial combat activities, he delivered this exhortation to his troops: "The time is now near at hand which must probably determine whether Americans are to be freemen or slaves; whether they are to have any property they can call their own; whether their houses and farms are to be pillaged and destroyed, and themselves consigned to a state of wretchedness from which no human efforts will deliver them. The fate of unborn millions will now depend, under God, on the courage of this army. Our cruel and unrelenting enemy leaves us only the choice of brave resistance, or the most abject submission. We have, therefore to resolve to conquer or die."

Henry Muhlenberg, pastor of a church located near the Army's Valley Forge camp, recognized the Providential care claimed and enjoyed by Washington: "I heard a fine example today, namely, that His Excellency General Washington rode around among his army yesterday and admonished each and every one to fear God, to put away the wickedness that has set in and become so general, and to practice the Christian virtues. From all appearances, this gentleman does not belong to the so-called world of society, for he respects God's Word, believes in the atonement through Christ, and bears himself in humility and gentleness. Therefore, the Lord God has also singularly, yea, marvelously, preserved him from harm in the midst of countless perils, ambuscades, fatigues, etc., and has hitherto graciously held him in His hand as a chosen vessel."

Congress approved the *Declaration of Independence* July 4, 1776. When the *Articles of Confederation* were ratified March 1, 1781, the Second Continental Congress became known as the Congress of the Confederation.

20.

Capture of Fort Ticonderoga

May 10, 1775

The battle that resulted in the capture of Fort Ticonderoga wasn't much of a battle, but the benefit it provided for the poorly-supplied, soon-to-be formed Continental Army had Providential ramifications. Without the weapons captured at the large but lightly-defended fort, the outcome of the consequential Siege of Boston could very well have turned out much differently to the overall disadvantage of the American Revolutionary War effort.

An account of the capture of Fort Ticonderoga included in *Chronicle of America*, a book of American history edited by Clifton Daniel and presented in the form of newspaper articles, told the story in this manner:

> *In a victory that was more comic than heroic, an irregular force of Americans captured this fort on Lake Champlain. Early this month, Ethan Allen led 200 members of his Green Mountain Boys to Hand's Cove, about two miles south of the fort. At the same time, Benedict Arnold, who had no troops, headed for Hand's Cove as well, and on arriving declared himself [their] leader. The men argued as they began loading the boat for a dawn attack, and it is unclear which of them was actually in command. It was probably not important because the dilapidated fort was indefensible.*
>
> *The members of the garrison, which consisted of two officers, 40 men and 24 women and children, were surprised in their beds. Allen caught Lieutenant Jocelyn Feltham standing sleepily*

with his breeches still in hand. "Come out of there, you damned old rat" said Allen. "By what authority are you acting?" asked Feltham. "In the name of the Great Jehovah and the Continental Congress," bellowed Allen. Presumably, Feltham was suitably impressed by these twin deities and surrendered immediately. Two days later, the garrison at Crown Point was also captured. There were no British or American casualties reported in either of these engagements.

While the *Chronicle* account may have tended to trivialize the events that took place on that morning in May, 1775, the results were anything but trivial. The capture of that strategically-located fort and, more importantly, the weapons stored in it took place less than a month after the Battles of Lexington and Concord and during the early stages of the Siege of Boston when more firepower would be desperately needed by the rebels. In a 1963 magazine article, historian Kenneth S. Davis described the captured materials as "an immense booty: upward of a hundred cannon (the figure is uncertain), several huge mortars and two or three howitzers, 100 stands of small arms, ten tons of musket and cannon balls, three cartloads of flints, a warehouse full of boat-building materials, thirty new carriages, and sundry other war supplies."

In November, men under the command of Colonel Henry Knox began moving the captured artillery to Dorchester Heights which overlooks Boston. From that advantageous location, they were able to effectively bombard British troops in the city and ships in the bay. Although the British attempted to return the fire, their cannons were unable to reach the American troops and their newly-acquired artillery located on the higher ground. The Providentially-provided British guns were instrumental in achieving an unlikely early-war victory for the Americans: On March 17, 1776, approximately 10,000 British troops and 1,000 civilians boarded 120 ships and abandoned the city. Their departure from Boston, for all practical purposes, brought an end to British military activities in the New England colonies. Boston remained in colonial hands for the duration of the war, an important benefit enjoyed by the colonies struggling for independence from the powerful British Empire.

Prior to the official creation of the Continental Army by the Second Continental Congress on June 14, 1775, the colonial forces were made up of a collection of state militias including the Green Mountain Boys. Formed in the late 1760s, the Green Mountain Boys were headed up by Ethan Allen, an outlaw in the eyes of the British governor of New York because of his opposition to British attempts to control and tax the territory known as the New Hampshire Grants, the area located between New York and New Hampshire that would become the state of Vermont in 1791 (the 14th state admitted to the union). Allen, one of the early leaders in the campaign to achieve statehood for the territory, and his militia were mostly successful in foiling the New York Governor's plan.

In a book he edited entitled *American Courage,* Herbert W. Warden III described Allen as "a tall man of Herculean strength. Stories had it that in an altercation with a New York sheriff and his six deputies, Ethan single-handedly knocked all seven unconscious. And that in a dispute with two land surveyors, he grabbed the pair, one in each arm, lifted them off the ground, and banged their heads together. He also had a sense of humor. When the British sought to arrest him and offered a twenty-pound bounty, he rode to Albany and tacked up his own poster offering a twenty-pound bounty for the arrest of the governor."

During the earliest stages of the American war for independence, state and territorial militias such as the Green Mountain Boys provided the only armed opposition to the well-trained, well-supplied, battle-tested army of the British Empire. That was necessary because Congress had not yet authorized a government-supported American army. While it took years for that army to become trained, funded, and effective as a fighting force, the militias stood in the gap.

Exceptionally dedicated and able men such as Ethan Allen and their collections of men who supplied their own guns and supplies should be a lesson to misguided people who would today deny the right for private citizens to own guns. Without those armed private citizens willing to fight against long odds for freedom, there may never have been a United States of America. The Second Amendment to the US Constitution says "A well regulated Militia, being necessary to the security of a free State, the right of the people to keep and bear Arms, shall not be infringed."

People can debate the meaning of "well regulated," but those who understand early American history know that traditionally the word "militia" has referred to an association of like-minded patriots who are willing to arm themselves to protect their rights, their families, and their property. The Founding Fathers understood that principle and memorialized it in the Bill of Rights of the US Constitution.

21.

British Lose While "Winning" At Bunker Hill

June 17, 1775

"A few more such victories would have shortly put an end to British dominion in America," said British General Henry Clinton when commenting on the outcome of the Battle of Bunker Hill fought near Boston on June 17, 1775.

Clinton was referring to the large number of casualties suffered by British forces as they temporarily forced the colonists, who had repulsed two attacks, to abandon their positions. After running out of ammunition, the colonists retreated when the British launched their third attack of the day but the British were not able to hold the ground nor to effectively break the land blockade. Although it was called a victory for the British, at the end of the day each side held the same territories they had controlled before the battle began. Because of heavy casualties the "victorious" British, unable to accomplish their goal, returned to Boston.

It was a major battle pitting British regulars against a band of inexperienced and inadequately trained militiamen who would soon provide the foundation for what would become the Continental Army. British General William Howe led 2,400 troops against approximately 1,500 militiamen under the command of American Generals Artemas Ward and Israel Putnam.

More than 1,100 British regulars were killed, wounded, or captured while the American casualties were estimated at around 450.

The militiamen fought from behind barricades while the British troops advanced without cover. While waiting behind their fortifications, legend has it, the militiamen obeyed, to a man, the famous command given by Colonel William Prescott: "Don't fire until you see the whites of their eyes." For both sides, the battle was a learning experience.

Two months earlier, during the battles of Lexington and Concord, the British had retreated to their Boston stronghold, under fire all the way, where they were soon besieged by the colonists who had pursued them from Concord.

Because the patriots had no navy, the British were able to provide supplies and reinforcements to Boston by sea but those provisions proved to be insufficient to meet the needs of the soldiers plus the civilian citizens who remained in the city. As rations dwindled, the British became aware that the patriots were putting cannons captured at Ft. Ticonderoga in place on Dorchester Heights with which they could bombard both the city and their ships located in Boston harbor. In an attempt to eliminate that threat, General Thomas Gage and his staff devised a plan by which they hoped to destroy the threatening artillery and to break the siege. Thus was hatched the plan to attack Bunker Hill.

The colonists' siege of Boston became a stalemate that lasted until March 17, 1776, when the British, without opposition, loaded 11,000 people and supplies on board 120 ships. Following the departure of the British, General Ward led an occupying force into the city which once again became an important port for the patriots as well as a center for revolutionary activities.

When King George III received a detailed report of the "victory," he understood it was no such thing and resolved to provide overwhelming military force in order to put a quick end to the rebellion. The British military leaders, he began to realize, were either over confident or incompetent and had consistently underestimated the resolve and the fighting ability of the colonists, a fact made abundantly clear to the king while reviewing results of fighting so far, especially at Bunker Hill.

While a Continental Army had been officially authorized by the Second Continental Congress three days prior to the Battle of Bunker Hill, George Washington, who was at the same time appointed Commander in Chief, didn't arrive in Massachusetts until July 2, 1775. He took command of what would become the nucleus of his Continental Army two weeks after the Bunker Hill hostilities.

His first task was to organize the disparate groups he inherited and train them to be a disciplined and effective fighting force. As a priority, he placed great importance and emphasis upon Godly behavior among those placed under his command. When nominating Washington to fill this vitally important position, John Adams praised Washington as the best man for the job: "This appointment will have a great effect in cementing the union of these colonies. The general is one of the most important characters of the world; upon him depend the liberties of America."

Washington's recorded words are laced with references to the necessity of dependence upon God and His Providence as his men prepared for combat against soldiers representing the world's most powerful empire. He was convinced the colonies could only be victorious with the help of almighty God and he didn't hesitate to say so. Nor did he hesitate later to state his conviction that it was God's plan and favor that provided the Americans with their freedom and independence.

"No people can be bound to acknowledge and adore the invisible hand which conducts the affairs of men more than the people of the United States,' said Washington. "Every step, by which they have advanced to the character of an independent nation, seems to have been distinguished by some token of Providential agency."

Best-selling author Tim LaHaye included in his well-researched book entitled *Faith of Our Founding Fathers* excerpts from Washington's personal prayer book with this lead-in: "That President George Washington was a devout believer in Jesus Christ and had accepted Him as His Lord and Savior is easily demonstrated by a reading of his personal prayer book (written in his own handwriting), which was discovered in 1891 among a collection of his papers. To date no historian has questioned its authenticity. It consists of twenty-four pages of his morning and evening prayers, revealing many of his theological beliefs about God, Jesus Christ, sin, salvation, eternal life, and himself as a humble servant of Christ."

By all authoritive accounts, Washington was a practicing Christian, a man of prayer, and one who walked humbly before his God. He was a patriot with a strong sense of calling and purpose to which he responded courageously. He was the right man at the right place at the right time.

22.

Congress Adopts *Articles of War*

June 30, 1775

Shortly after the battles of Lexington, Concord, and Bunker Hill, members of the Second Continental Congress came to the conclusion that a code of conduct for the newly authorized Continental Army should immediately be established "because successful armies are made up of disciplined men who know and understand the rules by which they must perform and be measured."

On June 30, 1775, Congress approved the *American Articles of War* as the first step necessary "to maintain discipline and secure justice" in the army. In addition to presenting sixty-nine rules and regulations to which all members of the army would have to comply, the document stated the reasons for taking up arms against the mother country as a reminder of the tyranny against which they were fighting. It was an internal exhortation as well as a code of military law developed specifically to instruct military personnel regarding personal behavior and the duties of a soldier. The emphasis was on personal behavior.

Article two, for example, said, "It is earnestly recommended to all officers and soldiers, diligently to attend Divine Service; and all officers and soldiers who shall behave indecently or irreverently at any place of Divine Worship, shall, if commissioned officers, be brought before a court-martial, there to be publicly and severely reprimanded by the President; if non-commissioned officers or soldiers, every person so offending shall, for his first offence, forfeit One Sixth of a Dollar, to be deducted out of his next pay; for the second offence, he shall not only forfeit a like sum, but be confined for twenty-four hours, and for every like offence, shall suffer and pay in like manner; which money so forfeited, shall be applied to the use of the sick soldiers of the troop or company to which the offender belongs."

Article three followed up with this declaration: "Whatsoever non-commissioned officer or soldier shall use any profane oath or execration, shall incur the penalties expressed in the second article; and if a commissioned officer be thus guilty of profane cursing or swearing, he shall forfeit and pay for each and every such offence, the sum of Four Shillings, lawful money."

A similar but separate document entitled *Rules for the Regulation of the Navy of the United Colonies* was adopted at the same time.

In the preamble to the *Articles*, Congress stated its case for establishing a standing army by reciting wrongs committed against the colonies by Great Britain.

The *Articles of War*, with but few revisions, remained in effect until 1950 when they were replaced by the *Uniform Code of Military Justice*. The original documents were primarily based on rules and regulations of the British Army and Navy.

John Adams was given the task of preparing the *Articles of War*. While Adams supported the growing resistance to the British government in the early 1770s, he had previously been in favor of reconciliation with Britain. In December of 1773, the Boston Tea Party changed Adams outlook irrevocably. From that point on, he was staunchly committed to the cause of American independence. By 1774, Adams was urging his fellow Americans to adopt "revolution principles," a resolve to do what had to be done in order to guarantee American rights and liberties.

The writings of John Adams attest to his personal devotion to principle, integrity, and self control, characteristics often reflected in the *Articles*. Weakness of character was anathema to him and he placed great demands on himself to conform to his own high ideals. Self improvement was an important goal from early in life as illustrated by this entry in his journal: "I resolve to rise with the Sun and to study the Scriptures on Thursday, Fryday, Saturday, and Sunday mornings, and to study some Latin author the other 3 mornings. Noons and Nights I intend to read English Authors. This is my fixt Determination, and I will set down every neglect and every compliance with this Resolution. May I blush whenever I suffer one hour to pass unimproved."

Evidence of John Adams' strong belief in the importance of the Christian religion and Biblical principles as the foundation upon which the United States of America rests appears over and over again in his writings. For example, an entry in his *Diary* dated July 26, 1796, said: "The Christian religion is, above all the Religions that ever prevailed or existed in ancient or modern Times, the Religion of Wisdom, Virtue, Equity, and humanity....it is Resignation to God, it is Goodness itself to Man."

"It is Religion and Morality alone which can establish the principles upon which freedom can securely stand," Adams said. "A patriot must be a religious man." He believed that applied to all military personnel as well as to all responsible citizens.

Richard Stockton wrote this tribute to Adams, his fellow delegate to the Second Continental Congress: "The man to whom the country is most indebted for the great measure of independence is Mr. John Adams .... I call him the Atlas of American independence. He it was who sustained the debate, and by force of his reasoning demonstrated not only the justice, but the expediency of the measure."

Americans who have not taken the time to learn about the exceptionalism of the men known as their Founding Fathers are denying themselves a source of pride, inspiration, and love of country because of America's inherent Bible-based goodness.

23.

Congress Authorizes the Continental Navy

October 13, 1775

After much talk, foot-dragging, and a prod by Commander-in-Chief George Washington, the Continental Congress passed a resolution authorizing construction of two-ships on October 13, 1775. That date has become recognized as the official birthday of what would someday become the world's largest and most powerful navy.

Several members of Congress felt building two small warships would pointlessly provoke the British even though their world class navy could hardly be affected by such a token move by the colonists. A majority of delegates apparently decided it was too late to worry about provoking the British and voted to take that small step. The shrinking number of delegates who still hoped for reconciliation with the mother country opposed the resolution because they felt that any movement toward the establishment of an American Navy would irrevocably remove that possibly.

The colonists' historic resolution began with these detailed instructions:

> *Resolved, That a swift sailing vessel, to carry ten carriage guns, and a proportionable number of swivels, with eighty men, be fitted, with all possible dispatch, for a cruise of three months, and that the commander be instructed to cruise eastward, for*

intercepting such transports as may be laden with warlike stores and other supplies for our enemies, and for such other purposes as the Congress shall direct.

That a Committee of three be appointed to prepare an estimate of the expence, and lay the same before the Congress, and to contract with proper persons to fit out the vessel.

Resolved, that another vessel be fitted out for the same purposes, and that the said committee report their opinion of a proper vessel, and also an estimate of the expence.

The "committee of three" as called for in the resolution was made up of John Adams, Silas Deane, and John Langdon. They were given the assignment of putting together a plan of operations for the ships of the new navy. American ships, according to the plan they produced, were to harass unarmed British merchant ships and transports in hopes of commandeering cargo and capturing vessels the colonists could convert to their own use. For obvious reasons, they were to avoid engaging the larger heavily armed British warships.

The vote to create at least a small maritime force had been helped along by Washington when he reminded his fellow patriots that an increased ability to interrupt British supply lines would be beneficial to his troops in the field. Leaders in several colonies had been thinking along the same lines. In August, the Rhode Island State Assembly had passed a resolution recommending "a fleet of sufficient force for the protection of these colonies and for employing them in such a manner and places as will most effectively annoy our enemies."

Before Congress passed the Navy Resolution, as it was called, Washington had begun to take matters into his own hands by enlisting seven privately owned American ships to help accomplish his goal of disrupting Britain's maritime supply line. Called privateers – some called them "legalized" pirates – the ships' captains were offered a percentage of the value of captured cargo as an inducement to attack vessels transporting supplies to the British army. In Massachusetts, John Hancock had been busy for some time assembling "vessels to be armed and manned for the purpose of intercepting transports daily arriving at Boston."

With ships already operating under Washington's control and with other influential colonists acting independently to arm ships for the purpose of interfering with British shipping, Congress could hardly have refused to support such a recommendation by their Commander-in-Chief.

As support for a Continental Navy increased, an enlarged naval committee was appointed by Congress on October 30. Made up of the three original members plus Christopher Gadsen, Joseph Hewes, Stephen Hopkins, and Richard Henry Lee, the committee soon recommended the addition of eleven more converted merchant ships to the fledgling navy. They also sent a recommendation to Congress calling for construction of thirteen new frigates with armaments ranging from twenty-four to thirty-two guns. Congress approved the committee's recommendation on December 13.

For some time, Adams had been intrigued with the idea of establishing an American Navy that could someday compete with the British for control of the seas. In anticipation of that day, he had written a document entitled *Rules for the Regulation of the Navy of the United Colonies of North America*. With America's navy becoming more of a factor in the war effort, Congress understood the need for such rules and accepted those proposed by Adams.

On December 22, Esek Hopkins was appointed Commander-in-Chief of the Navy. At the same time, other officers, including future navy hero John Paul Jones, were officially commissioned as U.S. Navy officers.

Eventually, the number of armed ships that harassed British shipping throughout the war is believed to have reached a high of approximately sixty-five. Navy ships and privateers are credited with capturing approximately two-hundred enemy ships, some carrying valuable munitions and other badly needed supplies that were put to good use by the Continental Army. The Navy lost twenty-four ships during the war including all thirteen of the frigates authorized by Congress. There is no official record of the number of privateers captured or sunk.

At the successful conclusion of the war, Congress decided the Continental Navy was no longer needed, calling it a luxury the colonies could not afford. Even though the war against Great Britain had demonstrated the importance of sea power, Congress felt they had other monetary priorities that prevailed over the substantial cost involved in maintaining a naval force. At that point in time, the westward overland expansion demanded more attention and more financial resources than the Atlantic area from which the threat had greatly diminished. The *USS*

Alliance was the last of eleven American Navy ships that survived the Revolutionary War. It was sold at auction August 1, 1778.

As the United States became more involved in international trade, it became obvious that the need for a permanent navy could not reasonably be denied. On April 30, 1798, they passed an act that established the *Department of the Navy.*

24.

Congress Establishes United States Marine Corps

<u>November 10, 1775</u>

Based on his extensive understanding of world military history, John Adams presented a resolution to the Second Continental Congress for the purpose of creating what is now known as the United States Marine Corps. Officially known at the time as the Continental Marines, members of the "amphibious army" (amphibious because they were ship-based), soon made their mark as an important part of the U.S. Navy and the growing U.S. military might. Adams resolution was approved November 10, 1775.

Adams was aware of the important role played by the British Royal Marines formed exclusively for service afloat in 1664. Many years earlier, American soldiers had served in a British regiment known as "Gooch's Marines." Under their commander, Colonel William Gooch, they had taken control of Guantanamo Bay, Cuba, in 1740 as a base for the Royal Navy. At least partially as a result of Adams' foresight, the United States Marine Corps has become a unique and universally respected military organization that "fights its countries battles in the air, on land, and sea," as their anthem proudly points out.

Adams resolution read as follows:

> *Resolved, That two Battalions of marines be raised,*
> *consisting of one Colonel, two Lieutenant Colonels, Two Majors,*

and other officers as usual in other regiments; and that they consist of an equal number of privates with other battalions; that particular care be taken, that no persons be appointed to office, or enlisted into said Battalions, but such as are good seamen, or so acquainted with maritime affairs as to be able to serve to advantage by sea when required; that they be enlisted and commissioned to serve for and during the present war between Great Britain and the colonies, unless dismissed by order of Congress; that they be distinguished by the names of the first and second battalions of American Marines, and that they be considered as part of the number which the Continental Army before Boston is ordered to consist of.

Captain Samuel Nicholas was named as the first commissioned officer of the newly-created Marine Corps on November 28, 1775. Though only a Captain at the time, Nicholas is considered to have been the first Commandant of the U.S. Marine Corps.

Nicholas established his recruiting headquarters in Philadelphia; by the end of December, he had signed up enough volunteers to create five companies of approximately 300 Marines each. Soon thereafter, the Marines, under Nicholas, successfully carried out an amphibious landing on New Providence Island in the Bahamas as part of the Continental Navy's first official action of the Revolutionary War.

Nicholas was in command of the 268-man Marine landing party aboard the *USS Alfred*, the U.S. Navy's first man-of-war. It was the flagship of a squadron under the command of Admiral Esek Hopkins, Navy Commander-in-Chief, who decided on his own to raid two forts located on New Providence Island where the British were known to have stored munitions that were a potential threat to the colonies. Hopkins knew they would be valuable to the desperately under-supplied American forces. It took two weeks to strip the forts and load the captured supplies that included eighty-eight artillery pieces.

Upon the *Alfred's* return from the Bahamas, Nicholas was promoted to the rank of Major and given the assignment of recruiting enough men to form four additional companies to fill the needs of four new frigates authorized by Congress.

The Continental Marines, along with the Continental Navy, were disbanded after the Treaty of Paris was signed in 1783 ending the war for independence. Soon, however, an undeclared war with France, now known as the Quasi War of 1798-1800, and on-going attacks upon American shipping by Barbary pirates made it clear to Congress that the U.S. Navy, including a Marine contingent, was needed to defend America's growing international interests.

In May of 1798, Congress formally reestablished the American Navy and in July, they reestablished the Marine Corps. The Navy and Marine Corps became major participants in many battles against the Barbary pirates. As a result of the Marines' conquering of Tripoli in 1804, the Arab states of North Africa became convinced it was no longer profitable to raid American shipping which motivated them to sign a peace treaty. The Marines' success at Tripoli is commemorated in the Marine Corps Hymn:

> *From the Halls of Montezuma*
> *To the Shores of Tripoli;*
> *We fight our country's battles*
> *In the air, on land and sea;*
> *First to fight for right and freedom*
> *And to keep our honor clean;*
> *We are proud to claim the title*
> *of United States Marine.*

Since its inception, the Marine Corps has been involved in more than 300 amphibious landings while fighting in all the wars in which the United States of America has been involved. *Semper Fidelis* (always faithful), the Marine Corps motto, is understood by Marines to mean they are to be faithful to God, Corps, and country.

25.

Thomas Paine Publishes *Common Sense*

January 10, 1776

Every event with potentially earth-shaking consequences needs a gifted agitator, one who has an uncommon ability to clarify issues, galvanize public opinion, and motivate people to take action. World history contains the names of many who, for better or for worse, filled that role at crucial times.

There were a number of rhetorically gifted men associated with the American Revolution – Patrick Henry and Samuel Adams come quickly to mind – but one name deserves special attention. The colonists' most often acknowledged *provocateur extraordinaire* turned out to be an Englishman named Thomas Paine who migrated from England to the American colonies in 1774 at the age of thirty-seven. Many consider Paine's timely arrival in America as Providential.

In 1775, a significant segment of the American public was still astraddle the proverbial fence regarding the independence issue; they needed the spark that only a highly skilled author/agitator could provide. Soon after arriving in Philadelphia on November 30 with a letter of recommendation from Benjamin Franklin in his pocket, Paine began writing *Common Sense*, a 48-page booklet that decidedly influenced the collective opinion of a large percentage of the remaining fence-sitting colonists. He hit exactly the right note at exactly the right time.

Common Sense was originally published anonymously because it clearly would have been considered treasonous by British King George III who Paine referred to as the "royal brute." The book quickly became a best seller in Europe as well as in the colonies. In three months, 120,000 copies had been purchased; more than 500,000 copies were sold within twelve months.

In his *Introduction*, Paine wrote, "The cause of America is, in a great measure, the cause of all mankind. Many circumstances have, and will arise, which are not local, but universal, and through which the principles of all lovers of mankind are affected, and in the event of which, their affections are interested." On another occasion, Paine expressed a similar thought: "Had it not been for America, there had been no such thing as freedom left throughout the whole universe."

Responding to the crystallizing of support provided by Paine's pamphlet, the *Continental Congress* appointed a committee to draft what would soon become known to the world as the American *Declaration of Independence*. Some historians have called the American Revolution the "first successful anti-colonial movement in modern history."

Being governed by a monarch was anathema to Paine who wrote: "Government by kings was first introduced into the world by the Heathens, from whom the children of Israel copied the custom. It was the most prosperous invention the Devil ever set on foot for the promotion of idolatry. The Heathens paid divine honors to their deceased kings, and the Christian world hath improved on the plan by doing the same to their living ones. How impious is the title of sacred majesty applied to a worm, who in the midst of his Splendor, is crumbling into dust!"

He was appalled by the idea a continent should be ruled by an island. "Small islands not capable of protecting themselves," Paine wrote, "are the proper objects for kingdoms to take under their care; but there is something very absurd in supposing a continent to be perpetually governed by an island. In no instance hath nature made the satellite larger than its primary planet, and as England and America, with respect to each other, reverses the common order of nature, it is evident they belong to different systems: England to Europe, America to itself. "

Following publication of *Common Sense*, Paine authored a series of articles published between December of 1776 and April of 1783. He wrote them for the purpose of generating ongoing support for an independent and self-governing America through the period of continuous crises that arose during the early stages of the fight for independence. So impressed was George Washington with Paine's series of articles that the

Commander-in-Chief ordered his officers to read them to their troops. The articles were later collected and published in a book entitled *The Crisis*.

The lead paragraph of the first of the thirteen *Crisis* articles provides an excellent example of Paine's powerful writing style:

> *THESE are the times that try men's souls. The summer soldier and the sunshine patriot will, in this crisis, shrink from the service of their country; but he that stands it now, deserves the love and thanks of man and woman. Tyranny, like hell, is not easily conquered; yet we have this consolation with us, that the harder the conflict, the more glorious the triumph. What we obtain too cheap, we esteem too lightly: it is dearness only that gives every thing its value. Heaven knows how to put a proper price upon its goods; and it would be strange indeed if so celestial an article as FREEDOM should not be highly rated. Britain, with an army to enforce her tyranny, has declared that she has a right (not only to TAX) but "to BIND us in ALL CASES WHATSOEVER," and if being bound in that manne, is not slavery, then is there not such a thing as slavery upon earth. Even the expression is impious; for so unlimited a power can belong only to God.*

He returned to Europe in 1787 where he divided his time between Britain and France eventually forsaking his English citizenship to become a French citizen in 1792. His two-part work entitled the *Rights of Man*, written in 1791-92, resulted in his getting kicked out of England and temporarily imprisoned in France. With the help of James Monroe, newly-appointed American Minister to France, Paine was released from prison and resumed his writing. In 1794, Paine began the first of his three-part deist manifesto entitled *The Age of Reason*. Because of the "radical" content of his writings, usually unabashedly anti-government in nature, Paine tended to wear out his welcome wherever he chose to live.

Benjamin Franklin, another influential friend and the reason Paine had originally decided to leave England for the colonies, gave him this prescient advice after reading a pre-publication draft of *The Age of Reason*: "At present, I shall only give you my opinion; the consequence of printing this piece will be a great deal of odium drawn upon yourself, mischief to you and no benefit to others. He that spits into the wind, spits in his own face."

Paine published the book anyway which subsequently cost him most of his American goodwill and a large part of his reputation. Considered blasphemous by many, its publication brought him widespread condemnation in both Europe and America. He said later, "I would give worlds, if I had them, if *The Age of Reason* had never been published. O Lord, help! Stay with me! It is hell to be left alone."

After calling Napoleon "the greatest charlatan that ever existed," he returned to America in 1802 in response to an invitation from his friend Thomas Jefferson. He died in New Rochelle, New York, in1809.

Perhaps reflecting a return to his earlier more conventional Christian beliefs, Paine said, "I die in perfect composure and resignation to the will of my Creator, God."

Although Paine spent few of his 72 years in America, he is usually designated by historians as one of America's Founding Fathers. Like so many others among the Founders, he was the right man at the right place at the right time.

26.

Adam Smith Publishes
Wealth of Nations

March 9, 1776

Although he was born in Scotland and never set foot on American soil, Adam Smith is credited with exerting a great deal of influence on America's economic system as a result of his landmark book entitled *An Inquiry into the Nature and Causes of the Wealth of Nations*. Published in March of 1776, it is now most often referred to simply as *The Wealth of Nations*.

In it, Smith argued against the predominant economic system of his day which was known as *mercantilism*. His book was an immediate success with the first edition selling out in six months. To most of America's Founding Fathers, *The Wealth of Nations* became a source of inspiration where economic theory was concerned. Adam Smith and the Founders were most certainly on the same page, especially where taxes and private property were concerned.

The mercantile system was based on control by the government through taxes and regulations that Smith believed were the antitheses of sound economic policy. The mercantilists believed that national prosperity can only be measured by the economic assets possessed by the state, a theory sometimes referred to as statism. Today, we would be correct in labeling it a form of socialism. Smith generally agreed with the Austrian School of Economics that opposed mercantilism on the grounds that it "employed economic fallacy to build up a structure of imperial state power, as well as special subsidy and monopolistic privilege to individuals or groups favored by the state."

After Parliament passed the Sugar Act in 1764, the American colonies became increasingly subjected to Britain's mercantilist economic system. The Sugar Act was soon followed by other acts that added to the list of goods flowing to or from the colonies that were required to go through Britain in order to be taxed. That kind of heavy-handed taxation became one of the major causes of the American Revolution.

Smith was opposed to *any* state control over economic systems. On the contrary, he believed that an individual "pursuing his own interest frequently promotes that of society more effectually than when he intends to promote it." Smith's now famous "invisible hand" concept was his way of illustrating the advantages of free market competition over the controlled and regulated economy of the mercantilists.

"By preferring the support of domestic to that of foreign industry," Smith said, "he [the individual entrepreneur] intends only his own security; and by directing that industry in such a manner as its produce may be of the greatest value, he intends only his own gain, and he is in this, as in many other cases, led by an invisible hand to promote an end which was no part of his intention." To further illustrate this point, Smith said, "It is not from the benevolence of the butcher, the brewer, or the baker that we expect our dinner, but from their regard to their own self-interest."

To paraphrase, Smith was saying that local entrepreneurs operating in a free market system are better suited to build the local [domestic] economy than the government because of a motivating desire to improve their own personal economic situations. They benefit others unintentionally when, in order to improve their own lot in life, they succeed in producing products and services their fellow citizens are willing to purchase because of the perceived advantages accruing to them.

When the entrepreneur becomes profitable, he is able to expand his business which often requires the purchase of additional land, the construction of new buildings, the purchase of more raw materials, and the hiring of more people. All those economic activities help other domestic businesses to grow and prosper which has a snowball effect throughout the economy. Successful "self-centered" business owners create vehicles through which their communities benefit. Since small businesses have a way of becoming big businesses, the role of enlightened government should be to create business-friendly environments rather than creating impediments to small business growth.

Smith understood that the basic component of free enterprise capitalism is the profit motive. And free enterprise almost always, sooner or later, creates competition. In order to grow his business and generate profits, each business owner must be competitive in his pricing which benefits the public by keeping prices as low as possible. Thus, Smith believed that the "invisible hand" does a much better job of regulating markets and prices than the heavy "visible hand" of government.

Most informed economists agree with Smith; too many mis-educated politicians and pundits don't.

Today, government controls in the form of unreasonable taxes, tariffs, quotas, price controls, and other counter-productive regulations sometimes make it irresistibly attractive for business owners to move their companies to off-shore locations where they don't have to deal with increasingly anti-business conditions. That, of course, results in a net loss to the short-sighted home country, a condition that can also have a snowball effect – in reverse.

Smith didn't use the phrase "laissez-faire," a French term that basically means "leave it be" in advancing his theory of economics even though it describes his theory in a nutshell. His friend Benjamin Franklin did use it in a book he co-authored in 1774, two years before Smith's seminal work was published. One of the most prominent and influential Founding Fathers, Ben Franklin was an outspoken devotee of free market capitalism including free trade.

Smith and the American Founding Fathers considered free trade and free enterprise, along with all other types of personal freedom, to be part of *natural law*, a term featured prominently in *The Declaration of Independence*. In the first paragraph, those who collaborated in writing the *Declaration* penned these famous words:

> *When in the course of human events, it becomes necessary for one people to dissolve the political bands which have connected them with another, and to assume among the powers of the earth, the separate and equal station to which the Laws of Nature and of Nature's God entitle them, a decent respect to the opinions of*

mankind requires that they should declare the causes which impel them to the separation."

From that powerful beginning, the authors went on to present their case for independence from the mother country. Economic freedom was a major justification for declaring their independence; Smith and his "invisible hand" concept provided the American Founding Fathers with a powerful rationale and a pattern for them to follow. Later, Smith's arguments helped to eliminate the mercantile system in Britain.

Smith and the Founding Fathers shared a distain for larger than necessary government and the corruption that always, sooner or later, accompanies over-arching political power. The *U.S. Constitution* was carefully written to give the power of government to the people in order to keep American leaders from behaving like royalty. "It is the highest impertinence and presumption in kings and ministers to pretend to watch over the economy of private people, and to restrain their expense," Smith wrote. "They are themselves, always, and without any exception, the greatest spendthrifts in the society." Does that ring a bell?

Was the publishing of Adam Smith's *The Wealth of Nations* in 1776 coincidental, coming as it did as the colonists were about to establish a new and different kind of society, or was it Providential? Based on the recorded words of the Founding Fathers, we can be certain they would have most assuredly seen it as the latter. Where their fight for freedom was concerned, they didn't believe in coincidences.

27.

Privateers Authorized to Attack British Ships

April 3, 1776

Going to war against the world's most powerful Navy with *no* real Navy of our own was a problem for the Second Continental Congress to contemplate. The best solution they could come up with was to enter into partnerships with privateers, in some minds a sanitized word for pirates. Members of the Continental Congress could hardly be blamed for feeling justified in thinking that desperate times sometimes require desperate measures.

Some colonists opposed such partnerships on moral grounds to which John Adams responded with this practical advice, perhaps with his tongue firmly planted in his cheek: "It is prudent not to put virtue to too serious a test. I would use American virtue as sparingly as possible lest we wear it out."

The tactic of privateering, sometimes referred to as "commerce raiding," had been practiced long before the colonists, out of necessity, adopted it as a strategy in their war for independence. Privateering began, according to some historians, in the Middle Ages and *is* permitted by international law. It's a practice by which private ship owners can be given incentives to arm their vessels for the purpose of capturing or destroying ships and supplies of an enemy wherever and whenever possible.

Traditionally, privateers have been offered a substantial percentage of the value of all properties captured, an enticing motivator. The practice could, according to international law, be authorized by Congress simply by issuing what were known as *Letters of Marque and Reprisal*, a practice they approved on April 3, 1776.

The legislation, officially entitled *Instructions to the Commanders of Private Ships or Vessels of War, which shall have Commissions of Letters of Marque and Reprisal, authorizing them to make Captures of British Vessels and Cargoes*, began with these instructions:

> *You may, by Force of Arms, attack, subdue, and take all Ships and other Vessels belonging to the inhabitants of Great Britain, on the High Seas, or between high-water and low-water Marks, except ships and Vessels bringing Persons who intend to settle and reside in the United Colonies, or bringing Arms, Ammunition of Warlike Stores to the said Colonies, for the Use of such inhabitants thereof as are Friends to the American Cause, which you shall suffer to pass unmolested, the Commanders thereof permitting a peaceable Search, and giving satisfactory Information of the Contents of the Ladings, and Destination of the Voyages.*
>
> *You may, by Force of Arms, attach, subdue, and take all Ships and other Vessels whatsoever carrying Soldiers Arms, Gun powder, Ammunition, Provisions, or any other contraband Goods, to any of the British Armies or Ships of War employed against these Colonies.*

The *Instructions* went on to lay out in some detail what the privateers could and could not do including this prohibition:

> *If you, or any of your Officers or Crew shall, in cold Blood, kill or maim, or by Torture or otherwise, cruelly, inhumanly, and contrary to common Usage and the Practice of civilized Nations in War, treat any Person or Persons surprised in the Ship or Vessel you shall take, the Offender shall be severely punished.*

Without *Letters of Marque*, privateers would continue to be treated as pirates under international law. For all practical purposes, privateers *were* licensed pirates. Once the war was concluded, the "license" was no longer valid.

American privateers soon appeared wherever British shipping was active, from the English Channel to the Colonies and everywhere in between. Most of the colonial privateers had learned their trade while still loyal subjects of the king, having served on British privateering vessels during the on going European wars.

The large number of American seaman who worked as privateers during the Revolutionary War became a valuable asset to George Washington who understood the vital military necessity of interfering with British supply lines. He also understood he had no other means by which he could accomplish that goal.

According to the *American Merchant Marine at War* web site, there may have been as many as 1,697 privately-owned ships operated by colonial privateers during the war. They are credited with capturing 2,283 enemy ships; Lloyds of London puts the number at 3,087. Congress kept the captured military supplies and pocketed the balance of any revenue received from the sale of other assets after the privateers had been paid.

Owners of ships converted to privateering use attracted crew members for their ships with advertisement like this one that appeared in Boston newspapers:

> *An invitation to all brave Seamen and Marines, who have an inclination to serve their Country and make their Fortunes.*
> *The grand Privateer ship DEANE, commanded by Elisha Hinman, Esq.; and prov'd to be a very capitol Sailor, will Sail on a Cruise against the Enemies of the United States of America, by the 20ᵗʰ instant. The DEANE mounts thirty Carriage Guns, and is excellently well calculated for Attacks, Defense and Pursuit – This therefore is to invite all those Jolly Fellows, who love their country, and want to make their fortunes at one Stroke, to repair immediately to the Rendezvous at the Head of His Excellency Governor Hancock's Wharf, where they will be received with a hearty Welcome by a Number of Brave Fellows there assembled, and treated with that excellent Liquor call'd Grog which is allow'd by all true Seamen, to be the Liquor of Life.*

Perhaps Providentially, ship owner John Hancock was president of the Second Continental Congress that enacted legislation providing for the issuing of *Letters of Marque and Reprisal*. In 1768, two of Hancock's ships, the *Lydia* and the *Liberty* had been seized by British officials who accused him of smuggling wine and other commodities. Hancock, who was well aware of the laws and customs of the sea, may have been the primary instigator of the *Marque and Reprisal* legislation and he, as president of that Congress, happily signed the bill.

Like most of his fellow Founders, Hancock believed in America's God-ordained future as a free nation: "I have the most animating confidence that the present noble struggle for liberty will terminate gloriously for America. And, having secured the approbation of our hearts by a faithful and unwearied discharge of our duty to our country, let us joyfully leave our concerns in the hands of Him who raiseth up and putteth down the empires and kingdoms of the earth as he pleaseth."

The power of *Congress* to issue *Letters of Marque and Reprisal* was included in the ratified version of the *U.S. Constitution* where it remains in Article 1, Section 8.

28.

Declaration of Independence Announced

July 8, 1776

"There! His Majesty can now read my name without spectacles, and can now double his reward of five hundred pounds for my head. That is my defiance!"

With those resolute words, John Hancock, as president of the Second Continental Congress, was first to sign *The Declaration of Independence* July 2, 1776. By July 4, all members had signed the historic document and four days after that, the first printed copy was read publicly prior to the ringing of what is now known as the Liberty Bell.

Hancock, along with the others signers of *The Declaration*, had been well aware that he may have just signed his own death warrant. After making his well known statement regarding the clarity of his over-sized signature, he went on to say, "There must be no pulling different ways; we must all hang together."

Rarely one to pass up a good straight line, Benjamin Franklin quipped, "Yes. We must all hang together, or most assuredly we shall all hang separately."

History has confirmed that uncommon courage, an uncompromising desire to be free, and faith in God characterized America's Founding Fathers. God and liberty were so tightly interwoven in their minds that their speeches and writings routinely included references to both. One of the best-remembered speeches that eventually inspired the writing of *The Declaration of Independence* and to the commencement of the war for independence was delivered by Patrick Henry just twenty-seven days prior to the battles of Lexington and Concord.

On March 23, 1775, Henry ended a fiery call to arms with these familiar words: "Is life so dear or peace so sweet as to be purchased at the price of chains and slavery? Forbid it, Almighty God. I know not what course others may take, but as for me, give me liberty or give me death!"

Most of the two hundred men generally considered to be worthy of the Founding Father label believed that a free and independent United States of America was ordained by the God of the Judeo-Christian Bible. John Adams, speaking to his fellow Continental Congress delegates July 1 said, "Before God, I believe the hour has come. My judgment approves this measure [*The Declaration of Independence*], and my whole heart is in it. All that I have, and all that I am, and all that I hope in this life, I am now ready here to stake upon it. And I leave off as I began, that live or die, survive or perish, I am for the *Declaration*. It is my living sentiment, and by the blessing of God it shall be my dying sentiment. Independence now, and independence for ever!"

The exceptional men who established American independence were supported by special women such as Abigail Adams whose letters to her husband John have become part of *Revolutionary War* history. While Adams was serving as a delegate to the Second Continental Congress in June of 1776, Abigail wrote, "I feel no anxiety at the large armament designed against us. The remarkable interpositions of heaven in our favor cannot be too gratefully acknowledged. He who fed the Israelites in the wilderness, who clothes the lilies of the field and who feeds the young ravens when they cry, will not forsake a people engaged in so right a cause, if we remember His loving kindness."

A majority of American Christians still agree with Samuel Adams statement regarding the *Declaration of Independence*: "The people seem to recognize this resolution as though it were a decree promulgated from heaven." Most patriotic Americans agree that these familiar opening words were heaven-inspired:

> *When in the Course of human events, it becomes necessary for one people to dissolve the political bands which have connected them with another, and to assume among the powers of the earth, the separate and equal station to which the Laws of Nature and of Nature's God entitle them, a decent respect to the opinions of*

mankind requires that they should declare the causes which impel them to the separation.

Those profound words were followed by this equally famous statement that expressed the colonists' right to rebel against despotic government:

> *We hold these truths to be self-evident, that all men are created equal, that they are endowed by their Creator with certain unalienable Rights, that among these are Life, Liberty, and the pursuit of Happiness. That to secure these rights, Governments are instituted among Men, deriving their just powers from the consent of the governed, That whenever any Form of Government becomes destructive of these ends, it is the Right of the People to alter or to abolish it, and to institute new Government, laying its foundation on such principles and organizing its powers in such form, as to them shall seem most likely to effect their Safety and Happiness. Prudence, indeed, will dictate that Governments long established should not be changed for light and transient causes; and accordingly all experience hath shewn, that mankind are more disposed to suffer, while evils are sufferable, than to right themselves by abolishing the forms to which they are accustomed. But when a long train of abuses and usurpations, pursuing invariably the same Object evinces a design to reduce them under absolute Despotism, it is their right, it is their duty, to throw off such Government, and to provide new Guards for their future security.*

After delineating their specific charges against the King, the colonists concluded with this statement of intent:

> *We, therefore, the Representatives of the united States of America, in General Congress, Assembled, appealing to the Supreme Judge of the world for the rectitude of our intentions, do, in the Name, and by Authority of the good People of these Colonies, solemnly publish and declare, That these United Colonies are, and of Right ought to be Free and Independent States; that they are Absolved from all Allegiance to the British Crown and that all political connection between them and the State of Great Britain, is and ought to be totally dissolved; and that as Free and*

> *Independent States, they have full Power to levy War, conclude*
> *Peace, contract Alliances, establish Commerce, and to do all other*
> *Acts and Things which Independent States may of right do. And*
> *for the support of this Declaration, with a firm reliance on the*
> *protection of divine Providence, we mutually pledge to each other*
> *our Lives, our Fortunes and our sacred Honor.*

Many misinformed people today have concluded the Founding Fathers and the foundational documents are merely relics that have no application to modern America. Andrew M. Allison, editor of *The Real Thomas Jefferson*, disagrees: "The nation these men [the Founding Fathers] built is now in the throes of a political, economic, social and spiritual crisis that has driven many to an almost frantic search for 'modern solutions.' Ironically, the solutions have been readily available for nearly two hundred years in the writings of our Founding Fathers. An honest examination of twentieth-century American history reveals that virtually every serious problem which has developed in our society can be traced to an ill-conceived departure from the sound principles taught by these great men. The citizen of today who turns back to the Founders' writings is often surprised by their timeless relevance – and perhaps equally dismayed that we have permitted ourselves to stray so far from such obvious truths."

The Liberty Bell that was used to call attention to the public reading of that foundational document was cast by Whitechapel Foundry in London in 1752. Many, but not all, believe that bell was originally ordered for the purpose of commemorating the 50th anniversary of Pennsylvania's *Charter of Privileges*. Because of a defect that resulted in the bell's cracking when first tested, it was recast by Pass and Stow of Philadelphia in 1753. The recast bell, currently on display in Independence National Historical Park in Philadelphia, was cracked in 1853 when rung at Chief Justice John Marshall's funeral.

Because references to God and His word were commonly part of the Founders' spoken and written words, it is no surprise that Isaac Norris, Pennsylvania Assembly Speaker who was in charge of ordering the Liberty Bell, had it inscribed with this portion of a Bible verse: *"Proclaim liberty throughout all the land unto all the inhabitants thereof – Lev. XXV, v. x."*

29.

Washington Crosses the Delaware River

December 25, 1776

George Washington's victory over Britain's mercenary troops at Trenton, New Jersey, on the morning of December 26, 1776, wasn't that big a deal as military victories go. But it was a very big deal psychologically for a number of reasons.

Most importantly, Washington's surprise victory broke a four-month losing streak that had begun with the Battle of Brooklyn. The Trenton victory came just a few days before the end of the year when his discouraged troops' enlistments were scheduled to expire and Washington was greatly concerned that large numbers of those troops could leave the army feeling the cause was lost; many had already deserted their units.

Many members of Congress had also begun to believe their dreams of independence were about to be shattered. And the general public, having heard nothing but bad news coming from the battle fields, was beginning to believe their Army was no match for the British regulars supported by the world's largest and most feared Navy.

A couple of weeks before the Trenton Victory, George Washington was so discouraged that he said, in a letter to his nephew, "In short, your imagination can scarce extend to a situation more distressing than mine. Our only dependence now is upon the speedy enlistment of a new army. If this fails, I think the game will be pretty well up, as, from disaffection and want of spirit and fortitude, the inhabitants, instead of resistance, are offering submission."

"I am resolved to take Trenton," Washington had said to one of his senior officers while preparing for the attack. To emphasize that resolve, Washington established an ominous password for the attack: "Victory or Death." He understood that his country desperately needed a military victory and he intended to provide it.

Washington's relatively small military victory negated all the negatives. Army morale immediately picked up and that had a positive effect on the looming re-enlistment crisis. Confidence in Washington's reputation as a military strategist and battlefield leader was re-established and increased the willingness of his demoralized troops to stay with him; it also helped to attract new recruits. Congress was encouraged to the point they offered cash bonuses for three-year enlistments and land grants to those who enlisted for the duration of the war. Soon, Washington had an army of 11,000 troops. A number of colonial militias were also available to augment his regulars.

News of the Trenton victory and other good news that soon followed provided a badly needed infusion of optimism into the spirit of the general public, an important factor in any war. It also sent a sobering message to the British: Under estimate us at your own peril. Military historians are pretty much in agreement that the Continental Army's victory at Trenton, closely followed by their victory at Princeton, was the turning point in America's war for independence.

Washington's victory was all the more remarkable because he achieved it with less than half of his Army. Due to extremely bad weather conditions, 3,000 of his 5,400 men and many of his artillery pieces were not able to make it across the Delaware River by the time designated for the attack to begin. The Hessian troops had been ready for an attack on Christmas Day after being alerted by loyalists and army deserters who somehow knew of Washington's plans.

Since that attack hadn't come when expected, Colonel Rahl, the Hessian commander, probably assumed it had been cancelled due to the bad weather that looked like it was going to continue for a while. In a Providential way, weather conditions caused him to decide not to send out patrols on December 26 which made it possible for Washington to greatly benefit from the element of surprise and undoubtedly contributed to the lopsided nature of his victory. While the Americans reported two soldiers killed and five wounded, the Hessian casualties were estimated at approximately twenty killed, ninety wounded and nine-hundred captured.

When people think of the Battle of Trenton, the first image that usually appears in their minds is that of the famous painting by Emanuel Leutze depicting Washington standing majestically in the bow of a boat as they crossed the icy Delaware River in the middle of that frigid winter night. What most people don't know is that the soldier depicted holding the flag is believed to be future president James Monroe, a Lieutenant in the Continental Army. Monroe suffered a serious wound from which he later recovered. Other notables who took part in the famous battle included future president James Madison, the future Chief Justice of the Supreme Court John Marshall, Aaron Burr, Alexander Hamilton, and William Washington.

Prior to accepting his appointment as Commander-in-Chief of the Continental Army, Washington had experienced sincere reservations regarding his ability to successfully fill that crucially important role. In a letter to his wife informing her of his appointment and his initial reluctance to accept it, he had explained that he felt "a consciousness of its being a trust too great for my capacity. I hope my undertaking this service is designed to answer some good purpose. I rely confidently on that Providence which has heretofore preserved and been bountiful to me."

Providence was often in the thoughts and on the lips of Washington before, during, and after the war. "It is the duty of all nations," he said, "to acknowledge the Providence of Almighty God, to obey His will, to be grateful for His benefits, and to humbly implore His protection and favor." On another occasion, he expressed a similar thought: "That man who refuses to see the hand of God in human events is worse than an infidel."

Washington's reputation for personally putting himself in danger at the forefront of the action in every battle was well known. Understanding his importance to the independence movement, Washington's men often tried to discourage him from taking such an exposed position. Perhaps to explain his seeming fearlessness, Washington said, "But by the all-powerful dispensations of Providence, I have been protected beyond all human probability or expectation; for I had four bullets through my coat, and two horses shot under me, yet escaped unhurt, although death was leveling my companions on every side of me."

An inscription at Mount Vernon pays this tribute to his many attributes:

Washington, the brave, the wise, the good,
Supreme in war, in council, and in peace.
Valiant without ambition, discreet without fear,
Confident without presumption.
In disaster, calm, in success, moderate;
In all, himself.
The hero, the patriot, the Christian.
The father of nations, the friend of mankind,
Who, when he had won all, renounced all,
And sought in the bosom of his family
And of nature, retirement,
And in the hope of religion, immortality.

30.

Marquis de Lafayette Joins the Patriots

June 13, 1777

One of the little-understood facts regarding the American Revolution is that hundreds of sympathizers, idealists, and adventurers from Europe joined the American patriots in their battle for independence against Great Britain. They realized something was going on in America that was unique in the history of the world, much of which had to do with freedom of religion, the bedrock of every individual freedom.

The Marquis de Lafayette and Baron de Kalb from France, Baron von Steuben from Prussia, and Casimir Pulaski from Poland are sometimes mentioned because each of them occupied important positions of leadership in the Continental Army. Pulaski, probably the least mentioned member of that group, eventually become known as the "father of the American cavalry." All four of the foreign-born patriots spent the awful winter of 1777-78 in or near Valley Forge, Pennsylvania, where they would have had contact with General George Washington and with each other.

Marquis (Marie Joseph Paul Yves Roch Gilbert du Motier) de Lafayette is the best known of the four primarily because of his close personal and official association with Washington. In addition to being a member of Washington's command staff, Lafayette is said to have loved his Commander-in-Chief as a father; he named his son George Washington Lafayette.

As a wealthy, idealistic nineteen-year-old nobleman and captain in the French Army, Lafayette made his decision, in defiance of the wishes of his prominent family *and* King Louis XVI, to offer his services to the Americans in their fight for freedom. His determination to join the patriots was based on his belief in the rights of man as promoted by the Masonic Lodge of which he was a member. It was through the Free Masons that Lafayette, Providentially, met Benjamin Franklin who recommended to Washington that he find a place on his staff for the experienced French Army officer.

Lafayette arrived in Georgetown, South Carolina, June 13, 1777, at what many historians consider the "darkest hour" of the colonists' fight for independence. So determined was Lafayette to join what he called the "holy cause of liberty," that he purchased his own ship, *La Victoire*, to make the voyage after King Louis had prevented his departure on another vessel.

Shortly after his arrival in the colonies, Lafayette, who was originally recruited by Silas Deane with the assurance of commissioned officer status in the Continental Army, traveled to Philadelphia expecting to receive the promised commission. Initially, Congress balked at the idea of making him superior in rank to experienced colonial officers. As a result of Lafayette's persistence, Congress became especially impressed with his offer to serve without pay which convinced them of his sincerity and his dedication to the cause of freedom. He received his commission, accompanied by this proclamation, on July 31:

> *"Whereas, the Marquis de La Fayette, out of his great zeal in the cause of liberty in which the United States are engaged, has left his family and connections, and, at his own expense, come over to offer his service to the United States, without pension or particular allowance, and is anxious to risk his life in our cause;*
> *"Resolved, that his services be accepted, and that in consideration of his zeal, illustrious family and connections, he have the rank and commission of a Major-General in the army of the United States."*

Lafayette fought in the Battle of Brandywine where he was wounded, commanded troops in the Battles of Barren Hill (now known as Lafayette Hill), and Monmouth, before spending the winter with Washington and his troops at Valley Forge.

Soon after the French signed a formal treaty of alliance with the Americans on February 6, 1778, Britain declared war on France leaving Lafayette in somewhat of a quandary. He asked for permission to return to France in order to clarify his position since both France and America were officially at war with Great Britain. The source of his quandary was that he considered himself a loyal citizen of both America and France.

During his stay in France, Lafayette was instrumental in obtaining much needed financial and military aid, including additional French troops, for the colonial cause, winning praise from his friend Benjamin Franklin. After being given permission to return to America in 1780, he rejoined Washington's forces.

Lafayette was extensively involved in the campaign that eventually brought about the surrender of British General Cornwallis at Yorktown, Virginia, October 19, 1781. Two months after that decisive victory, which, for all practical purposes successfully ended the American war for independence, Lafayette returned to France where he worked with Thomas Jefferson in establishing trade agreements between France and America.

When the French Revolution began in 1789, Lafayette was commander of the French National Guard and a member of the *Estates General*. As vice president of the legislative body, Lafayette proposed the *Declaration of the Rights of Man* which defined the individual and collective rights of French citizens and states. When the violently radical anti-Christian Jacobins led by Robespierre prevailed, Lafayette attempted to leave the country but was apprehended and imprisoned in Austria for five years. In 1797, Napoleon freed Lafayette who then returned to France. After the downfall of Napoleon, Lafayette resumed his political career as a member of the French Chamber of Deputies.

Lafayette occupied a warm spot in the hearts of Americans that erupted, much to his astonishment, when he accepted an invitation "to be the nation's guest" from President James Monroe in 1824 during which he visited all twenty-four of the existing states. Here's how Henry W. Elson, in his book entitled *Sidelights on American History*, described the public outpouring of admiration that overwhelmed Lafayette:

> *The joyful welcome, the universal homage, with which General Lafayette was received by the American people have never been equaled before nor since in our history. The few remaining*

soldiers of the Revolution, now tottering with age, gathered around him, and their eyes were bathed in tears as they beheld his benignant face and recalled the memories of the past. Men and women, youths and maidens, left their homes and hastened to the cities which he visited to look upon the countenance of this hero of a past generation, and to join in the universal shout of welcome.

"Lafayette had been cordially invited to visit our country, and he expected a warm welcome; but he had not counted on such an unreserved outburst of joyful acclamation from the whole people. He had expected to land quietly and engage private lodgings; but when he found that he was to be a public guest, that the people had made the most elaborate preparations to do him honor, he was overcome with emotion. His eyes flowed with tears, and pressing both hands upon his heart, he exclaimed, 'it will burst.'"

During his visit to Boston, Lafayette was publicly honored with this short but fitting poem by Charles Sprague:

Our fathers in glory shall sleep
That gathered with thee to the fight;
But their sons will eternally keep
The tablet of gratitude bright.
We bow not the neck and we bow not the knee,
But our hearts, Lafayette, we surrender to thee.

Lafayette returned to Paris in 1825 where he remained until his death in 1834.

31.

Articles of Confederation Approved By Congress

November 15, 1777

On July 12, 1776, John Dickinson presented Congress with his draft of a plan entitled the *Articles of Confederation and Perpetual Union*. It was the colonists' first attempt at designing a governing document that would bind the colonies together, a sensitive piece of business.

Dickinson's draft had provided for a strong Federal government with the power, among others, to levy taxes. On November 15, 1777, after sixteen months and much wrangling, Congress approved a watered-down version that was eventually ratified in March of 1781. Although, the *Articles of Confederation* became the first constitution of the United States of America, the seeds of its own eventual destruction were sewn into it by its originators because of their fear of a strong Federal government. Members of Congress were trying to be very careful to design a governing document that would prevent the possibility of a British-style monarchy ever being established in America.

The *Articles* gave Congress no power to impose taxes on the individual states, a condition that severely impacted the confederation's effectiveness, especially regarding its ability to properly maintain the Continental Army. Lack of money to pay soldiers at times made it difficult to enlist or retain adequate numbers of fighting men and often made it impossible to properly equip them. Without the power to tax, the Federal government basically had to rely on donations from the states. George

Washington called the confederation as described in the *Articles* as "little more than a shadow without substance." History proved the accuracy of Washington's characterization.

Congress was given the power to borrow money, declare war, and enter into treaties but only after securing the consent of nine states. The *Articles* did not include a provision for an independent executive nor did it establish a judicial branch. Far too often individual states ignored Congress, especially after the conclusion of the war, which reduced it in many ways to an advisory body with no power to enforce its edicts. Most of the thirteen colonies, while recognizing a common interest in separating themselves from Great Britain, still thought of themselves first and foremost as independent states and often acted accordingly.

History has proven that the reservations of both the Federalists and the anti-Federalists were justified. The Federalists, with whom Dickinson sided, were correct in that the *Articles of Confederation* did not provide for a central government with enough power to carry out its responsibilities. The anti-Federalists were correct in that they were convinced a Federal government with too much power could someday trample on the states' rights they were trying so hard to preserve. Most of the Founders, including the Federalists, would be aghast at the power today's gargantuan Federal government exercises over states and individuals.

Dickinson had been appointed by the Second Continental Congress to head up a thirteen-member committee given the assignment of writing the *Articles* because of his well-known writing abilities. Some historians have speculated that Dickinson, had he been convinced sooner that armed conflict was the only way to throw off the ever-increasing economic shackles imposed on the colonies, might have been given the assignment of producing the *Declaration of Independence* rather than Thomas Jefferson. He had initially established his reputation as an expositor in 1765 with his prominent role in producing the *Declaration of Rights and Grievances* protesting the Stamp Tax. In 1775, he added to his reputation by authoring the *Declaration on the Causes and Necessity of Taking up Arms*. Dickinson's many important writings earned him the title "Penman of the Revolution."

Dickinson's *Farmer's Letters to the Inhabitants of the British Colonies* has been recognized as one of the most effective expressions of colonial rights generated during the pre-war period. "But while Devine Providence, that gave me existence in a land of freedom, permits my head to think, my lips to speak, and my hand to move, I shall so highly and gratefully value the blessing received as to take care that my silence and inactivity shall not give my implied assent to any act, degrading my brethren and myself from the birthright, wherewith heaven itself 'hath made us free,'" he wrote, placing himself among his fellow Founders who believed a free and independent America was God ordained.

In 1775, he had alienated many of the "patriots," as those who believed war was the only acceptable alternative were called, by authoring the *Olive Branch Petition* and other written and spoken public utterances favoring reconciliation if at all possible. Once firmly convinced that reconciliation with the mother country was not possible, Dickinson dedicated himself to the cause, including enlisting in the Pennsylvania militia. The British, perhaps more than his own countrymen, recognized his prominence in generating the rebellion when they burned his house to the ground in 1776.

By 1786, realization had set in that the *Articles of Confederation* as written were much less than adequate as the governing document for an emerging nation taking its place as a major player on the world stage. What later became known as the Constitutional Convention was convened in Philadelphia in May of 1787 ostensibly to revise the *Articles* but most of the delegates understood they were there to produce a new constitution. Dickinson was selected as a delegate to the Convention by his fellow Pennsylvanians.

The *Articles* were officially replaced by the U.S. Constitution June 21, 1788.

32.

France Recognizes U.S. as An Independent Nation

December 17, 1777

Still smarting from the loss of his lucrative foothold in the American colonies to the British as a result of the *Seven Years' War*, French King Louis XVI was very much inclined to openly assist the colonists in their fight for independence from his nemesis King George III. He didn't, however, believe during the early months of the fighting that the colonists' chances of success were very good. At that point, he thought it was unwise to gamble money, military assets, and manpower on what could turn out to be a losing cause.

While King Louis understood that declaring a formal alliance with the colonies would be tantamount to a declaration of war against Britain, he surreptitiously authorized unofficial financial and military aid. Prominent French citizens also assisted an American delegation in generating individual and group financial contributions that were forwarded to the American rebels. That delegation, appointed by the Second Continental Congress in 1776, was composed of Benjamin Franklin, Silas Deane, and Arthur Lee.

Watching developments in the colonies carefully, the King was encouraged by George Washington's victories at Trenton and Princeton at the end of 1776. When Washington defeated General John Burgoyne's army at Saratoga in the fall of 1777, the French government became convinced it was time to take the step of recognizing the United States as an independent nation. Charles Gravier, the French Foreign Minister, announced that recognition on December 17, 1777.

The next step, a formal *Treaty of Alliance* between France and America, was signed February 6, 1778. As expected, that treaty provoked a declaration of war against France by England. King George III had, for all practical purposes, already declared war on the colonies in August of 1775 when he proclaimed them to be in a state of rebellion.

In conjunction with the *Treaty of Alliance*, France and America entered into the *Treaty of Amity and Commerce* that officially established a mutually advantageous commercial relationship between the two nations. Those two pacts were the first foreign treaties entered into by the American government.

The most important economic provision in the *Commerce Treaty* was the establishment of Most Favored Nation status between the U.S. and France. Other major points of agreement included a declaration of peace and friendship, a pledge of safe harbor for each other's ships while in the other's territory, and an agreement to protect U.S. and French ships from privateers. The *Treaty* also stated that neither country would reconcile with the British before American independence was officially recognized. Franklin signed both of the vitally important treaties for America.

When informed that Franklin had been successful in getting the treaties signed, Washington said, in a letter to Congress, that "no event was ever received with a more heart felt joy." Washington celebrated the new alliance with France by issuing this general order to his army: "Upon a signal given, the whole Army will Huzza! Long Live the King of France!"

French support for the American cause proved to be a major factor in shortening the war and in winning the colonists' fight for independence. In addition to providing desperately needed financial aid, the French government sent an estimated 12,000 soldiers and 32,000 sailors to assist the American armed forces. Franklin's French connections had finally paid off handsomely for the colonists.

Before the American Revolution began, Franklin had already enjoyed an international reputation for "down home" wisdom through his highly popular serial publications known as *Poor Richard's Almanack.*

The *Almanack*, described by Franklin as "the wisdom of many ages and nations," eventually became second only to the Bible in popularity. Published in the colonies from 1732 to 1758, and reprinted in France and England, *Poor Richard* was familiar to many Frenchmen who assumed the fictional Richard represented the philosophy of the author. They often referred to Franklin as "le bon Quaker" (the good/clever Quaker). During the Revolutionary War, the French King named a ship he gave to John Paul Jones the *Bonhomme Richard.*

When Franklin had first arrived in France in 1767, his social charms and witty conversational skills had helped to project him into a position of respect among an influential element in French society that included many who occupied high positions in government. When he returned to France after signing the *Declaration of Independence* he was honored as a leader of the American Revolution and welcomed back by those influential friends.

Franklin, born and raised in a Puritan family, had been instilled early in life with strong beliefs in self-government, personal freedom, and vigorous opposition to tyranny. Josiah Franklin, Benjamin's father, had a favorite Bible quote, (Proverbs 22:29) that greatly influenced the way his son lived his life: "Seest thou a man diligent in his calling, he shall stand before Kings." Benjamin Franklin stood confidently before the powerful of his day, a standing that may have served a Providential purpose.

In concert with most of his fellow Founding Fathers, Franklin believed that the establishment of a free and independent America was foreordained. During an exasperatingly unproductive time during the 1787 *Constitutional Convention* in Philadelphia, Franklin delivered this sobering admonition that many feel saved the Convention from disbanding before they could accomplish their mission:

> *In the beginning of the contest with Great Britain, when we were sensible of danger, we had daily prayer in this room for the Divine protection – Our prayers, Sir, were heard and they were graciously answered. All who were engaged in the struggle must have observed frequent instances of a superintending Providence in our favor. To that kind Providence, we owe this happy opportunity of consulting in peace on the means of establishing our future national felicity. And have we now forgotten this powerful Friend? Or do we imagine we no longer need His assistance?*

I have lived, Sir, a long time, and the longer I live, the more convincing proofs I see of this truth – that God governs in the affairs of men. And if a sparrow cannot fall to the ground without His notice, is it probable that an empire can rise without His aid? We have been assured in the Sacred Writings that except the Lord build the house, they labor in vain that build it. I firmly believe this. I also believe that, without His concurring aid, we shall succeed in this political building no better than the builders of Babel.

With Franklin's admonition in mind, the convention delegates went back to work with renewed determination and soon completed the U.S. Constitution that many have called *The Miracle of Philadelphia*.

Franklin died April 17, 1790. From his estate, a walking stick that had been presented to him in France was willed to his friend and fellow Founding Father George Washington. Franklin's message to Washington that accompanied the bequeathal read: "My fine crab-tree walking-stick, with a gold head curiously wrought in the form of a cap of liberty, I give to my friend, and the friend of mankind, General Washington. If it were a scepter, he has merited it and would become it."

In turn, Washington included these words of praise in a eulogy when informed of Franklin's death:

Venerated for benevolence, admired for talents; esteemed for patriotism; beloved for philanthropy.

33.

Baron von Steuben Joins Washington at Valley Forge

February 23, 1778

During their difficult struggle for independence, American rebels often received timely help from unexpected sources, occurrences that reinforced a generally held belief that the invisible hand of Providence was advancing their cause.

One of the unexpected *human* resources who became especially valuable to the colonists' fight for independence was a former Prussian Army officer who arrived in America when his expertise was badly needed. Today, most Americans aren't familiar with his name: Baron Friedrich Wilhelm Rudolf Gerhard August von Steuben.

Steuben, as a young officer in the Prussian Army, had served with distinction in the *Seven Years' War* in Europe and had risen quickly to the rank of Captain. Based on his combat record, Steuben had been selected to serve on the General Command staff of Frederick the Great where he had an opportunity to learn military strategy while working closely with the renowned warrior-king. But his budding military career was ended abruptly when, as a result of differences with a fellow officer more favored by the King, Steuben was discharged from the army.

Upon becoming dissatisfied with the bureaucratic career he had pursued after leaving the army, Steuben traveled to Paris in 1777 in search of employment in a foreign army. It was there that he was introduced to Benjamin Franklin by Count Claude Louis, French Minister of War, who happened to mention Steuben's quest to his American friend. Based on background information provided by the Count, Franklin understood how a man of Steuben's experience could provide the struggling Continental Army with an unusually well-qualified source of training in how to fight a war against a modern European army. Because Steuben understood the American Army could offer him the kind of opportunity he was seeking, he let it be known he was more than interested.

Perhaps Providentially, a year earlier George Washington had been experiencing feelings of exasperation that he described in a letter to Lund Washington, his nephew: "I am wearied to death all day with a variety of perplexing circumstances, disturbed at the conduct of the militia, whose behavior and want of discipline has done great injury to the other troops, who never had officers, except in a few instances, worth the bread they eat. In confidence I tell you that I never was in such an unhappy, divided state since I was born." Unbeknownst to Washington, the "invisible hand" in which he put so much stock, was already at work on his behalf. After his meeting with Steuben, Franklin sent a letter to Washington in which he recommended that America's overworked and understaffed Commander-in-Chief make the experienced Prussian Army officer a member of his staff, a recommendation Washington quickly acted upon.

Steuben and his entourage landed in Portsmouth, New Hampshire, in December; he arrived at Valley Forge in February and immediately went to work. Washington was so impressed with Steuben's abilities that he appointed him Inspector General of the Continental Army with the rank of Major General. One of Steuben's first assignments was to prepare a formal training plan.

A few months later, Steuben's plan was expanded and published as *Regulations for the Order and Discipline of the Troops of the United States*. They replaced a variety of existing field manuals and provided much-needed unity in training procedures and standards. His *Blue Book*, the soldiers' shortened name for the *Regulations*, was based on standards established by Frederick the Great whose army was considered by most military historians as the best in Europe at that time.

Prior to Steuben's arrival, Washington's tactics had been based on a hit and run strategy as the only option available to him. As the weaker force, the Continental Army had, in the early stages of the war, mostly fought a series of guerrilla strikes, hitting the British where they were the weakest to try to wear them down while buying time. That strategy had begun to change in February of 1778 when France joined the war on the side of the colonists and later when Steuben's training methods began to have their desired effect.

Working together, Steuben and Washington were able to convert the raw material of a ragtag army into a well trained and disciplined fighting force that, along with their new French allies, would eventually pursue the war to a successful conclusion. Steuben's *Regulations* remained in use as the American Army's drill manual until the War of 1812.

When he arrived in America, Steuben was able to speak little, if any, English which made it necessary for him to have translators available at all times. He wrote his *Regulations* in French; historians have written that Alexander Hamilton and Nathanael Greene assisted Steuben in translating his manual into English.

During the early days of his on-field training drills, Steuben frequently became impatient and frustrated with the lack of progress demonstrated by his men which often prompted him to beckon his translator to "Come here and swear for me!"

Once again, the right man was available at the right time to fill a vital need.

34.

Cornwallis Surrenders at Yorktown

<u>October 19, 1781</u>

The decisive battle in the American colonies' long war for independence ended October 19, 1781, when British General Earl Cornwallis surrendered his remaining forces of approximately 7,000 soldiers and 1,000 seamen to a numerically superior combined American and French army supported by a fleet of French ships. Although the war wouldn't be officially concluded until the *Treaty of Paris* was signed two years later, the Battle of Yorktown was the last major Revolutionary War battle fought on American soil.

In August, General Cornwallis, after fighting a series of resource-draining battles with various American forces in the Carolinas, moved his troops into Yorktown, Virginia. A combination of experienced guerilla warfare leaders, including Francis (the Swamp Fox) Marion, Thomas Sumter and Nathanael Greene, had chased Cornwallis out of the Carolinas with their effective harassing tactics. Against the advice of fellow British General Sir Henry Clinton, Cornwallis selected Yorktown as a sanctuary and a base with the idea in mind of fortifying the existing port town and securing control of Chesapeake Bay. History has proven that he should have listened to Clinton; that fateful decision set the stage for British capitulation.

When Washington was informed that Cornwallis and his troops were encamped at Yorktown, he, with input from French General Jean-Baptiste Rochambeau, recognized an opportunity to strike a major blow against the British. He ordered General Lafayette and his 5,000-man army already present in Virginia to do everything possible to eliminate any chance of Cornwallis escaping by land while Washington, Rochambeau and French Admiral Francois de Grasse set a land-sea trap. Washington needed time to move his troops from New York and Rochambeau's troops from Rhode Island while at the same time coordinating his plan with the operations of de Grasse's fleet operating just off the American coast.

The combined armies of Washington and Rochambeau began their march south on August 14; by September 14 there were an additional 12,000 allied troops and militiamen in the Yorktown area including 8,000 of Rochambeau's French regulars. With the American and French troops in place surrounding the British Army, Washington began the siege of Yorktown with a heavy artillery bombardment.

An objective vital to the October 19 victory had been successfully accomplished September 5 when a French fleet of twenty-eight ships had prevented a nineteen-ship British fleet from delivering supplies and fresh troops to Cornwallis. Under the command of Admiral de Grasse, the superior French fleet also stood in the way of a rescue of the British army by their navy. For a welcome change, everything was working to the advantage of the forces under Washington's command. Lord Cornwallis and his officers were suddenly left with the realization that the only prudent option available to them was to ask for terms of surrender.

American, French, and British leaders signed the *Articles of Capitulation* on October 19. The gentlemanly-worded agreement contained fourteen articles detailing the terms of surrender, many of which guaranteed humane and respectful treatment of British personnel and "loyalists" (colonists who had remained loyal to the mother country). The language of the preamble is typical of the diplomatic language of its time:

> *Settled between his Excellency General WASHINGTON, Commander-in-Chief of the combined Forces of America and France; his Excellency the Count de ROCHAMBEAU, Lieut. General of the armies of the King of France, Great Cross of the Royal and Military Order of St. Louis, commanding the auxiliary Troops of His Most Christian Majesty in America; and his Excellency the Count de GRASSE, Lieut. General of the naval Armies of His Most Christian Majesty, Commander of the Order*

of St. Louis, commander-in-chief the naval Army of France in the Chesapeake, on the one Part

AND

The Right Hon. Earl CORNWALLIS, Lieut. General of his Britannic Majesty Forces, commanding the Garrisons of York and Gloucester; and THOMAS SYMONDS, Esq; commanding his Britannic Majesty naval Forces in York river in Virginia, on the other part.

For the formal surrender ceremony, French and American troops lined up facing each other with a space between them through which the British soldiers marched to lay down their arms. Appropriately, a British band played "The World Turned Upside Down." When that part of the ceremony was completed, an American band played "Yankee Doodle Dandy" as the victorious troops jeered the humiliated British soldiers – during the war, British troops had often referred to American soldiers as Yankee Doodles. While dignitaries on both sides tried to maintain a proper decorum, the American troops enjoyed the last laugh.

After the *Articles of Capitulation* were formerly signed, the two sides began to discuss a treaty of peace that would declare the United States of America to be a free and independent nation. There were many issues yet to be settled, including territorial ones, but the shooting that had begun April 19, 1775, with "the shot heard 'round the world" had officially come to an end.

35.

Great Seal of the U.S. Adopted by Congress

June 20, 1782

As early as 1774, independence-minded colonists had begun thinking about national symbols and ideas for a motto that would appropriately represent the American spirit and the growing desire for freedom they believed was their destiny. But it wasn't until 1782 that a symbol and motto were finally combined in the form of a dignified and meaningful design that Congress could enthusiastically accept.

Before the independence movement, America was symbolized most often in Europe by various Indian caricatures; the earliest symbol was an Indian child. As the country increased in stature, that symbolism was replaced by caricatures of Indians, usually female, progressing in age and maturity.

After America became an independent nation, Europeans often symbolized America as an Indian Chief taking his place among caricatures of various old world countries. Drawings of animals – buffalo, deer, beaver (usually chopping down an unusually large tree symbolizing England), and rattlesnakes – later replaced the Indian as symbols of America.

As part of the historic meeting of the Second Continental Congress, the same meeting during which the delegates had approved a motion to declare independence from Great Britain, a three-man committee was appointed to prepare a Great Seal to graphically represent the independent country they foresaw. After some time and many attempts, committee members John Adams, Thomas Jefferson, and Benjamin Franklin were unable to produce an overall design acceptable to Congress, but their work did produce one element that eventually became part of the finished product. The words *E pluribus unum* (out of many, one), suggested by Jefferson, would later become the official national motto for an independent America.

When a second committee also failed to come up with an acceptable design, Congress assigned Charles Thomson, permanent secretary of the Continental Congress and a friend of Benjamin Franklin, the task of coming up with ideas for a Great Seal. Thomson enlisted his friend William Barton, an attorney who was familiar with "the laws of heraldry," to assist him.

After reviewing all previous attempts to design a national "Coat of Arms," Thomson and Barton put together a powerful combination of elements that would satisfy the desires of most members of Congress. The center of their design was an eagle with a shield of thirteen alternating red and white stripes covering its breast. One claw held an olive branch and the other held a bundle of arrows. In the eagle's beak is a banner on which is written *E pluribus unum*; above its head is a gold circle around a blue field with thirteen white stars.

Congress immediately, if not unanimously, saw the desirability of the eagle as a strong symbol of freedom and power with its huge, powerful wings, legendary eyesight, fearsome talons, and ability to soar majestically above the earth. Christian members of Congress, and that included most of them, were reminded of Isaiah 40:31: "Yet those who wait for the Lord will mount up with wings like eagles, they will run and not get tired, they will walk and not become weary."

Franklin, who got most things right regarding the founding of the United States, didn't agree that an eagle was the best choice as a symbol. Modern day Americans may be amused to learn that he preferred the turkey which has come to symbolize anything but majesty and power.

"I wish that the bald eagle had not been chosen as the representative of our country," Franklin said. "He is a bird of bad moral character; he does not get his living honestly. You may have seen him perched on some dead tree where, too lazy to fish for himself, he watches the labor of the fishing-hawk, and when that diligent bird has at length taken a fish, and is bearing it to its nest for the support of his mate and young one, the bald eagle pursues him and takes it from him...For a truth, the turkey is in comparison a much more respectable bird, and a true original native of

America…a bird of courage, and would not hesitate to attack a grenadier of the British guards, who should presume to invade his farmyard with a red coat on." Franklin's dim view of eagles didn't impress his fellow members.

Although most Americans today are not familiar with Thomson, his credentials as a Founding Father are verified in a number of ways including the little-known fact that he, in his official capacity as Secretary to the Continental Congress, along with John Hancock, as President of the Congress, were the only people who signed the original *Declaration of Independence*. The others added their signatures at a later date.

Besides the prominence he earned as Secretary to Congress from 1774 to 1789, Thomson, was known for having translated the *Old Testament* from Greek to English. His many other writings included *A synopsis of the Four Evangelists, or a Regular History of the Conception, Birth, Doctrine, Miracles, Death, Resurrection, and Ascension of Jesus Christ, in the Words of the Evangelists."*

An entry in *Appleton's Cyclopædia of American Biography* described Thomson as "the soul of that political [the Continental Congress] body. It went on to say, "He visited Philadelphia, met Benjamin Franklin there, and was brought to the notice of many other eminent men. His reputation for veracity was spread even among the Indian tribes, and when the Delawares adopted him into their nation in 1756, they called him in their tongue 'man of truth.' In his autobiography, Reverend Ashbel Green said it was common to say that a statement was 'as true as if Charles Thomson's name was to it.'"

Born in Ireland, Thomson was said to have been "one of the first to take his stand with the colonists, and he exercised immense influence, owing to the confidence of the people in his ability and integrity."

John Adams paid him this tribute: "He was the Sam Adams of Philadelphia, the life of the cause of liberty."

As is true of so much early American history, the story of Charles Thomson again points out how often Providence provided the right man at the right place at the right time to perfectly accomplish an important task.

36.

Treaty of Paris Signed Ending Revolutionary War

<u>September 3, 1783</u>

Because of the number of major powers involved to various degrees, the treaty granting freedom and independence to America required uncommon diplomatic skills and some additional time to complete. It was negotiated concurrently with other interrelated treaties among Britain, France, Spain, and the Netherlands,

Following the October 19 American victory at Yorktown, the British people and their Parliament had concluded the war was no longer worth the considerable cost, especially since their treasury had been depleted earlier by the Seven Years' War. Providentially, the British government of Lord Frederick North had recently been replaced by one much more favorably disposed toward America. In April of 1782, Parliament voted to end the war and began preparation of a preliminary peace agreement that was signed in November.

The treaty that formally ended the war, called the *Second Treaty of Paris* (the *First Treaty of Paris* ended the Seven Years' War in 1763) was signed September 3, 1783. John Adams, Benjamin Franklin, and John Jay signed for America. It was ratified by the Continental Congress on January 14, 1784.

That all parties to the treaties were primarily Christian in faith and believers in God's Providential role in world events was made clear by the following unmistakable language included in the preamble:

In the name of the most holy and undivided Trinity.

It having pleased the Divine Providence to dispose the hearts of the most serene and most potent Prince George the Third, by the grace of God, king of Great Britain, France, and Ireland, defender of the faith, duke of Brunswick and Lunebourg, arch- treasurer and prince elector of the Holy Roman Empire etc., and of the United States of America, to forget all past misunderstandings and differences that have unhappily interrupted the good correspondence and friendship which they mutually wish to restore, and to establish such a beneficial and satisfactory intercourse, between the two countries upon the ground of reciprocal advantages and mutual convenience as may promote and secure to both perpetual peace and harmony; and having for this desirable end already laid the foundation of peace and reconciliation by the Provisional Articles signed at Paris on the 30th of November 1782, by the commissioners empowered on each part, which articles were agreed to be inserted in and constitute the Treaty of Peace proposed to be concluded between the Crown of Great Britain and the said United States, but which treaty was not to be concluded until terms of peace should be agreed upon between Great Britain and France and his Britannic Majesty should be ready to conclude such treaty accordingly; and the treaty between Great Britain and France having since been concluded, his Britannic Majesty and the United States of America, in order to carry into full effect the Provisional Articles above mentioned, according to the tenor thereof, have constituted and appointed...to be plenipotentiaries for the concluding and signing the present definitive treaty; who after having reciprocally communicated their respective full powers have agreed upon and confirmed the following articles.

Ten articles were listed that provided details of the agreement, the most important of which included British recognition of U.S. independence and the delineation of boundaries established by the peace treaty. Those boundaries were defined as the Mississippi River on the west, Canada on the north, and Florida and the Gulf of Mexico on the south. All the unsettled land between the Appalachian Mountains and the Mississippi River were henceforth to be under the authority of the United States as a whole rather than divided up between individual states. That large area was primarily occupied by various Indian tribes loosely allied with Britain. Even though they had not been previously consulted, those tribes formally recognized U.S. control, a concession by the British that set the stage for many years of often-times violent conflict as America expanded to the west.

Britain, in a separate but related treaty with Spain, had ceded Florida to Spain and the Bahamas had again become the property of Great Britain. Also in a separate treaty, Britain and France had exchanged captured territories and redefined some disputed fishing rights.

At last, the colonists' dream of independence was memorialized in the form of an international treaty. The United States of America was now poised to assume an expanding role on the world stage.

In announcing his decision to step down as commander-in-chief of the Continental Army, Washington wrote an open letter to the nation in which he reminded his fellow citizens of the opportunities and responsibilities lying in wait for them on that stage:

> *The citizens of America, placed in the most enviable condition, as the sole Lords and Proprietors of a vast Tract of Continent, comprehending all the various soils and climates of the World, and abounding with all the necessaries and conveniences of life, are now by the late satisfactory pacification, acknowledged to be possessed of absolute freedom and Independency; They are, from this period, to be considered as the Actors on a most conspicuous Theatre, which seems to be peculiarly designated by Providence for the display of human greatness and felicity; Here, they are not only surrounded with every thing which can contribute to the completion of private and domestic enjoyment, but Heaven has crowned all its other blessings, by giving a fairer opportunity for political happiness, than any other Nation has ever been favored with. Nothing can illustrate these observations more forcibly, than a recollection of the happy conjuncture of times and circumstances, under which our Republic assumed its rank among the Nations...At this auspicious period, the United States came into existence as a Nation, and if their Citizens should not be completely free and happy, the fault will be entirely their own.*
>
> *I now make it my earnest prayer, that God would have you, and the State over which you preside, in his holy protection, that he would incline the hearts of the Citizens to cultivate a spirit of subordination and obedience to Government, to entertain*

a brotherly affection and love for one another, for their fellow Citizens of the United States at large, and particularly for their brethren who have served in the Field, and finally, that he would most graciously be pleased to dispose us all, to do Justice, to love mercy, and to demean ourselves with that Charity, humility and pacific temper of mind, which were the Characteristicks of the Divine Author of our blessed Religion, and without an humble imitation of whose example in these things, we can never hope to be a happy Nation.

The world would never be the same. The geopolitical center of gravity shifted on September 3, 1783.

37.

Constitutional Convention Begins in Philadelphia

May 25, 1787

When delegates to the Constitutional Convention that first convened on May 25, in Philadelphia finally completed their work in September, two key members of that eminent group, George Washington, convention President, and James Madison, often called "the Father of the Constitution," pronounced it a miracle. Many still refer to the Convention that produced the *U. S. Constitution*, the oldest written national constitution still in use today, as the *Miracle of Philadelphia*.

Generating a document that leaders of thirteen separate "republics," as they saw themselves, could accept as the supreme law of the land would seem to meet *Webster's Dictionary* definition of a miracle – "an event or action that apparently contradicts known scientific laws and is hence thought to be due to supernatural causes, esp. to an act of God." We know from the Founding Fathers' writings that is exactly what they believed had happened.

By 1783, it had become more and more obvious to a growing number of American leaders that there were serious defects built into the *Articles of Confederation*, America's first "constitution," that needed to be rectified in order to protect the security and economic well-being of the new nation. Alexander Hamilton, an early supporter of a strong federal government, described the problem as he and his fellow Federalists saw it: "The fundamental defect is a want of power in Congress...But the

Confederation itself is defective, and requires to be altered. It is neither fit for war nor peace. The idea of an uncontrollable sovereignty in each State over its internal police will defeat the other powers given to Congress, and make our union feeble and precarious."

Those weaknesses did not go unnoticed by existing world powers including America's immediate neighbors – England to the north and Spain to the South – who, many suspected, could very well have been awaiting the right time to reassert their power over a loose confederation of vulnerable states.

The Massachusetts uprising known as Shays' Rebellion provided ammunition for the Federalists to use in making their point about the need for a strong central government, one that would have the power to deal with external threats or internal insurrections. They pointed out that a hastily-assembled local militia had been the only tool available to quell the rebellion in Massachusetts.

On paper, the *Articles* gave Congress power to act as a national governing body, but that document provided Congress with no effective way to enforce those "paper" powers. In matters requiring a military response, Congress could only *request* money or troops from the states, a weakness forcefully brought to the attention of Congress by the 1783 *Newburgh Conspiracy.* It had also become obvious that Congress had no power to regulate commerce nor did it have the power to enforce settlements in an increasing number of quarrels between states. At least one historian described Congress as "penniless and powerless."

Acting on a recommendation by Madison in January of 1786, the Virginia General Assembly had called for a meeting of leaders from each of the thirteen states to be held in Annapolis, Maryland, to address these issues. Only twelve delegates representing five states – Delaware, New Jersey, New York, Pennsylvania, and Virginia – attended the proposed meeting that was finally held in September. Representatives from Massachusetts, New Hampshire, North Carolina and Rhode Island, for various reasons, didn't show up and Connecticut, Georgia, Maryland, and South Carolina didn't even appoint delegations.

Those who did attend the Annapolis Convention sent a report of the results of their meetings to Congress and to each state legislature. As part of their report, they requested that all the states appoint delegations to attend a meeting "to devise such further provisions as shall appear to them necessary to render the constitution of the Federal Government adequate to the exigencies of the Union." They suggested that the proposed meeting be held May 14, 1787, in Philadelphia.

Twelve of the thirteen states responded favorably; only Rhode Island declined their invitation. Fifty-five delegates attended the Convention supposedly to discuss making changes to the *Articles of Confederation*. The meeting was finally convened May 25 in the building now known as Independence Hall. Soon after the meeting was called to order, it became obvious that the real purpose of the convention was to write a new constitution that would replace the existing confederation with a national government.

As the first item of business, the delegates selected Washington as convention President and then established rules by which business would be conducted. According to those rules, all deliberations would be transacted in closed door secrecy. The copious but unofficial Convention notes taken by Madison have provided the most reliable record of those deliberations and they weren't published until many years later.

Over a period of sixteen weeks, delegates worked their way through often times disputatious debates over a range of issues many of which were finally resolved through compromise. The most hotly-debated issue, and the one that nearly destroyed any hope of success, came after it was decided the new government should be made up of three branches, Executive, Legislative, and Judicial. The method by which states would be numerically represented in the Legislative branch became a highly contentious issue. The issue was advanced when the delegates agreed that the new Congress would include two legislative bodies, an upper and a lower house. But when it came time to decide how the individual states would be represented in each of those houses, the lid nearly blew off. The position of the large states was that representation should be based on population; the small states' position was that all states should be represented equally regardless of size.

Four different approaches were presented – the Virginia Plan, the Pinckney Plan, the New Jersey Plan, and Hamilton's Plan – none of which were acceptable. Nearly two months after the opening gavel, Roger Sherman and Oliver Ellsworth of Connecticut, presented a plan by which representation in the House of Representatives would be determined by population; in the Senate, each state would have an equal number of representatives. That plan, known as the *Connecticut Compromise*, won approval and allowed the convention to move ahead.

During the next two months, delegates found ways to compromise on other issues that mostly had to do with regional differences. By September 17, the new constitution had taken a form that a majority of the delegates could sign with the assurance that amendments guaranteeing basic individual rights including freedom of speech and religion could soon be added. The first ten amendments to the Constitution are now known as the Bill of Rights; it was submitted in 1789 and ratified in 1791.

To become binding, the document had to be ratified by nine of the thirteen states which was accomplished June 21, 1788. The delegates then selected March 4, 1789 as the date on which the *U. S. Constitution* would become effective.

In commenting on the finished work of the Constitutional Convention, Benjamin Franklin undoubtedly spoke for many of his fellow delegates when he said, "There are several parts of this constitution which I do not at present approve, but I am not sure I shall never approve them. I doubt too whether any other Convention we can obtain, may be able to make a better constitution. It therefore astonishes me, Sir, to find this system approaching so near to perfection as it does; and I think it will astonish our enemies."

William Ewart Gladstone, one-time British Chancellor of the Exchequer, offered an even more positive assessment: "The American Constitution is the greatest work ever struck off at any one time by the mind and purpose of man."

38.

Congress Enacts the *Northwest Ordinance*

July 13, 1787

When the thirteen states located along the east coast were declared an independent nation in 1783, they occupied only a small percentage of the land that would someday become a fifty-state republic. Land located to the west of the original colonies now includes thirty-five additional contiguous states. That expansion and consolidation was accomplished in a relatively short period of time through a series of inspired negotiations, legislative activities, and military actions.

Enactment by Congress of the *Northwest Ordinance* on July 13, 1787, was one of the key legislative accomplishments that opened the way for the next phase in westward expansion. Before that historic piece of legislation could be enacted, the existing states, some of which had previously laid claim to portions of the land in question, had to agree to relinquish those claims. Recognizing the need to cooperate for the greater good, all effected states did eventually agree to cooperate.

Most historians consider the *Declaration of Independence*, the *U.S. Constitution*, the *Articles of Confederation*, and the *Northwest Ordinance* to be the founding documents most important to the successful launching and expansion of the emerging nation. Enactment of the *Ordinance* served notice to the world that the Northwest Territory was part of the United States and that the land included in it would soon be converted into additional states.

By establishing federal control over 650-million acres of wide open land, the *Northwest Ordinance* provided an orderly procedure under which five states would be added to the union between 1803 and 1848. Ohio, Indiana, Illinois, Michigan, and Wisconsin were the states carved out of land located north of the Ohio River and extending west to the Mississippi River. Organization of the region within the Northwest Territory became a pattern for the establishment of additional territories and states as the westward expansion picked up momentum in its Providential march toward the Pacific Ocean.

The *Northwest Ordinance* altered and added powers to the *Land Ordinance of 1785* that had been passed earlier by an impoverished Congress. Operating under the toothless *Articles of Confederation*, Congress saw the *Land Ordinance* as a way to raise money by enabling the government to sell land located in the unsettled area. In order to prepare the land for sale, Congress added provisions ordering it to be surveyed and partitioned into townships. Each township was to be six miles long by six miles wide. The townships were then to be divided into thirty-six sections of one square-mile (640 acres) in size. Once the sections were platted, they could be subdivided for sale in portions of any size.

Because the *Land Ordinance* didn't spell out how the Northwest Territory would be governed, nor did it include a clear procedure for establishing new states within the territory, Congress, still operating under the *Articles of Confederation*, enacted the *Northwest Ordinance* not only to cover those shortcomings but also to cover other issues that, fortunately, provide us with insight into the original intent of the Founding Fathers regarding individual freedoms. Many of those added provisions were soon included in amendments to the Constitution known as the *Bill of Rights*.

Non-land issues addressed in the *Northwest Ordinance* include religious freedom, morality, education, treatment of Native Americans, the right of *habeas corpus* and slavery.

Article One made it clear that religious freedom was to be a fundamental right of everyone settling in the territory: "No person shall ever be molested on account of his mode of worship or religious sentiments in the said territory."

Article Two covered the right of *habeas corpus* and trial by jury. It guaranteed "a proportionate representation of the people in the legislature" and that "no law ought ever to be made, or have force in the said territory, that shall, in any manner whatever, interfere with or affect private contracts or engagements, bona fide and without fraud, previously formed."

Article Three began by identifying the ingredients that provide a proper foundation for government: "Religion, morality, and knowledge, being necessary to good government and the happiness of mankind, schools and the means of education shall forever be encouraged." It's apparent that the Founding Fathers linked religion and morality with public education, a point frequently lost on modern day judges and politicians. Article Three went on to prohibit the taking of lands and property from Indians "without their consent" and further stated "that they shall never be invaded or disturbed, unless in just and lawful wars authorized by Congress."

Article Four declared that the land and states formed therein "shall forever remain a part of this Confederacy of the United States of America" and that land owners within the territory would be required to pay their proportionate share of taxes "levied by the authority and direction of the legislatures of the district or districts, or new States, as in the original States, within the time agreed upon by the United States in Congress assembled."

Article Four also addressed rights of settlers where rivers within the territory were concerned: "The navigable waters leading into the Mississippi and St. Lawrence, and carrying places between the same, shall be common highways and forever free, as well to the inhabitants of the said territory as to the citizens of the United States, and those of any other States that may be admitted into the confederacy, without any tax, impost, or duty therefore."

Article Five addressed the land issues and spelled out how the territory was to be governed.

Article Six would have far-reaching future implications because it dealt with the increasingly sensitive and provocative issue of slavery: "There shall be neither slavery nor involuntary servitude in the said territory, otherwise than in the punishment of crimes whereof the party shall have been duly convicted: Provided, always, that any person escaping into the same, from whom labor or service is lawfully claimed in any one of the original States, such fugitive may be lawfully reclaimed and conveyed to the person claiming his or her labor or service as aforesaid."

Because it banned slavery in the territory, the *Northwest Ordinance* essentially designated the Ohio River as the official boundary between free and slave territories from the Appalachian Mountains to the Mississippi River.

At the same time, an equally large territory south of the Ohio River remained unsettled until Georgia and the Carolinas ceded their interests in it to the federal government. Slavery *would* be permitted in the states eventually formed within that territory – Kentucky, Tennessee, West Virginia, Georgia, Alabama, and Mississippi.

As more states were created and added to the union, determining which new states would be free and which would permit slavery was almost always an issue and it remained a divisive issue that wouldn't be resolved nationally until the end of the Civil War.

Even though the *U.S. Constitution* replaced the *Articles of Confederation* after the *Northwest Ordinance* became law, its provisions are still a part of federal law; Congress affirmed it under the new Constitution on August 7, 1789.

39.

Government Under the Constitution Begins

March 4, 1789

March 4, 1789, the day specified by the old Confederate Congress as the day the new *U.S. Constitution* would go into effect, came and went with no official meeting of Congress. For a variety of reasons, only nine of the twenty-two Senators and thirteen of the fifty-nine House members were present which represented much less than a quorum. And, although no one doubted who it would be, the president, was yet to be officially elected, and wouldn't be until the Electors could meet on April 4.

Even though Congress couldn't convene on the appointed day, it was nevertheless celebrated with bells and cannons by the city of New York, the newly designated seat of government. It was April 1 before a quorum of House members was able to gather in New York; the Senate wasn't able to begin conducting business until April 6.

After getting organized, the first order of business for the new Congress was to meet with the Electors for the purpose of certifying the election winners. When that was done, and a messenger had been dispatched to Mount Vernon to inform George Washington of his election as President, Congress turned its attention to the task of producing a *Bill of Rights* as promised during the campaign to ratify the Constitution.

Historians have generally acknowledged James Madison as the Founding Father most responsible for passage of the *Bill of Rights*, although early on he didn't see the need for one. The Federalist position was that the people retained all powers not specifically delegated to the federal government by the proposed Constitution. The anti-Federalists rejected this logic as wishful thinking. Madison made this short, powerful statement that should be a basic tenet observed by every electorate: "All men having power ought to be distrusted."

As early as 1776, Madison, as a delegate to the Virginia Constitutional Convention, had served on a committee that produced a state declaration of rights based on a concept developed by George Mason. Madison's assertion that the right "to the free exercise of religion according to the dictates of conscience" was a foreshadowing of his efforts to have the *Bill of Rights* added to the U.S. Constitution, especially the religious freedom provision that eventually became the First Amendment. He is credited with originating this famously-worded clause included in the Constitution: "Congress shall make no law respecting an establishment of religion, or prohibiting the free exercise thereof."

Through perseverance, the Antifederalists finally made their case that without a bill of individual rights, efforts to ratify the Constitution could very well fail. During the debate, Madison said he believed that "the great mass of the people who opposed [the Constitution], disliked it because it did not contain effectual provision against encroachments on particular rights, and those safeguards which they have been long accustomed to have interposed between them and the magistrate who exercised the sovereign power: nor ought we to consider them safe, while a great number of our fellow citizens think these securities necessary."

The *Bill of Rights* protected freedom of speech, religion, and the press; guaranteed citizens the right to keep and bear arms; prevented the quartering of troops in private homes, and provided an assortment of judicial protections and remedies. The last two amendments were general in nature: The ninth made it clear that citizens' rights were not limited to those specifically mentioned in the Constitution and the tenth stated that any powers not granted to the Federal government were "reserved to the states respectively, or to the people."

Madison presented the *Bill of Rights* to the House on June 8. After much debate and several changes, it became part of the Constitution on September 25.

With the new president and his cabinet in place and Congress functioning as designed, the 1787 *Miracle of Philadelphia* was now a reality. Many Founding Fathers used the word *miracle* in speeches or writings to describe what they believed to be the Providential nature of their achieving independence and the successful formulation and ratification of the Constitution.

George Washington expressed his feelings on the subject to Marquis de Lafayette in a letter dated February 8, 1788: "It appears to me little short of a miracle that the delegates from so many States, differing from each other, as you know, in their manners, circumstances, and prejudices, should unite in forming a system of national government so little liable to well-founded objections. It will at least be a recommendation to the proposed Constitution that it is provided with more checks and barriers against the introduction of tyranny, and those of a nature less liable to be surmounted, than any government hitherto instituted among mortals. We are not to expect perfection in this world; but mankind in modern times have apparently made some progress in the science of government."

Time has validated Washington's reputation as a good judge of character and talent as reflected by the makeup of his initial cabinet that included bright and courageous men including Thomas Jefferson as Secretary of State, Alexander Hamilton as Secretary of the Treasury, Edmund Randolph as Attorney General, and Henry Knox as Secretary of War. Washington selected John Jay as the first Chief Justice of the Supreme Court.

Few, if any, of the Founding Fathers believed their success happened by accident. Benjamin Franklin, who may have been a deist earlier in his life, summed up his position with this clear statement: "I have so much faith in the general government of the world by Providence that I can hardly conceive a transaction of such momentous importance [as the framing of the *Constitution*] to the welfare of millions now in existence and to exist in the posterity of a great nation, should be suffered to pass without being in some degree influenced, guided, and governed by that omnipotent, omnipresent, and beneficent Ruler in whom all inferior spirits live and move and have their being."

March 4, 1789 was an appropriate day to celebrate, but the hard work of building a unique nation was just beginning. The Founding Fathers felt confident in the country's future because they believed the Providence to whom they attributed their success so far would continue to work in their behalf.

40.

Washington Sworn In As First President

April 30, 1789

America's first presidential election was an election in name only; George Washington was a shoo-in because of the level of trust and admiration his fellow citizens felt towards him. The only issue to be decided by the casting of ballots was who would occupy the office of vice president.

Prior to ratification of the *United States Constitution*, what passed for a national government was the Continental Congress operating under the *Articles of Confederation*. The only position remotely resembling that of a chief executive officer was a figurehead position with no real executive power; the leader of each session of Congress was referred to as President.

The almost universal assumption that Washington, a Federalist, would become president under the newly adopted Constitution had provided assurance to many state ratifying convention delegates that they had little to fear from creating a strong executive position. Although some Antifederalists worried that *president* might be a code word for *king*, most of his fellow citizens were certain Washington had no such intention.

Washington is the only American president to be elected unanimously by the Electors who make up the Electoral College. The system whereby presidents are elected by Electors rather than by direct vote was codified in Article II, Section 1 of the Constitution. In 1789, those Electors were chosen by popular vote, a process that took some time due to the difficulties involved in traveling from their homes to their polling places. Voting for Electors began December 15, 1788 and ended January 10, 1789.

The number of Electors per state was determined then, just as it is now, by a formula included in Article II of the Constitution. The number allotted to each state is established by the total of its Senators and House Members. A state, for example, with five House Members (determined by population) plus its two Senators would have seven Electors or electoral votes.

The purpose of the Electoral College was to set up a system by which the President of the United States would be elected by a "polling" of states rather than by a national popularity vote by individuals. The Electoral College system was intended to hinder the possibility of a president being elected by a majority vote of individuals in a few large states. It is a states' rights issue and one that is a mainstay of Republicanism as opposed to a "pure" Democratic system. The establishment of a Republic is exactly what the Founding Fathers intended as was often revealed in their own words.

The Electoral College was originally scheduled to meet on February 4 in New York City, designated the nation's capital during the final meeting of the 1788 Confederate Congress. They also designated March 4, 1789, as the date on which the new *Constitution* would go into effect.

Since there were no official political parties with lineups of opposing candidates in 1789, each Elector was to cast a vote for two candidates from what was basically a list of self-nominated candidates; the candidate receiving the most votes was elected president and the candidate receiving the next highest number of votes was elected vice president.

When they met in New York on April 4 – the meeting was delayed for two months due to unanticipated circumstances – every Elector cast a vote for Washington. Receiving the next highest number of votes, John Adams was elected vice president.

Word didn't reach Washington at his Mount Vernon home informing him of his election until April 14. On April 16, Washington recorded these thoughts in his diary: "About ten o'clock I bade adieu to Mount Vernon, to private life, and to domestic felicity; and with a mind oppressed with more anxious and painful sensations than I have words to express, set out for New York with the best disposition to render service to my country in obedience to its call, but with less hope of answering its expectations."

Washington's procession to New York provided his fellow citizens many opportunities along the way to enthusiastically demonstrate their gratitude and respect. The essence of that seven-day trip was beautifully captured and recorded by Henry W. Elson in his *Sidelights on American History*:

> *Washington's journey to New York was one continuous ovation. It was like the triumphal march of a Roman conqueror. Men, women, and children of all ages thronged the highways to shout their glad welcomes, and show their love to this first citizen of the land. He preferred a quiet, unostentatious journey, but public feeling was too strong to be suppressed. In every city through which he passed, there was great preparation for his reception, and large numbers of citizens and soldiers escorted him through their respective States. At Alexandria he was given a public dinner presided over by the mayor, whose happy address was answered by Washington in a few choice words showing the deepest emotion. He was received with high honors at Baltimore and Chester; but it was left for Philadelphia and Trenton to make the greatest display in doing homage to this civilian hero…The procession was two days crossing New Jersey to Elizabethtown Point, where they were met by a reception committee from both houses of Congress. Here a fine barge, built for the occasion, was waiting to take the President elect to the New York harbor. It was manned by thirteen pilots in white uniform, and was accompanied by many other vessels highly decorated and bearing many distinguished citizens. These formed a nautical procession and swept up the beautiful bay, cheered on by instrumental music and by the firing of salutes from the ships lying at anchor along the harbor.*
>
> *It was Thursday, April the 23rd, 1789. New York City had donned its holiday dress. Flags were floating over the principal buildings, bells were ringing, and the people were in a flutter of excitement. Soldiers in bright uniform stood along the side walks, mounted aids galloped to and fro amid the surging crowd, while bands of music enlivened the scene. The bay was full of vessels with flaunting flags and streaming pennants. The crowd along the Battery was dense, and, as the people stood gazing down the bay, the barge in which Washington had embarked hove in sight, when the boom of cannon from the anchored vessels announced the fact, and was answered by thirteen guns from the city.*

At length the day came – April 30, 1789. At nine o'clock religious services were held in all the churches in the city. Before noon the streets about Federal Hall were packed with a solid mass of people, the windows of the surrounding buildings were filled with eager faces, and the roofs were covered with anxious sight-seers.

A few minutes after twelve o'clock, Washington, accompanied by John Adams and Chancellor Livingston, and followed by both Houses of Congress, stepped forth on the balcony in the presence of the vast assemblage of people. The shout of welcome that rose seemed to pour forth the whole heart of the Nation. Washington placed his hand upon his heart and bowed again and again to the cheering multitude. He then sank back into an arm-chair, and the crowd, seeming to understand that he was overcome with emotion, was instantly hushed into silence. He soon rose again and stepped forward between Adams and Livingston, while in the rear stood Alexander Hamilton, Roger Sherman, Baron Steuben, and two Revolutionary generals, Knox and St. Clair.

The secretary of the Senate stood by with an open Bible, on which Washington laid his hand while Chancellor Livingston pronounced the oath of office. At its conclusion Washington replied in solemn, stifled words: "I swear – so help me God."

While those words are not officially part of the oath of office as it appears in Article II of the *U.S Constitution*, a number of presidents have followed Washington's lead in completing their swearing in ceremonies by voluntarily adding "so help me God."

41.

U.S. Capital Founded

<u>July 16, 1790</u>

Before the nation's capital was permanently located in Washington, DC, Congress had, for a variety of reasons, met at different locations. Wherever Congress met was, for all practical purposes, the seat of government at the time. Those locations included Philadelphia, Lancaster and York, Pennsylvania, Princeton and Trenton, New Jersey, Annapolis, Maryland and New York City.

It took the threat of a mutiny by unpaid Revolutionary War soldiers to focus the minds of members of Congress on the issue of a permanent location for the capital in a separate federal district formed specifically for that purpose.

Taking the threat of the *Pennsylvania Mutiny of 1783* seriously, Congress decided to quickly move from Philadelphia to Princeton. They took that threat seriously because five hundred angry soldiers with control of a munitions depot presented a serious threat, especially since the only force available to oppose the mutineers was a local militia. Local authorities weren't sure whose side the militia would come down on.

Because many members of the Executive Council of the Commonwealth of Pennsylvania sympathized with the plight of the irate soldiers, they refused to even attempt to stop the mutiny. Failure on the part of Pennsylvania officials to protect Congress became a major factor in generating support for the idea of establishing a district in which the government could be located and protected by federal security forces rather than by state militias. The mutiny was defused by Alexander

Hamilton who persuaded the soldiers to allow Congress time to meet later and address their concerns. Eventually, most of the soldiers were paid at least part of what they were owed.

Determining where the nation's capital should be permanently located took a back seat for a few years to other more urgent issues including alterations to or replacement of the *Articles of Confederation.* The issue, though, did remain on the minds of a number of leaders, especially George Washington and James Madison.

During the Constitutional Convention of 1787, the importance of the issue was acknowledged by a provision included in Article I of the new *Constitution* that gave Congress power "to exercise exclusive Legislation in all Cases whatsoever, over such District (not exceeding ten Miles square) as may, by Cession of particular States, and the Acceptance of Congress, become the Seat of the government of the United States, and to exercise like Authority over all places purchased by the Consent of the Legislature of the State in which the Same shall be, for the Erection of Forts, Magazines, Arsenals, dock-Yards, and other needful Buildings – And to make all Laws which shall be necessary and proper for carrying into Execution the foregoing Powers, and all other Powers vested by this Constitution in the government of the United States, or in any Department or Officer thereof."

For those not yet convinced of the need, Madison, in 1788, wrote *Federalist No. 43* in which he explained the reasoning behind the movement to establish a separate district in which the national government would be located.

Congress solved their problems of itinerancy and lack of security on July 16, 1790, with passage of *An ACT for Establishing the Temporary and Permanent Seat of the Government of the United States*, also known as the *Residence Act of 1790.* It said:

> BE *it enacted by the Senate and House of Representatives of the United States of America in Congress assembled, That a district of territory, not exceeding ten miles square, to be located as hereafter directed on the river Potomack, at some place between the mouths of the Eastern-Branch and Connogochegue be, and the same is hereby accepted for the permanent seat of the government of the United States: Provided nevertheless, That the operation of the laws of the state within such district shall not be*

affected by this acceptance, until the time fixed for the removal of the government thereto, and until Congress shall otherwise by law provide.

The *Residence Act* gave President Washington authority to choose the exact location "on the River Potomac" within the prescribed area. It also established a deadline of the first Monday in December of 1800 as the date upon which the government would begin to operate in its new location.

When Washington determined his choice of locations, the land, after being surveyed, was ceded to the federal government by the states of Maryland and Virginia. On September 9, 1791 the one hundred square mile district was officially named the Territory of Columbia, after a female figure by that name often used to represent America; the city was named in honor of war hero and first president George Washington.

On April 15, 1791, the first cornerstone of the District of Columbia was laid at Jones Point near Alexandria. During the dedication ceremony, Rev. James Muir reaffirmed the generally-held belief among the Founders that the United States of America had been the recipient of Providential guidance and protection: "May this stone long commemorate the goodness of God in those uncommon events which have given America a name among nations. Under this stone may jealousy and selfishness be forever buried. From this stone may a superstructure arise whose glory, whose magnificence, stability, unequalled hitherto, shall astonish the world, and invite even the savage of the wilderness to take shelter under its wings."

Shortly after the city of Washington became the permanent seat of American government, the *District of Columbia Organic Act of 1801* was passed placing the cities of Washington, Georgetown, and Alexandria under the jurisdiction of Congress. Since that time, the area has been known as the District of Columbia.

42.

Alexander Hamilton Outlines Economic Plan

January 9, 1791

When Alexander Hamilton was appointed Secretary of the Treasury in 1789, the new U.S. government was worse than broke. Interest was growing daily on almost $12,000,000 owed to foreign creditors and over $27,000,000 of domestic debt. The country was looking to Hamilton, the man George Washington once labeled a financial genius, to figure out what to do about it. Hamilton proved to be equal to the task. He understood America was a wealthy country; it was just the government that was broke.

Article 1, Section 8 of the new Constitution gave Congress the power to "lay and collect Taxes, Duties, Imposts and Excises, to pay the Debts and provide for the common Defence and general Welfare of the United States" and "To borrow Money on the credit of the United States." But it didn't say how that was to be done. Someone had to translate those general powers existing only on a piece of paper into a workable, real-world program.

On January 9, 1791, Hamilton presented his *First Report on Public Credit* that analyzed the financial situation and then recommended actions he believed would lead to financial stability and economic growth. A student of British and French political systems, he based much of his thinking on what he considered to be their established and proven tools including tariffs and excise taxes. Many of those tools could only be obtained and put to work by a strong central government, a fact that had greatly influenced his Federalist leanings.

According to Hamilton's plan, the U. S. government would have to find a way to pay foreign and domestic creditors rather than repudiating those debts which would have destroyed the young country's credit and hindered development opportunities, perhaps fatally, before it had a chance to get up and running. He devoted the first part of his report to stating the desireable advantages of establishing good credit and the potentially diastrous consequences of being unable to obtain credit on favorable terms. He was convinced that a creditworthy America would attract investors from all over the world which would provide capital needed to build the economy.

Hamiliton's plan began with a recommendation that the Federal government assume war debts of the states and combine them with existing Federal debt to create a permanent national debt. That debt would be security-based and backed by a combination of the government and wealthy Americans thereby creating a way to generate funds to retire debt and, he was convinced, to make America highly creditworthy.

Many of his fellow Federalists, including James Madison, thought his push for that kind of strong central government went too far and joined Secretary of State Thomas Jefferson and other Antifederalists in opposing Hamilton's recommendations. Along with reluctance to go so far in giving such sweeping powers to an overarching national government, there were other issues separating Federalists and Antifederalists. Among them was the unresolved dispute regarding where the nation's capital would be located.

At that point, the stage was set for a little legislative gamesmanship. In general, the northern states were okay with Hamilton's financial plan and weren't nearly as concerned as the southern states about where the capital should be located. Southern members of Congress very much wanted the seat of government to be established in a southern state and were willing to do a little horse trading to get their way on that issue.

In a deal worked out over dinner at Jefferson's home, Madison agreed to support Hamilton's financial plan in exchange for Hamilton's backing the location of the capital in a southern state. Both issues were then able to advance with the capital relocation bill being approved by Congress July 16 and Hamilton's *Assumption Bill*, as it was sometimes called, gaining approval on July 26.

Hamilton's plan quickly became successful in establishing excellent credit for what, in the eyes of the world, had been a financial mess. The newly established credit standing provided immediate as well as far-reaching benefits for the United States of America.

His *Second Report on Public Credit* resulted in the founding of *The First Bank of the United States*, and, later, to creation of the Federal Reserve System. Another Hamilton report led to the establishment of the U. S. Mint. A fourth, and final, report to Congress had to do with government involvment in manufacturing. To a country with a free enterprise tradition, Hamilton's recommendations provided too much opportunity for government control over business matters to be acceptable to most of Congress or the American people. It was the only one of his recommendations that was rejected.

Hamilton resigned as Secretary of the Treasury in 1795 but maintained a close relationship with Washington as a friend and occasional advisor.

As opposing political philosophies further crystalized, a concensus began to evolve favoring the establishment of political parties that would represent sharply differing ideas regarding the science of government. Hamilton is generally seen by historians as the titular head of what became known as the Federalist Party. Jefferson is recognized as leader of the Democratic-Republican Party also known as the Antifederalists. Hamilton continued to take an active role in partisan politics until his untimely death in 1804. That partisanship, especially an acrimonious on-going political battle with Aaron Burr, led to the duel that ended Hamilton's life.

The story of Alexander Hamilton is another example of the right man appearing at the right time in the right place during the foundational period of the United States of America. Hamilton arrived in New York from the island of Nevis in the British West Indies in 1772 as a teenager. A few years after his father had left the family, his mother died leaving him to provide for himself. Recognizing the young Hamilton's obvious intellectual potential, his employer, with the help of a Presbyterian minister, made arrangements with acquaintances in New York to look after the young Hamilton while he attended school there.

Upon graduating from King's College in 1775, Hamilton had become associated with the New York militia which led to his Providential long term relationship with George Washington two years later. As a twenty-year-old artillery captain, he was introduced to Washington by General Nathanael Greene. Serving under Greene in the battles of Long Island, White Plains, Trenton, and Princeton, Hamilton's courageous service had been noted. Upon Greene's recommendation, he was promoted to the rank of Lieutenant Colonel and appointed to serve as Washington's aide-de-camp and personal secretary, positions he held until 1781.

Hamilton's Revolutionary War experience with Washington, his staff, and his confederates, including many of the most powerful and influential men in the colonies, had provided Hamilton at an early age with contacts that enabled him to take a prominent role in the independence movement. Later, those contacts made it possible for him to help shape the newly emerging republic, especially in the vitally important areas of finance and commerce. His out-of-nowhere arrival on the scene in pre-Revolutionary War America as an unknown fifteen-year-old boy from the West Indies with a natural talent for writing and political insight seems more like a supernatural plan than a highly unlikely coincidence.

Founding Father Fisher Ames wrote this tribute to Hamilton: "It is difficult in the midst of such varied excellences, to say in what particular the effect of his greatness was most manifest. No man more promptly discerned truth; no man more clearly displayed it: It was not merely made visible; it seemed to come bright with illumination from his lips. He thirsted only for that fame which virtue would not blush to confer, or time to convey to the end of his course. Alas! The great man who was at all times the ornament of our country is withdrawn to a purer and more tranquil region. May Heaven, the guardian of our liberty, grant that our country may be fruitful of Hamiltons and faithful to their glory."

43.

Treaty of Greenville **Is Signed**

August 3, 1795

General Anthony Wayne, who signed the *Treaty of Greenville*, was know as "Mad Anthony" because of his temper, not because he was crazy. Far from it. He was one of the most effective military leaders of the Revolutionary War period about whom most modern day Americans know little or nothing unless they happen to live near Ft. Wayne, Indiana, originally the site of an Army fort named after the general. What little is accurately taught about early American history in public schools today is usually included in something called "social studies."

For the same reason, most Americans know little if anything about the treaty Wayne signed with the twelve-tribe Western Indian Confederacy August 3, 1795. It was an important document that helped to clear the way for the westward expansion of the United States. For a period of time, the treaty established a workable boundary, known as the *Greenville Treaty Line*, between Native American territory and areas open to white settlers. The land covered by the treaty was bounded on the north by the Great Lakes and on the south by the Ohio River. Its western boundaries were the western borders of the original northern colonies and the Mississippi River, a territory of huge economic potential.

While the Northwest Territories had been ceded to the United States by the 1783 *Treaty of Paris*, native American tribes living in that area had not been parties to it and refused to abide by its terms. Also, in violation of the terms of the treaty, the British still occupied a few forts in the Great Lakes area and often allied themselves with the Indians. Pioneers trying to settle the territory were in constant danger of being attacked by members of the various hostile Indian tribes operating throughout the area. They needed protection. In 1790 and again in 1791, President George Washington had sent military expeditions into the territory to rid it of the Indian threat. Both attempts ended in humiliating defeats that cast doubt in the minds of Americans as well as the leaders of other nations regarding the effectiveness of the new government and its military arm.

A big part of the problem was a deep-seated distrust of a standing army by many Americans. Unrealistically, many political leaders operated under the overly optimistic assumption that state militias would be adequate to meet the security needs of the young country. The defeats of 1790 and 1791 had advanced the point of those who understood that the state militias weren't the answer. Those defeats also played into the hands of the Commander-in-Chief who had long understood the country's need for a professional army.

Washington, realizing he had to get control of the Northwest Territory, called upon Secretary of War Henry Knox to help him assess the situation. Poor military leadership, inadequate training, and a shortage of manpower and supplies, they decided, had sealed the doom of earlier expeditions. Knox devised a plan that Washington accepted and then presented to Congress along with his recommendation for approval.

When Congress approved it in 1792, Washington and Knox began to implement their plan that called for the formation of a new branch of the Army known as the *Legion of the United States*, a specially trained force of 5,000 men. Washington chose General Wayne to head this new branch of the Army being raised for the specific purpose of defeating the Indian Confederation and thereby nullifying the twelve tribes as a hindrance to settlement of the territory. Washington was determined to end what historians call the Northwest Indian War that began in the mid 1780s.

Wayne is credited with creating the first military basic training camp as the initial step in implementing the plan. The camp was located at Legionville, Pennsylvania, where he began to prepare a professional fighting force for the dual purposes of winning the war and protecting the reputation of the U.S. government. After two years of intensive training, the legion prevailed in a number of battles with Indian forces culminating with the battles of Fort Recovery and Fallen Timbers. It was at Fallen Timbers that Wayne's forces won what most historians recognize as the last battle of the Northwest Indian War.

Wayne's victory also led to Britain's giving up their slim hope of maintaining a presence south of the Great Lakes. In 1796, they surrendered all their remaining forts on American soil to Wayne.

In *A History of the American People*, Paul Johnson provides this politically-incorrect insight into the sociological-cultural forces at play between native Americans and the newly independent American government:

> *The prevailing American view was that the Indians must assimilate or move west. This was a constitutional rather than a racist viewpoint. The United States was organized into parishes, townships, counties, and states. The Indians were organized not geographically but tribally. So organized, they lived in pursuit of game. But the game was gone, or going. They therefore had to detribalize themselves and fit into the American system. If they chose to do so, they could be provided with land (640 acres a family was a figure bandied about) and US citizenship. This was, in fact, the option countless Indians chose. Many settled, took European names, and, as it were, vanished into the growing mass of ordinary Americans. In any case there was no clear dividing line between "redskins" and whites. There were scores of thousands of half-breeds, some of whom identified with the whites, and others who remained tribal. The bulk of the pure-bred Indians seem to have preferred tribalism when they had the choice. In that case, said the settlers, you must move west, to where there is still game and tribalism is still possible.*

The *Treaty of Greenville* was an agreement that represented a general desire to get along and provided some specific terms to which each side was to be bound. The preamble read as follows:

> *To put an end to a destructive war, to settle all controversies, and to restore harmony and friendly intercourse between the said United States and Indian tribes, Anthony Wayne, major general commanding the army of the United States, and sole commissioner for the good purposes above mentioned, and the said tribes of Indians, by their sachems, chiefs, and warriors, met together at Greenville, the headquarters of the said army, have agreed on the*

> *following articles, which, when ratified by the President, with the advice and consent of the Senate of the United States, shall be binding on them and the said Indian tribes.*

How successfully those desires were realized is subject to interpretation, but the treaty provided a way to continue the inevitable goal of civilizing and developing the future contiguous American states on the North American continent.

44.

Washington Delivers *Farewell Address*

September 19, 1796

When George Washington invited his Continental Army officers to a meeting on December 4, 1783, he planned to inform them of his longed-for plan to retire and to bid them a fond farewell. He *did* bid them a very fond farewell – all of them were overcome with emotion, especially Washington – but that retirement turned out to be a short one.

In May of 1787, he was called out of retirement from his comfortable Virginia estate to preside over the Constitutional Convention that didn't end until September. Less than seventeen months later, he was elected the first President of the United States. His short retirement announced in 1783 officially ended April 30, 1789, when he was sworn-in to office.

When his first term as President ended in 1793, he would again have preferred to retire permanently but he felt an obligation to remain in office another four years rather than subject the country to the potential risk of major disruptions involved in a change of leadership. America's position in the world was still in a developmental and perhaps perilous stage. It was clear his countrymen wanted and needed him to continue to serve as their President and Commander-in-Chief.

Nearing the end of his second term, and faced with failing health, Washington was resolute in his desire to retire to his beloved Mount Vernon. On September 19, 1796, he was able to confidently announce his decision to permanently retire from public service. Rather than deliver his famous *Farewell Address* orally, Washington had it published in *The* [Philadelphia] *American Daily Advertiser*. A few days later, it was published by *The Independent Chronicle* in Boston, then in newspapers and pamphlets throughout the country.

Washington devoted the first part of his formal announcement to a lengthy explanation of the reasons behind his decision to step down:

> *The period for a new election of a citizen, to administer the executive government of the United States, being not far distant, and the time actually arrived, when your thoughts must be employed designating the person, who is to be clothed with that important trust, it appears to me proper, especially as it may conduce to a more distinct expression of the public voice, that I should now apprize you of the resolution I have formed, to decline being considered among the number of those out of whom a choice is to be made.*
>
> *I beg you at the same time to do me the justice to be assured that this resolution has not been taken without a strict regard to all the considerations appertaining to the relation which binds a dutiful citizen to his country; and that in withdrawing the tender of service, which silence in my situation might imply, I am influenced by no diminution of zeal for your future interest, no deficiency of grateful respect for your past kindness, but am supported by a full conviction that the step is compatible with both.*
>
> *The acceptance of, and continuance hitherto in, the office to which your suffrages have twice called me, have been a uniform sacrifice of inclination to the opinion of duty, and to a deference for what appeared to be your desire. I constantly hoped, that it would have been much earlier in my power, consistently with motives, which I was not at liberty to disregard, to return to that retirement, from which I had been reluctantly drawn. The strength of my inclination to do this, previous to the last election, had even led to the preparation of an address to declare it to you; but mature reflection on the then perplexed and critical posture of our affairs with foreign nations, and the unanimous advice of persons entitled to my confidence impelled me to abandon the idea.*
>
> *I rejoice, that the state of your concerns, external as well as internal, no longer renders the pursuit of inclination incompatible with the sentiment of duty, or propriety; and am persuaded, whatever partiality may be retained for my services, that, in the*

present circumstances of our country, you will not disapprove my determination to retire.

He went on to remind his "friends and fellow-citizens," as he began his address, of the advantages of and need for unity; warned them against foreign entanglements; cautioned them against the potential dangers inherent in partisan politics; exhorted them to be weary of overly ambitious, self centered leaders; and advised them to avoid public debt and its potentially disastrous economic consequences. He asked them to honor his service by adhering to those basic concepts important to the health of the republic.

One of Washington's most firmly-held beliefs had to do with the importance of morality and religion to national success. It was natural that he would address that core concept in his remarks:

Of all the dispositions and habits, which lead to political prosperity, Religion and Morality are indispensable supports. In vain would that man claim the tribute of Patriotism, who should labor to subvert these great pillars of human happiness, these firmest props of the duties of Men and Citizens. The mere Politician, equally with the pious man, ought to respect and to cherish them. A volume could not trace all their connexions with private and public felicity. Let it simply be asked, Where is the security for property, for reputation, for life, if the sense of religious obligation desert the oaths, which are the instruments of investigation in Courts of Justice? And let us with caution indulge the supposition, that morality can be maintained without religion. Whatever may be conceded to the influence of refined education on minds of peculiar structure, reason and experience both forbid us to expect, that national morality can prevail in exclusion of religious principle.

It is substantially true, that virtue or morality is a necessary spring of popular government. The rule, indeed, extends with more or less force to every species of free government Who, that is a sincere friend to it, can look with indifference upon attempts to shake the foundation of the fabric?

Relying on its kindness in this as in other things, and actuated by that fervent love towards it, which is so natural to a man, who views it in the native soil of himself and his progenitors for several generations; I anticipate with pleasing expectation that retreat, in which I promise myself to realize, without alloy, the sweet enjoyment of partaking, in the midst of my fellow-citizens, the benign influence of good laws under a free government, the ever favorite object of my heart, and the happy reward, as I trust, of our mutual cares, labors, and dangers.

After spending all of his adult life in the midst of earth-shaking events that often put his life in danger, Washington said he just wanted to "make a little flour annually, to repair houses (going fast to ruin), to build one for the security of my papers of a public nature, and to amuse myself in agricultural and rural pursuits [which] will constitute employment for the years I have to remain on this terrestrial globe."

On December 14, 1799, George Washington died at his Virginia home. One of many glowing eulogies was delivered by Colonel Henry Lee at the request of Congress:

Methinks I see his august image, and hear falling from his venerable lips these deep-sinking words – "Cease, sons of America, to lament our separation; go on and confirm by your wisdom the fruits of our joint councils, joint efforts, and common dangers; REVERENCE RELIGION; patronize the arts and sciences; let liberty and order be inseparable companions; control party spirit, the bane of free government; observe good faith to, and cultivate peace with all nations; shut up every avenue to foreign influence; contract rather than extend national connection; rely on yourselves only; be American in thought, word and deed. Thus will you give immortality to that union which was the constant object of my terrestrial labors; thus will you preserve undisturbed to the latest posterity the felicity of a people to me most dear; and thus will you supply (if my happiness is aught to you) the only vacancy in the round of pure bliss high Heaven bestows."

When Washington used the word *religion*, it always referred to the Christian religion which had been a prominent part of his life.

45.

Thomas Jefferson Officially Becomes President

World attention was focused on the American presidential election held November 4, 1800, because many considered it a test of republicanism. World leaders watched to see if political power really could be transferred peacefully between regimes with significantly different political views.

By the time America's third presidential election rolled around, two opposing political parties, much to George Washington's chagrin, had become a reality that had to be recognized. Washington was adamantly opposed to political parties because he saw them as divisive and as a potential threat to national unity.

In other areas of the world, major political/philosophical differences had most often been resolved through intrigue often leading to bloody revolution rather than by putting those differences to a vote of the general public. To most European leaders, the idea that a ruling regime would peacefully hand over control of government to any group with whom they were in strong disagreement was difficult to imagine.

In 1797, the transition of power from President George Washington to President-elect John Adams didn't attract much interest among foreign rulers because Washington and Adams were both members of what officially became known as the Federalist Party. Thomas Jefferson, eventual winner of the 1800 election, was a member of the emerging

Democratic-Republican Party that basically represented the interests of people known as Antifederalists.

Jefferson ran on a platform of substantial change including smaller, less powerful government and a less aggressive foreign policy. His party wanted no standing army because they believed state militias were adequate as a land force and that a navy was a luxury they couldn't afford. Also, the Federalists' policies had been more directed toward restoring a friendly relationship with England while the Democratic-Republican Party preferred a closer relationship with France.

Due to a glitch in the system, the outcome of the 1800 presidential election wasn't determined until February 17, 1801, when the House of Representatives, after thirty-five votes, finally named Jefferson the winner. It had been left for the House members to decide the election when the electoral vote finished in a tie. Eventually, Federalists in the House provided Democratic-Republican Jefferson with his margin of victory over Burr because they considered him the lesser of two evils. In any case, the outcome of the third American presidential election proved that the "experiment" in republicanism could work. Under the new American Constitution, the losing Party was guaranteed their chance to rebound in four years, a relatively short period of time in the overall scheme of things. A precedent -- ballots rather than bullets -- was thereby set that has successfully met the test of time.

During a post-election meeting with Jefferson, Adams also established another American political tradition we call the "loyal opposition." Adams reportedly said, "Well I understand that you are to beat me in this contest, and I will only say that I will be as faithful a subject as any you will have."

In his first Inaugural Address, Jefferson spoke in conciliatory terms of the need for unity and expressed his desire to work with the Federalists:

> *During the contest of opinion through which we have passed the animation of discussions and of exertions has sometimes worn an aspect which might impose on strangers unused to think freely and to speak and to write what they think; but this being now decided by the voice of the nation, announced according to the rules of the Constitution, all will, of course, arrange themselves under the will of the law, and unite in common efforts for the common good. All, too, will bear in mind this sacred principle,*

that though the will of the majority is in all cases to prevail, that will to be rightful must be reasonable; that the minority possess their equal rights, which equal law must protect, and to violate would be oppression. Let us, then, fellow-citizens, unite with one heart and one mind...But every difference of opinion is not a difference of principle. We have called by different names brethren of the same principle. We are all Republicans, we are all Federalists.

In accord with his fellow Founding Fathers, Jefferson also made reference to their commonly held belief in the providential nature of the establishment of the United States of America:

Let us, then, with courage and confidence pursue our own Federal and Republican principles, our attachment to union and representative government. Kindly separated by nature and a wide ocean from the exterminating havoc of one quarter of the globe; too high-minded to endure the degradations of the others; possessing a chosen country, with room enough for our descendants to the thousandth and thousandth generation; entertaining a due sense of our equal right to the use of our own faculties, to the acquisitions of our own industry, to honor and confidence from our fellow-citizens, resulting not from birth, but from our actions and their sense of them; enlightened by a benign religion, professed, indeed, and practiced in various forms, yet all of them inculcating honesty, truth, temperance, gratitude, and the love of man; acknowledging and adoring an overruling Providence, which by all its dispensations proves that it delights in the happiness of man here and his greater happiness hereafter – with all these blessings, what more is necessary to make us a happy and a prosperous people?

History revisionists routinely refer to Jefferson as a deist or atheist rather than as a Christian. In his own words, here is how he responded to those false and misleading charges in a letter to Benjamin Rush: "My views are the result of a life of inquiry and reflection, and very different from the anti-Christian system imputed to me by those who know nothing of my opinions. To the corruptions of Christianity I am, indeed opposed; but not to the genuine precepts of Jesus himself. I am a

Christian in the only sense in which he wished any one to be; sincerely attached to his doctrines in preference to all others."

Jefferson reaffirmed his belief in the validity of republicanism, the Constitution, and the electoral process in the last paragraph of his inaugural address:

> *Relying, then, on the patronage of your good will, I advance with obedience to the work, ready to retire from it whenever you become sensible how much better choice it is in your power to make. And may that Infinite Power which rules the destinies of the universe, lead our councils to what is best, and give them a favorable issue for your peace and prosperity.*

46.

Second Great Awakening Gains Momentum

August 6, 1801

During the first half of the nineteenth century, across-the-board change was happening fast in America. Between 1800 and 1850, the population increased from seven million to nearly twenty-five million. Fifteen new states were carved out of the Louisiana Purchase territory more than doubling the land area of the United States.

The rapid growth in population and territory was accompanied by an expansion of industrialization made possible by technological advances along with improvements in transportation and communication infrastructure, all of which combined to initiate massive socio-economic changes. Also, a feeling of uneasiness over the issue of slavery as a moral issue was increasingly permeating the public consciousness.

Extensive and rapid change is almost always accompanied by general feelings of anxiety and confusion, feelings that usually prompt large numbers of people to look beyond themselves for help in coping. Thus, those huge changes in secular demographics and economics were undoubtedly major contributing factors in a significant increase in church attendance and to the large number of churches constructed during the first half of the century.

Many historians refer to the first half of the nineteenth century as the period of time when the *Second Great Awakening* was at its zenith in America. The *First Great Awakening,* dated from around 1739 and well into the 1740s and beyond, was a major force in uniting the colonies and preparing them for the Revolutionary War. The *Second Great Awakening* may very well have been a contributing factor in bringing about the Civil War that began in 1861.

Those historians who have written about such things seem to agree that the "Great Revival," as it was labeled at the time, began in Kentucky's Cumberland, Logan, and Bourbon Counties in 1799 and eventually provided the spark that led to an explosion of evangelistic activity in the western territories. When Kentucky had become a state in 1792, the population was approximately 75,000; by 1800, it had nearly tripled. To say many frontier territories needed a good dose of evangelization would be a huge understatement in almost anyone's estimation; the western territories weren't called "the wild, wild West" without good reason.

By 1800, the European *Enlightenment*, described by Johann Friedrich Zoellner as "a movement which devoted itself to undermining the basics of morality and to denying the value of religion, turning hearts away from God," had influenced American society, especially on the frontier. Recognizing the scope of the problem, Rev. James McGready and several of his fellow Presbyterian, Methodist, and Baptist preachers in Kentucky felt the need to take action. McGready became well known for his fiery preaching style and sermons with titles like "The Character, History and End of the Fool" in which he talked about "the furnace of hell with its red-hot coals of God's wrath" and other similar attention-getters. Because of the instrumental role he played in initiating the revival movement that quickly spread from Kentucky throughout the western territories, McGready is frequently labeled "Father of Revivalism in the American West."

A camp meeting revival that lasted seven days began August 6, 1801. It was held near a Kentucky town called Cane Ridge. Attendance figures vary but some historians have pegged attendance as high as 25,000 people which would make it the largest outdoor revival meeting ever held prior to revival meetings held in modern day sports arenas.

Camp revivals were scheduled to last several days to make it worth the while of potential participants many of whom lived in sparsely-populated areas many miles from the events – the typical frontier area had a population density of less than two people per square mile. In addition to traveling significant distances, attendees had to come prepared to sleep in tents, covered wagons, or whatever kind of shelter they could provide for themselves.

To reach those who couldn't, or wouldn't, attend camp meeting revivals, some denominations established a system of "circuit riders," preachers who traveled assigned circuits to preach and teach in remote areas. Their assigned work included encouraging the establishment of Sunday Schools in which they were to teach reading, writing and arithmetic along with the Gospel.

Many frontiersmen were so impacted by the Cane Ridge event and others like it that they were motivated to build churches in their own communities when they returned to their homes. It has been estimated that one thousand new churches were constructed every year from 1800 throughout the antebellum period. In many instances, circuit riders served as pastors of the newly-constructed rural churches until each could afford its own permanent pastor.

As part of the *Second Great Awakening*, a phenomenon labeled the *Restoration Movement* also gathered a following that led to the establishment of a number of interdenominational societies with mission statements based on Christian principles. The *Restorationists'* goal was to return to "primitive" Christianity, i.e., Biblical precepts stripped of denominational disputes based on differences of interpretation.

Out of the *Restoration Movement* emerged an offshoot called the *Benevolent Empire*. It was made up of nondenominational benevolent organizations concerned with helping to advance the public good while at the same time advancing the Christian religion in general. Many organizations were formed to exclusively address such issues as the abolition of slavery, women's rights, penal reform, temperance, public education, and the establishment of missionary societies. Typical of the benevolence groups formed during the first half of the nineteenth century were the *American Bible Society*, the *American Tract Society*, the *American Sunday School Union*, the *American Education Society*, the *Society for the Promotion of Temperance*, the *American Board of Foreign Missions,* and the *American Home Missionary Society.*

Elias Boudinot, first President of the *American Bible Society*, may have been speaking for all laymen involved in the formation of the *Benevolence Empire* when he said, "I am so convinced that the whole of this business is the work of God himself, by his Holy Spirit, that even hoping against hope I am encouraged to press on through good report and evil report, to accomplish His will on earth as it is in heaven. So apparent is the hand of God in this disposing the hearts of so many men, so diversified in their sentiments as to religious matters of minor importance, and uniting them as a band of brothers in this grand object that even infidels are compelled to say, 'It is the work of the Lord, and it is wonderful in our eyes!' Having this confidence, let us go on and we shall prosper."

Revivalism has always been an important part of the story of America dating back to the early seventeenth century. The first settlements were intended as places for the revival of religious freedom in a world in which true religious freedom was rare; many have said that in the beginning, America was a fundamentalist church relocation project. Some Christian historians are on record as saying revivals of varying intensity have happened in America every quarter century.

French author and historian Alexis de Tocqueville also recorded this observation regarding the Christian religion in America: "The Americans combine the notions of Christianity and of liberty so intimately in their minds that it is impossible to make them conceive the one without the other...I have known of societies formed by Americans to send out ministers of the Gospel into the new Western states, to found schools and churches there, lest religion should be allowed to die away in those remote settlements, and the rising states be less fitted to enjoy free institutions than the people from whom they came."

Many of our Founding Fathers warned of the predictably undesirable consequences of unbridled freedom without the self restraint taught throughout the Judeo-Christian Bible, a book with which they were all familiar. Typical of their thinking on the subject is this statement by Samuel Adams: "The sum of all is, if we would most truly enjoy the gift of heaven, let us become a virtuous people; then shall we both deserve and enjoy it. While, on the other hand, if we are universally vicious and debauched in our manners, though the form of our Constitution carries the face of the most exalted freedom, we shall in reality be the most abject slaves."

It's time for another "primitive Christianity" revival in America.

47.

Jefferson Writes to Danbury Baptists

January 1, 1802

Why is a letter written by Thomas Jefferson to a Baptist group more than two hundred years ago an important event in early American history? Because radical left wing legal organizations, in concert with liberal Supreme Court Justices, have turned the contents of that letter inside-out and stood it on its head as a tool to advance the disingenuous issue of separation of church and state. The issue is deceitful because those promoting it base their argument on twisted facts.

In *Everson v. Board of Education (1947)*, a case brought by Catholic parents seeking reimbursement of public education tax money, the U. S. Supreme Court, in a 5-4 decision said: "The First Amendment has erected a wall between church and state. That wall must be kept high and impregnable. We could not approve the slightest breach." They claimed as their authority words that had appeared 145 years earlier in a letter Jefferson had written in response to one he had received from the Danbury Baptist Association of Connecticut. The Baptist group, a religious minority, had appealed to the President to protect the church from the state.

In remarks intended to assure them of his whole-hearted support for religious freedom, Jefferson said, ""Believing with you that religion is a matter which lies solely between Man & his God, that he owes account to none other for his faith or his worship, that the legitimate powers of government reach actions only, & not opinions, I contemplate with sovereign reverence that act of the whole American people which declared that their legislature should 'make no law respecting an establishment of religion, or prohibiting the free exercise thereof,' thus building a wall of separation between Church & State."

The words "building a wall of separation between church and state" do not appear in any part of the Constitution nor do they appear in the recorded history of debates leading to the passage of the First Amendment. They were inserted into the 1947 *Everson* decision by a left wing attorney and became the basis of the liberal campaign to marginalize Christians and Christianity.

Along with other Founders involved in producing the First Amendment, Jefferson clearly intended for the government to be *completely* neutral where religious issues were concerned and that there would be no state sponsored denomination as there had been in England and in the early days of some colonies. The radical left has been successful in getting many uninformed people to believe Jefferson was advocating protection of the state from the church, the exact opposite of Jefferson's intended meaning. Evidence is incontrovertible that Jefferson never imagined a time when the church would not be looked to by the people and their government for moral and ethical leadership.

Justice Joseph Story, recognized as an authority on the Constitution and the framers, wrote in his *Commentaries on the Constitution of the United States,* "The real object of the First Amendment was not to countenance, much less advance, Mohammedanism, or Judaism, or infidelity, by prostrating Christianity; but to exclude all rivalry among Christian sects, and to prevent any national ecclesiastical establishment which should give to a hierarchy the exclusive patronage of the national government. It thus cut off the means of religious persecution (the vice and pest of former ages), and the subversion of the rights of conscience in matters of religion which had been trampled upon almost from the days of the Apostles to the present age."

Those whose goal is to reverse the meaning of the First Amendment in order to promote an anti-Christian agenda ignore this lesser known unambiguous statement by Jefferson: "I consider the government of the United States as interdicted by the Constitution from intermeddling with religious institutions, their doctrines, discipline, or exercises. This results not only from the provision that no law shall be made respecting the establishment or free exercise of religion, but from that also which reserves to the states the powers not delegated to the United States. Clearly, no power to prescribe any religious exercise, or to assume authority in religious discipline, has been delegated to the general government."

In commenting on *Wallace vs. Jaffree* in 1985, Supreme Court Justice William Rehnquist stated his opinion on the true purpose of the First Amendment: "The Framers intended the Establishment Clause to prohibit the designation of any church as a 'national' one. The clause was also designed to stop the Federal government from asserting preference for one religious denomination or sect over others. There is simply no historical foundation for the proposition that the framers intended to build a wall of separation that was constitutionalized in *Everson*. But the greatest injury of the 'wall' notion is its mischievous diversion of judges from the actual intentions of the drafters of the Bill of Rights... [N]o amount of repetition of historical errors in judicial opinions can make the errors true. The 'wall of separation between church and State' is a metaphor based on bad history...It should be frankly and explicitly abandoned...Our perception has been clouded not by the Constitution but by the mists of an unnecessary metaphor."

"No great American," says historian Clyde N. Wilson [referring to Jefferson] "has been put to so many contradictory uses by later generations of enemies and apologists, and therefore none has undergone so much distortion. In fact, most of what has been asserted about Jefferson in the last hundred years – and even more of what has been implied or assumed about him – is so lacking in context and proportion as to be essentially false. What we commonly see is not Jefferson. It is a strange amalgam or composite in which the misconceptions of each succeeding generation have been combined until the original is no longer discernible."

Secular humanists who label Jefferson an atheist, an infidel, a skeptic, and an infrequent church attendee, ignore convincing evidence to the contrary including the documented history of his regular attendance of worship services his entire life, having been born into a devout Anglican family. Many of the Christian church services he attended while in Washington were held in courthouses, the chambers of the U.S. House of Representatives, and the Capitol Rotunda, with music often supplied, at Jefferson's request, by the U.S. Marine Corps Band. He approved money out of the Federal Treasury for the support of a Christian missionary program to the Indians and for the construction of a Christian church in which they could worship. So much for Jefferson's alleged creation of the phony issue known as the "wall of separation between church and state."

At times during his life, Jefferson was quoted as saying he doubted the doctrine of the Triune God which puts him in the company of many Christians who have sometimes questioned the Trinity and other basic Christian doctrine. Secular humanists who use those occasional statements as proof that Jefferson was not a Christian ignore this straight forward statement: "A more beautiful or precious morsel of ethics [the Bible] I have never seen; it is a document in proof that I am a real Christian; that is to say, a disciple of the doctrines of Jesus."

His writings contain so many references to the rightful place of religion, especially the Judeo-Christian religion, in government that the secularists have nothing to stand on except their carefully-designed and perverted version of the First Amendment. "It yet remains a problem to be solved in human affairs," Jefferson emphasized, "whether any free government can be permanent, where the public worship of God, and the support of religion, constitutes no part of the policy or duty of the state in any assignable shape."

As Samuel Butler wisely observed, "Though God cannot alter the past, historians can." If he were writing today, he may well have added, "as can anti-Christian radicals acting in tandem with activist judges."

48.

Military Academy Established at West Point

<u>March 16, 1802</u>

Because of America's location on the globe, protected on two sides by the world's largest oceans, sages have speculated that an initially weak United States benefited from natural, which many have called Providential, protection. Otto von Bismarck put it this way: "The Americans have contrived to be surrounded on two sides by weak neighbors and on two sides – *by fish*!" It was also Bismarck who said, "There is a Providence that protects idiots, drunkards, children, and the United States of America."

In the early days of the republic, most Americans were more concerned about the presence of a large standing army and the possibility of its evolving into a military dictatorship than they were of foreign invasion. American leaders preferred to rely on a collection of state militias rather than a national army led by a professional officer corps to protect the country from invasion which they considered an unlikely possibility.

Not all leaders completely agreed with that assessment, especially the men who had experienced the battlefield hazards of the war for independence. While a few may have harbored minor reservations about standing armies, most understood from first hand experience that lack of a well-trained officer corps had been a problem for the Continental Army. They didn't want to see that disadvantage reappear in some future national emergency.

After the war, Federalist army veterans George Washington, Henry Knox, and Alexander Hamilton led a movement to create an institution by which an officer corps could be established, maintained, and trained in the art and science of war. A few years later, Congress took a major step in that direction.

Understanding the widely-held reservations regarding the establishment of a professional army, Congress authorized President Thomas Jefferson to establish a "Corps of Engineers" that would "constitute a Military Academy" on March 16, 1802. Thus, with just bit of subterfuge, was the first of America's military academies established. Technically, the U.S. Military Academy remained part of the Corps of Engineers until 1866.

The COE was to be housed at West Point, New York, location of the oldest continuously occupied fort in the United States, where a few young army officers, members of the "Corps of Artillerists and Engineers," had been trained since 1794. Seeking to downplay the military training aspect of the institution, Jefferson appointed civilian businessman Jonathan Williams as its first superintendent. Williams, who happened to be Benjamin Franklin's grandnephew, was a man of vision and competence in several fields. He is credited with founding the U.S. Military Philosophical Society and originated its prescient motto: "Science in war is the guarantee of peace."

In 1817, the Academy underwent a transformation under the direction of a new superintendent, Colonel Sylvanus Thayer, an 1808 Academy graduate. During the two years prior to his appointment, Thayer had studied at the French *Ecole Polytechnique*, the foremost French engineering school of its day. He was able to introduce advanced engineering practices he learned in France to the Academy curriculum which, along with his experience as an army engineer, enhanced the educational experience by combining newly-developed theory with practical know-how.

Because of the advances in education and professionalism he initiated, Thayer is now remembered as the "Father of the Military Academy." He made the Academy a model upon which engineering schools established their curricula for the next fifty years when construction of the young nation's infrastructure was creating a rapidly growing need for well-trained civil engineers.

Thayer's increased overall academic standards and military-style discipline led to the Academy's written mission statement: "To educate, train, and inspire the Corps of Cadets so that each graduate is a commissioned leader of character committed to the values of Duty, Honor, Country and prepared for a career of professional excellence and service to the Nation as an officer in the United States Army."

In 1919, one of Thayer's successors as superintendent of the U.S. Military Academy, Brigadier General Douglas MacArthur, further advanced Thayer's honor principle by forming a Cadet Honor Committee. MacArthur is known for the emphasis he placed on an honor code intended to guide the behavior of every USMA student and graduate: "A cadet will not lie, cheat, steal, or tolerate those who do."

"Duty, honor, country," said MacArthur, "reverently dictate what you ought to be, what you can be, what you will be. They are your rallying point to build courage when courage seems to fail, to regain faith when there seems to be little cause for faith, to create hope when hope becomes forlorn. Your guidepost stands out like a ten-fold beacon in the night: Duty, honor, country."

MacArthur also broadened the curriculum to include additional instruction in the areas of history, liberal arts, and economics. To underscore his belief in the importance of physical fitness, he encouraged all cadets to become involved in either varsity or intramural athletics: "Every cadet an athlete" was one of his axioms. "Upon the fields of friendly strife are sown the seeds that, upon other fields, on other days, will bear the fruits of victory."

A member of the Long Gray Line, as Academy graduates are known, MacArthur shares that tradition with some of America's most famous military leaders including Robert E. Lee, Ulysses S. Grant, William T. Sherman, John J. Pershing, George S. Patton, Dwight D. Eisenhower, and Omar Bradley along with many others who have helped to shape American history as both military and political leaders.

History has proven the Founding Fathers had nothing to fear and much to respect about what has become the proud military tradition of the American citizen soldier and the officer corps created to lead them. Motivated by a love of freedom and a love of country, American military personnel, whether as volunteers or draftees, have met every challenge with confident courage and ability. Washington, Knox, Hamilton, and others understood that excellent training generates competence and confidence.

G. K. Chesterton, an Englishman, may have best described what makes the American patriot soldier, sailor, marine, and airman the most respected in the world: "The true soldier fights not because he hates what is in front of him, but because he loves what is behind him."

49.

Louisiana Purchase Treaty Signed

When thirteen small English colonies located along the eastern coast of the North American continent became the free and independent United States of America, they occupied only 375,000 square miles of land area. How they expanded to fifty states that now include a land area of approximately 6,700,000 square miles is quite an involved story. The *Louisiana Purchase* was a major part of that story.

With the stroke of a pen, the land area obtained from France at a bargain price more than doubled the size of the United States. It included what would become all or part of the states of Louisiana, Arkansas, Oklahoma, Kansas, Missouri, Iowa, Nebraska, Colorado, New Mexico, Wyoming, Montana, North Dakota, South Dakota, and Minnesota.

It was a transaction that appeared to Thomas Jefferson and his designated negotiators to be a Providential event because it certainly hadn't happened as the result of some clever and well-designed plan. What began as a rather timid attempt to purchase control of the city of New Orleans from France soon resulted in America's gaining ownership over all the French controlled land west of the Mississippi River.

Jefferson was motivated to gain control of New Orleans because it was by far the best and most strategically located port on the southern coast of North America. That port, important in itself, was also the gateway to the Mississippi River which had become vitally important to America because it was an essential natural resource for transportation and trade in its westward expansion.

In 1762, Spain had been given control of the territory, known then simply as Louisiana, by the French government before the treaty ending the French and Indian War was signed in 1763. Even though a 1795 treaty with Spain, formally titled the *Treaty of Friendship, Limits, and Navigation Between Spain and the United States*, had guaranteed America access to the Mississippi River, Jefferson wasn't entirely comfortable with the situation.

The reason for his discomfort could have been validated in 1800 when a weakened Spain returned control of the area to France as the result of a treaty called the *Preliminary and Secret Treaty between the French Republic and His Catholic Majesty the King of Spain, Concerning the Aggrandizement of His Royal Highness the Infant Duke of Parma in Italy and the Retrocession of Louisiana*. Jefferson's discomfort was based on Spain's weakened position in the world and on the suspicion that at some point France or Britain would someday attempt to resume a major role in the development of the western territories of the United States. If a new owner of the territory should choose to renounce the 1795 treaty with Spain, they would be in a position to block American access to New Orleans and the Mississippi River.

Jefferson had no way of knowing about the secret treaty between Spain and France until word leaked out in 1801. When informed about the treaty, he sent Robert Livingston, U.S. Minister to France, to Paris with orders to discuss the possibility of purchasing New Orleans. French Foreign Minister Charles Maurice de Talleyrand told Livingston they had no interest in discussing the matter.

Unbeknownst to Jefferson and Talleyrand, Napoleon was concerned with other problems and those problems, as it turned out, were working to the advantage of American interests in securing control of New Orleans. A combination of events, including France's inability to put down a rebellion in Haiti and a looming war with Great Britain, influenced a decision Napoleon announced to his Foreign Minister and his Treasury Minister on April 10, 1803: He instructed Talleyrand to open negotiations with the Americans regarding the possible sale of the entire Louisiana territory. Napoleon needed money to support his ambitions in Europe more than he needed a large chunk of New World real estate he might have to defend from the Americans or the British at some point in the future.

At the same time Napoleon was moving toward that conclusion, Jefferson had decided to send James Monroe to join Livingston in Paris with instructions to offer $10 million for the port of New Orleans and the area immediately surrounding the strategically located city. To their astonishment, the American emissaries were informed by Talleyrand that France was only willing to sell all of the Louisiana territory, not just New Orleans and the price was $15 million; $11.25 million in cash plus cancelled debts totaling $3.75 million. While that was a huge sum in 1803, it translated into approximately three-cents per acre. Livingston and Monroe couldn't believe their ears.

Fearing that Napoleon might change his mind, the American emissaries agreed to the terms and signed the document April 30, 1803. When word of the successful negotiations reached him, Jefferson was thrilled. He announced the land purchase on July 4, the Senate ratified it October 20, and the treaty was implemented December 20.

Providing a little insight into his thinking, Napoleon said, "This accession of territory affirms forever the power of the United States, and I have given England a maritime rival who sooner or later will humble her pride."

At no point during the process did the negotiators on either side know the exact boundaries of the land area included in the Louisiana territory. The treaty describes it as "the Same extent that it now has in the hand of Spain, & that it had when France possessed it; and Such as it Should be after the Treaties subsequently entered into between Spain and other States." When pressed for specifics, Talleyrand said, "I can give you no direction. You have made a noble bargain for yourselves, and I suppose you will make the most of it."

The boundary issue wasn't settled until 1819 when the *Treaty with Spain*, also known as the *Adams-Onis Treaty*, put it to rest. That treaty finally established the territorial boundaries of the U.S. through the Rocky Mountains and west to the Pacific Ocean. Negotiated by John Quincy Adams, the treaty also added Florida and some disputed areas in Texas to the United States. In 1804, a territorial government was established and in 1812, Louisiana, the first of the fourteen states to be carved out of the Louisiana territory, was admitted to the Union.

As a strict constitutionalist, Jefferson had harbored reservations regarding the constitutionality of purchasing land from foreign governments. But he felt that getting control of the Mississippi River was important enough to transcend his Antifederalist roots.

The Louisiana Purchase established a precedent that would guide the American government in future land acquisitions as the young nation systematically expanded toward the Pacific coast.

50.

Lewis and Clark Depart From St. Louis

May 14, 1804

The "invisible hand" of Providence seems to have been active throughout the story of the Lewis and Clark Expedition, an exploratory adventure that began in 1804 in St. Louis, Missouri, and ended, to great acclaim, back where it started in September of 1806.

How the leading characters in the drama – President Thomas Jefferson, Meriwether Lewis, William Clark, a teenage Shoshone Indian girl named Sacagawea, a Shoshone Indian Chief, plus a highly competent supporting cast – all came together at just the right time appears to have been coordinated by a "director" possessing supernatural capabilities and a plan. Coincidences do sometimes occur, but usually not in bunches.

Traveling through thousands of miles of topographically difficult country inhabited primarily by Indian tribes, whose response to itinerant Europeans was often unpredictable, presented a formidable challenge, to say the least. In addition to those hazards, members of the *Corps of Discovery*, as the expedition was called, didn't have any idea what they were going to experience when it came time to cross the Rocky Mountains. Because no one had mapped their chosen route, the group had no way of knowing how far they would have to travel through unknown mountainous terrain to arrive at their destination, the Pacific Ocean.

Fifteen years earlier, a west-bound Canadian expedition had turned north at the Continental Divide, eschewing a trip through the Rockies, and proceeded west to the Pacific by way of Canada. Future explorers therefore would have no maps or information regarding the more direct route through the rugged, uncharted mountain range and beyond to the Pacific Ocean. The *Corps* began their journey knowing they would have to rely on hunters, trappers, and Indians to provide regional information as they went along.

Although it couldn't fulfill one of the main hoped-for objectives of the mission – to find a Northwest Passage via water to the Pacific Ocean – the expedition did succeed in providing a valuable description of the northwest portion of the land included in the *Louisiana Purchase*. As a result of Clark's detailed *Voyage of Discovery* journal, future explorers and settlers were provided with information on geology, wildlife, Indian tribes, natural resources, and other general facts that would make westward expansion a much less daunting challenge. The information they provided also helped later to strengthen U.S. claims to the Oregon Territory.

Knowing that the French had at one time considered sending an expedition into the area may have influenced Jefferson's thinking about sending one of his own as early as 1802, a year before the *Louisiana Purchase* seemed likely to happen. He may have felt some urgency to do that when he learned in 1801 that Spain had recently ceded the area, then known simply as Louisiana, back to France. Jefferson began talking to his personal secretary, Meriwether Lewis, about the possibility of his leading a "scientific expedition" through the territory. Even though Lewis was only twenty-eight years old at the time, he had known his President and fellow Virginian socially for many years during which they had developed a mutual respect. Lewis had been commissioned as a Lieutenant in the U.S. Army in 1795; since 1801, he had served as a military aid to Jefferson.

An avid outdoorsman since his youth, Lewis was intrigued by the idea and began working on a plan for such an expedition. An important part of that plan included finding the right man to complement and assist him as leader of the contingent and to help him select men with the talents, skills, and character needed to accomplish the arduous task. Early in 1803, Lewis selected his former Army commanding officer William Clark to be his co-leader.

As a youngster, Clark was taught how to survive in the wilderness by an older brother who had fought in the Revolutionary War, mostly against Indian tribes allied with the British. In 1792, the younger Clark had enlisted in the 5,000-man *Legion of the United States*, the first unit of what was to become a professionally-trained standing American army. Under the command of "Mad Anthony" Wayne, the *Legion* was originally formed to clear hostile Indian tribes from what was then known as the Northwest Territory.

Early in his Army career, Lieutenant Clark had been personally recognized by Wayne for his abilities as a leader of men. At the Battle of Fallen Timbers, Clark and the men under his command had played a major role in achieving a decisive victory. His familiarity with Indian customs and behaviors along with his possession of wilderness survival skills would prove to be of great value to the success of the Lewis and Clark expedition. Having retired from the army, Clark was available and ready to accompany his former comrade in arms on the historic journey.

Plans and preparations continued, mostly in secret, to the point that when the *Louisiana Purchase* was announced July 4, 1803, strategy for the mission had pretty much been determined. Lewis and Clark could then turn their attention to staffing and logistics. Lewis ordered construction of a fifty-five-foot keel boat, then set up a camp on the Illinois side of the Mississippi River near St. Louis where they spent the winter of 1803-04 assembling supplies and training personnel.

On May 14, the *Corps of Discovery* debarked on the first leg of their exploratory trip up the Missouri River. They intended to proceed by boat to the headwaters of the River which they hoped would connect with the Columbia River thereby providing a water route all the way from St. Louis to the Pacific Ocean.

On October 24, the expedition arrived in central North Dakota, an area dominated by the Mandan Indian tribe. They decided to build a fort and spend the winter there due to the severe weather they knew would soon set in. It was at Ft. Mandan that Lewis and Clark met a fur trapper named Toussaint Charbonneau who they hired to guide them through the territory over which they would have to travel when Spring arrived. Fortuitously, Charbonneau's young wife Sacagawea, a Shoshone Indian, would become invaluable to the explorers as a translator when they passed through Shoshone and Nez Perce territory. She was the daughter of a respected Shoshone chief and the sister of Cameahwait, another Shoshone chief whose friendship would also become invaluable, especially in the procurement of horses vital to the success of their mission.

In February, Sacagawea gave birth to a son, Jean Baptiste, who became an asset in convincing suspicious Indians that the expedition was on a peaceful mission; it was contrary to Indian custom for a war party to include a mother and small child. Charbonneau, Sacagawea, and Jean Baptiste would stay with the expedition all the way to the Pacific Ocean and back to Ft. Mandan where they would part company in 1806.

Departing from their winter quarters in April of 1805, the explorers proceeded west and arrived at the headwaters of the Missouri River in Montana in August. On August 26, they crossed the Continental Divide on horseback at Lemhi Pass and, finding no connection to the Columbia River, a disappointed Lewis and Clark realized that there was no way to complete their trek to the west coast completely by water.

Proceeding west on horseback, and by boat when possible, they finally were able to see the Pacific Ocean at the mouth of the Columbia River on November 20. Writing in his journal, Clark memorialized the occasion with this entry: "Great joy in Camp we are in view of the Ocean, this great Pacific Ocean which we've been so long anxious to see and the roaring or noise made by the waves breaking on the rocky shores (as I suppose) may be heard distinctly."

Members of the expedition spent the winter at Ft. Clatsop near modern day Portland, Oregon working on their maps and journals. They began the journey home on March 23, 1806. Six months later, they arrived back in St. Louis having secured an important place in American history.

51.

War of 1812 Declared

June 18, 1812

Avoiding entanglement in European hot and cold wars, one of the tenets of the American government since achieving independence in 1783, was a constant challenge since the major European powers, especially Britain and France, were almost always fighting over something. Because American interests were often affected, a policy of neutrality, while it may have been desirable, was not an easy one to maintain. In 1812, it became impossible.

Congress attempted a number of alternatives in hopes of avoiding hostilities, one of which was an embargo that nearly destroyed the American economy before reality finally set in. By June of 1812, it had become clear to President James Madison and a majority of Americans that the on-going European wars, generally known from 1799 to 1815 as the *Napoleonic Wars*, had placed the U.S. in an untenable position and that there was no possible way to avoid getting dragged into them other than by abandoning vital American economic interests.

European belligerents were interfering with America's growing economy by attacking U.S. commercial vessels and denying them access to European ports. The British Navy attacked the ships of any country doing business with France and the French Navy attacked the ships of any country doing business with England. Both the British and the French offered immunity from attack to countries that would do business exclusively with them, but accepting an exclusivity deal would only have solved half the problem for America. Like it or not, it was time to pick a side.

The British had the larger and more powerful navy, especially after defeating a combined French and Spanish fleet during the Battle of Trafalgar in 1805, but that also meant they needed more sailors than they could provide for themselves. They created part of their personnel problem by mistreating their own seamen who often deserted in American ports where they then signed on to American ships. The British *solution* was to impress (capture) the crews of foreign ships, especially American, to fill out the crews of their warships. American leaders, as well as the American public, found that practice to be more than unacceptable.

In 1810, the election to Congress of a group known as "war hawks," tipped the scales in favor of doing what had to be done to protect American interests and that meant declaring war against Britain, the more menacing threat. With the Democratic Republican Party in control of Congress, Madison finally had the political muscle he needed to secure a declaration of war. It was approved June 18, 1812, by a vote of 79-49 in the House of Representatives. The ensuing war, which lasted until 1815, is often called America's Second War for Independence against England.

Getting that declaration of war had not been easy primarily because of regional differences of opinion. Federalists, who were prevalent in the northeast, tended to favor England because of shared mercantile interests. Antifederalists, now called Democratic-Republicans, tended to favor France because they still felt a debt of gratitude for the vital assistance France had provided during the Revolutionary War. The states of Massachusetts and Connecticut called the declaration unconstitutional because the U.S. had not been invaded.

Backing Madison, former President Thomas Jefferson, who originally favored neutrality at almost any cost, had come to believe it was time to take a stand and, at the same time, settle some old scores with England. Especially annoying to Jefferson was British failure to live up to an obligation to remove their troops from a few outposts in the Northwest Territory, one of several accords included in the 1783 *Treaty of Paris*. In addition to the impressment of American seamen and the damage they were doing to the U.S. economy, the British were also known to have been assisting American Indian tribes in forming alliances to oppose America's westward expansion. Jefferson, Madison, and others also believed another war with England could possibly result in an American takeover of Canada and the end of English influence on the North American continent.

A three-pronged attack on Canadian targets from Detroit to Montreal launched in July of 1812 by General William Hull quickly proved that an easy takeover of Canada was an ill-conceived theory. The results of those attacks also proved that poorly-trained state militiamen were no substitute for a professionally trained army as Hull's ragtag forces were routed and forced to surrender in August. Native Americans fighting for the British were instrumental in providing that British victory. Other American attacks on Canadian targets produced similar results as the militiamen, lacking in training and motivation, were routinely defeated.

While the militiamen were taking their lumps, the U.S. Navy was enjoying unexpected success against British warships on the high seas. The most famous of those victories occurred August 19, 1812, off the coast of Nova Scotia when the *USS Constitution*, under the command of Captain Isaac Hull, defeated *HMS Guerriere*, becoming the first American warship to force the surrender of a British man o'war. As a result of that victory, the *Constitution* became know as *"Old Ironsides"* when eye witnesses reported that *Guerriere's* projectiles bounced off its wooden hull "as if it were made of iron."

An American Navy squadron operating in Lake Erie under the command of Captain Oliver Hazard Perry achieved a major victory September 10, 1813, by defeating a six-ship British flotilla giving America control of Lake Erie. That victory led to the retaking of Detroit by General William Henry Harrison who was then able to drive the British back into Canada. An important ally of the Canadians, Shawnee Chief Tecumseh, died in the fighting which resulted in diminished participation in the war by a Native American confederation. The victories won by Perry and Harrison also removed a threat of attack on the Northwest Territories.

Early in 1814, the British Navy was able to blockade the entire east coast of America. In August, they captured Washington which they burned before reboarding their ships. They then sailed down the Patuxent River and up Chesapeake Bay to Baltimore where they bombarded Fort McHenry on September 14, an event that was described by Francis Scott Key's poem originally entitled *Defence of Fort McHenry*. When the British ships were unable to destroy the fort, they withdrew and abandoned the

Chesapeake area. A musical version of Key's poem, later retitled *The Star Spangled Banner*, became the American national anthem in 1931.

A naval battle fought on Lake Champlain September 11, 1814, is believed to have been the turning point in a war that both sides were ready to bring to an end. Also known as the Battle of Plattsburgh, New York, the American naval victory in the Battle of Lake Champlain ended British attempts to control a strategic location from which they could launch land attacks on the U.S. An American flotilla under the command of Master Commandant Thomas MacDonough defeated a powerful British naval squadron while American General Alexander Macomb's regular Army troops, who had replaced the militiamen, were winning their campaign against a much larger British Army.

Those American victories led to the signing of the *Treaty of Ghent* concluded in Ghent, Belgium (formerly part of the Netherlands), on December 24, 1814, that officially brought the *War of 1812* to an end.

As it turned out, the *official* and the *actual* ending dates of the war varied by two weeks. Due to the lack of long distance methods of communicating, one more major battle was fought before news of the treaty reached General Andrew Jackson and his British counterpart General Edward Pakenham. Capturing New Orleans, America's greatest port, had been a major British objective during the war. On January 8, 1815, Jackson and his Army achieved the greatest victory of the war when they repulsed an attack on New Orleans by a 10,000-man British Army killing 2,000 of them while losing less than 100 of their own.

In commenting on the Battle of New Orleans, Jackson later said, "It appears that the unerring hand of Providence shielded my men from the shower of balls, bombs, and rockets, when every ball and bomb from our guns carried with them a mission of death."

His spectacular victory in the Battle of New Orleans vaulted Andrew (Old Hickory) Jackson into national prominence. In 1829, he became the seventh President of the United States of America.

52.

USS Constitution Defeats *HMS Guerriere*

August 19, 1812

That the United States of America was guided and protected by the God of the Judeo-Christian Bible throughout the perilous times of its founding was a conviction frequently expressed in the spoken and written words of most of those recognized as Founding Fathers. The story of how *Old Ironsides* got its name is one of those often cited as an example.

Providence is the word our Founders often used as a metaphor for God's pre-established and inevitable plan. It seems to have been at work August 19, 1812 as the *USS Constitution*, with Commander Issac Hull as her skipper, battled the *HMS Guerriere* off the coast of Nova Scotia. According to eye witness reports, cannon balls fired by the *Guerriere* failed to penetrate the wooden hull of the *Constitution* as the two ships engaged in a fierce thirty-minute sea battle. While cannon balls were bouncing off the *Constitution*, the *Guerriere* was being systematically destroyed by the American frigate's cannon fire. Because the *Guerriere's* projectiles bounced off its wooden hull as if it were made of iron, the *Constitution* became known as "*Old Ironsides*."

It was a historic victory for the American Navy because, as the *London Times* reported: "Never before in the history of the world did an English frigate strike to an American." Later that year the upstart U.S. Navy continued to raise eyebrows when *Old Ironsides* captured the *HMS Java* and when the *USS United States*, under the command of Captain Stephen Decatur, captured the *HMS Macedonian*. Those victories gave credibility to the U.S. Navy as a fighting force and confidence to the officers and men manning American combat ships. Before the war ended, *Old Ironsides* had destroyed or captured five more British war ships.

Built in a Boston shipyard and launched in 1797, the *Constitution*, a three-masted frigate, was given her name by President George Washington. In 1798, she was ordered to protect American commercial shipping from French pirate ships operating along the coast from New England to Florida. After the *Quasi War* with France ended in 1800, she was taken out of service until 1803 when she was recommissioned by Captain Edward Preble. For the next two years, the *Constitution* was Preble's flagship as he commanded a squadron in fighting Barbary Pirates and in blockading the Tripolitan coast. The Barbary War peace treaty with Tripoli was signed on board the *Constitution* June 3, 1805.

Captain Preble, a disciplinarian, later became influential in establishing rules and regulations that helped to shape a professional navy that was beginning to win recognition as an important part of America's growing importance in international commerce and geopolitics. He also trained many of the young officers who went on to make names for themselves as American Navy heroes. "Preble's boys," as they were called, included Stephen Decatur, James Lawrence, Thomas MacDonough, and Issac Hull.

Captain Hull, who had previously served aboard the *Constitution* as a young Lieutenant under Preble, took command of the frigate in 1810 and remained in command throughout the War of 1812. The training he had received under Preble's supervision served him well throughout the war and especially in his famous victory over the *Guerriere*.

After the war, *Old Ironsides* remained in service many years beyond what was considered to be the normal useful life of a wooden-hulled warship. But a plan by the Navy to scrap the 33-year-old frigate in 1830 was strongly opposed by an aroused public leading instead to a refurbishing of the historic ship and its subsequent return to an active role in the fleet. A poem entitled *Old Ironsides* by Oliver Wendell Holmes is credited with rallying the public to protest the ship's proposed destruction.

Writing about his poem, Holmes explained: "This [*Old Ironsides*] was the popular name by which the frigate *Constitution* was known. The poem was first printed in the *Boston Daily Advertiser*, at the time when it was proposed to break up the old ship as unfit for service. I subjoin the paragraph which led to the writing of the poem. It is from the *Advertiser* of Tuesday, September 14, 1830:"

> *Old Ironsides – It has been affirmed upon good authority that the Secretary of the Navy has recommended to the Board of Navy Commissioners to dispose of the frigate Constitution. Since it has been understood that such a step was in contemplation we have heard but one opinion expressed, and that in decided disapprobation of the measure. Such a national object of interest, so endeared to our national pride as Old Ironsides is, should never by any act of our government cease to belong to the Navy, so long as our country is to be found upon the map of nations. In England it was lately determined by the Admiralty to cut the Victory, a one-hundred gun ship (which it will be recollected bore the flag of Lord Nelson at the battle of Trafalgar), down to a seventy-four, but so loud were the lamentations of the people upon the proposed measure that the intention was abandoned. We confidently anticipate that the Secretary of the Navy will in like manner consult the general wish in regard to the Constitution, and either let her remain in ordinary or rebuild her whenever the public service may require. – New York Journal of Commerce.*

Here is Holmes' poem entitled *Old Ironsides* written September 16, 1830:

Ay, tear her tattered ensign down!
Long has it waved on high,
And many an eye has danced to see
That banner in the sky;
Beneath it rung the battle shout,
And burst the cannon's roar;
The meteor of the ocean air
Shall sweep the clouds no more.
Her deck, once red with heroes' blood,
Where knelt the vanquished foe,
When winds were hurrying o'er the flood,
And waves were white below,
No more shall feel the victor's tread,
Or know the conquered knee;

The harpies of the shore shall pluck
The eagle of the sea!
Oh, better that her shattered bulk
Should sink beneath the wave;
Her thunders shook the mighty deep,
And there should be her grave;
Nail to the mast her holy flag,
Set every threadbare sail,
And give her to the god of storms,
The lightning and the gale!

Old Ironsides can be seen today at the Charlestown Navy Yard in Boston.

53.

Francis Scott Key writes
Star Spangled Banner

<u>September 14, 1814</u>

August 24, 1814, was a very bad day for America. It was on that date during the War of 1812 that members of British forces under the command of General Robert Ross and Admiral George Cockburn, following their victory at the battle of Bladensburg, were given orders to burn the White House, the Capital Building, and other buildings in Washington, DC. The British met so little resistance that they felt confidant victory was within their grasp as they raised their flag over the conquered city. Ross and Cockburn began quickly to plan an attack on their next strategic target.

On September 12, they left their command headquarters in Upper Marlboro, Maryland, to return to the *HMS* Tonnant, Cockburn's flagship that was to lead a coordinated land and sea attack on Ft. McHenry in Baltimore Harbor the next day. The British officers took Dr. William Beanes, whose home they had used as their area headquarters, with them as a prisoner, claiming he was a spy. Perhaps Providentially, the elderly and respected Dr. Beanes was an acquaintance of a well-connected and socially prominent lawyer-poet named Francis Scott Key.

As part of a family with close ties to England, Key had been philosophically opposed to the idea of going to war with the mother country. But those misgivings quickly disappeared when he became aware of the deliberately malicious act of the Brtitish in destroying the

U.S. capital. When mutual friends requested his help in getting Dr. Beanes released from British captivity, Key, with his access to President James Madison, accepted what could have been a dangerous assignment.

Madison made a sloop available and assigned Colonel John Skinner, a prisoner exchange agent, to accompany Key to the British ship under a flag of truce that would allow them to safely approach the enemy vessel. When the Americans reached the *Tonnant*, they were received cordially and invited to dine with the Admiral and his staff. Key and Skinner presented their case during which they showed their hosts letters from wounded British prisoners who had good things to say about the care they had received from American doctors including Dr. Beanes.

Eventually, the British officers agreed to release their prisoner but, fearing that Key and Skinner had heard too much about their plans, they said the three Americans could not leave until their attack on Fort McHenry was completed. Key and Skinner had become prisoners themselves and were not too sure about how they would be treated if the British attack turned out to be successful. The decision by the British to hold them put Key exactly where he needed to be in order to produce what would officially become America's national anthem 117 years later. From the deck of the truce ship that had been secured to the British warship, he nervously watched the event he would soon memorialize.

Key was able to see the Stars and Stripes flying above the fort when the British bombardment began at 6 a.m. The flag they would watch through 25 hours of furious shelling had been specially made at the request of Major George Armistead, commanding officer of Fort McHenry. When requesting the flag, Armistead said he wanted it to be so big "the British would have no trouble seeing it from a distance." The flag delivered to Armistead measured 42 feet by 30 feet!

As darkness fell, Key, Skinner, and Beanes watched the fort and kept their focus on that huge flag as best they could through the darkness and smoke. Throughout the night, occasional flashes of "bombs bursting in air" revealed that the "flag was still there." They were comforted by the realization that as long as the bombing continued, they knew Major Armistead had not surrendered.

At one point, the British shelling stopped and Key imagined the worst. Later, he learned the shelling had been stopped to allow the launching of a British amphibious attack on the fort by British troops.

It had been repulsed by an assortment of poorly trained but highly motivated Maryland militiamen. When the "dawn's early light" of September 14 revealed the flag still flying above Fort McHenry, the British ships stopped the attack due to lack of ammunition. As the British began preparing to withdraw in frustration, Key and his party were given their freedom.

Inspired and thrilled by the sight of Armistead's flag flying above Fort McHenry in the morning breeze and by the miraculous nature of what he had just witnessed, Key began to write his thoughts on the back of a letter while sailing back to Baltimore. After checking into a hotel, he completed a rough draft of what he had entitled *The Defence of Fort M'Henry*. He gave a copy to his brother-in-law, Judge J. H. Nicholson, who quickly had it printed as a handbill. On September 20, it was featured in a Baltimore newspaper. Within a month's time, it was printed under its new title, *The Star Spangled Banner*, in newspapers all over the country.

Many historians believe it was Nicholson who originally suggested Key's poem be sung to the tune of *Anacreon in Heaven* because the words seemed to fit. Sometimes described as a British drinking song, it originated with London's AnacreonticSociety named for a sixth century Greek poet who focused his artistry on love and merry-making. While their members may have done a little drinking, the Society was known as an amateur musical group whose stated purpose was to promote an interest in music.

Unofficially, *The Star Spangled Banner* quickly became recognized as the national anthem by many groups, including the military, but it wasn't proclaimed as such until 1916 when President Woodrow Wilson signed an executive order to that effect. Finally on March 3, 1931, Congress issued a proclamation, signed by President Herbert Hoover, that made it official: "Be it enacted by the Senate and House of Representatives of the United States of America in Congress assembled, That the composition known as *The Star Spangled Banner* is designated as the National Anthem of the United States of America."

In addition to his poetry, Key wrote a book entitled *The Power of Literature and Its Connection with Religion* in 1834. As a patriot and Christian, Key observed: "The patriot who feels himself in the service of God, who acknowledges Him in all his ways, has the promise of Almighty direction, and will find His Word in his greatest darkness, 'a lantern to his feet and a lamp unto his paths.' He will therefore seek to establish for his country in the eyes of the world, such a character as shall make her not unworthy of the name of a Christian nation."

Today, the over-sized flag that survived the bombardment of Fort McHenry can be seen at the Smithsonian Institution's Museum of American History.

54.

U.S. Acquires Spanish Florida

Spanish-controlled Florida had been a problem for America for many years. By 1817 the solution to that problem had become obvious but no one in Washington could bring themselves to do what needed to be done. Andrew Jackson, who courageously led the American Army to victory in the 1815 battle of New Orleans, understood the problem *and* the solution but his common sense method of thinking made the "elites" of his day nervous.

Jackson got his first taste of military action when he, as a teenager during the Revolutionary War, was part of his uncle's South Carolina militia. Both he and his brother were captured by the British in 1781 and held until the end of the war. When he was released, Jackson returned to South Carolina before moving to North Carolina where he studied Law. He was admitted to the bar in 1787 at the age of twenty.

The following year, with the help of a law school contact, Jackson was appointed Attorney General in a portion of western North Carolina that would become part of the new state of Tennessee in 1796. In Nashville, he also became a successful attorney and a member of the local militia. Jackson served in the U.S. Congress from 1796 to 1798.

In 1802, Jackson was selected to be commander of the Tennessee Militia and given the rank of Major General. When the War of 1812 was declared and with Indian wars heating up in the area, Jackson activated the militia and began doing battle with Creek Indians who had massacred a large group of settlers at Fort Mims in the Mississippi Territory (now the states of Mississippi and Alabama) on August 30, 1813.

Jackson's first major military victory was achieved during the battle of Horseshoe Bend when his Tennessee militia soundly defeated the Creek Indians responsible for the Fort Mims bloodbath. Creek survivors fled into Spanish Florida that had become a sanctuary for Indians and escaped slaves who frequently attacked American settlers on both sides of the border. The *Treaty with the Creeks* (also know as the *Treaty of Fort Jackson*), signed August 9, 1814, ended Jackson's successful action against the Creeks. According to the terms of that treaty, the Creeks ceded twenty-three million acres of land in Alabama and Georgia to the U.S. government.

The victory over the Creeks made "Old Hickory" a folk hero among the frontiersmen and earned him a Major General commission in the regular U.S. Army. A few months later, Jackson added to his fame by driving the British out of Pensacola and destroying Spanish Forts in the area. From there, he moved his troops to Mobile to protect it from the possibility of a British attack but was told to advance to New Orleans to help in its defense. His reputation as a military leader was firmly established on January 8, 1815, with his overwhelming victory over a powerful British Army at New Orleans.

Jackson turned down an offer to become Secretary of War because he felt there was unfinished work to be done where he was as long as Florida remained under Spanish control. As military commander of the area along the Florida/U.S. border, he knew the territory better than any who might be named to replace him. In 1817, Jackson sent a letter to President James Monroe in which he said he would "gladly defeat the Seminoles and capture Spanish Florida" if given the go-ahead in any form. For good measure, Jackson also told Monroe he would "ensure you Cuba in a few days" if provided with a warship." Monroe passed on the warship idea but, in a rather ambiguous way, seemed to go along with the other part of Jackson's proposal.

In December, Jackson received the response he was waiting for from John Calhoun, Secretary of War: Neutralize the Seminoles using whatever "necessary measures" might be required to get the job done. The order was subject to interpretation and many believe Calhoun knew exactly how it would be interpreted by his territorial military commander.

Jackson had made it clear he believed any foreign control of Florida was a threat to the security of the United States. That order plus sporadic Seminole attacks on southern U.S. territories gave him the excuse he needed to militarily remove the threat in a campaign now known as the First Seminole War.

Jackson's victories over the Seminoles, along with a few Spanish forts in the process, caused some consternation in Washington because many feared those attacks would trigger a war with Spain. But Secretary of State John Quincy Adams successfully argued that Jackson's campaign had revealed Spain's weakness in the area and had strengthened America's bargaining position in possibly negotiating the U.S. purchase of Florida. Adams followed up by suggesting to Spanish Foreign Minister Luis de Onis that they should consider selling Florida to the U.S. if they were unable to control people populating the area. Also, Adams knew, Spain had bigger problems than Florida to deal with as their colonies in South America and Mexico were in various stages of revolt at the time. Peacefully getting rid of their Florida problem apparently made sense to the Spanish government.

By forcing the issue with Spain while his superiors in Washington dithered, Jackson had laid the groundwork for the *Adams-Onis Treaty*, also known as the *Transcontinental Treaty*, through which the United States obtained another huge and strategically important piece of real estate at a bargain price. Actually, the U.S. paid nothing directly to Spain but did assume responsibility for a maximum of $5,000,000 in claims filed against them by American citizens. Also, Spain relinquished their claim to the Oregon country north of California and agreed to recognize the American description of the land area included in the Louisiana Purchase. The treaty was signed February 22, 1819, but not ratified until February 22, 1821, at which time Jackson became the first Territorial Governor of Florida.

In 1829, Jackson was elected President of the United States for the first of two terms. He believed in a strong presidency and a strong union. "Without union our independence and liberty would never have been achieved; without union they never can be maintained. The loss of liberty, of all good government, of peace, plenty, and happiness, must inevitably follow a dissolution," Jackson warned.

As president, Jackson evoked strong feelings in reaction to many of his policies, especially his determined campaign to do away with the Bank of the United States. That issue may or may not have been the reason he became the first president to experience an attempt on his life. In 1835, a potential assassin approached Jackson, pulled out a pistol, and pulled the trigger. According to a report on the event, the gun misfired. Pulling out another pistol, the assassin pulled the trigger with the same result. Jackson beat the man with a cane before aids were able to take control of his assailant.

Authorities who later tested the weapons found nothing wrong with either of them which confirmed for Jackson his belief in God's involvement in human affairs. When the King of England sent a letter in which he expressed his concern, Jackson replied with this statement: "A kind of Providence had been pleased to shield me against the recent attempt upon my life, and irresistibly carried many minds to the belief in a superintending Providence."

Jackson died at his home June 8, 1835. His last will and testament included this statement by which he wanted to be remembered: "The Bible is true. Upon that sacred Volume I rest my hope of eternal salvation through the merits of our blessed Lord and Savior Jesus Christ."

"Faults he had, undoubtedly," said William Cullen Bryant, "such faults as often belong to an ardent, generous, sincere nature – the weeds that grow in rich soil. Notwithstanding, he was precisely the man for the period, in which he well and nobly discharged the duties demanded of him."

55.

Congress Passes the *Missouri Compromise*

<u>March 3, 1820</u>

When Missouri became the first territory west of the Mississippi River to seek statehood, the long simmering controversy over slavery policy became a "hot potato" political issue. At that time, there were eleven "slave" states and eleven "free" states giving each side equal representation in the U.S. Senate – twenty-two Senators representing "slave" states and twenty-two Senators representing "free" states.

The Missouri statehood issue also brought into play competing concerns regarding a larger long term question: Which side would control slavery policy in states that would soon be carved out of the western land area included in the Louisiana Purchase?

Since many of the settlers of Missouri had migrated from the south, it was assumed the new territory would enter the Union as a "slave" state which would tilt the balance of power in the Senate to the pro-slavery states, a possible turn of events that was unacceptable to the northern states. The House of Representatives was already controlled by the anti-slavery states of the north because they held a huge population advantage over the southern states. That advantage automatically gave the anti-slave states a much larger number of representatives in the House which made the possibility of accepting Missouri into the union as a "free" state unacceptable to the "slave" states.

Slave owners in the south were adamant about having freedom to expand their plantation system into states that would soon be coming into the Union, a condition that was anathema to abolitionists of the north.

But southern planters were convinced that slave labor was necessary to their continued prosperity. Feelings were so strong on both sides that many members of Congress believed the existence of the Union hung in the balance; some southern states had even begun to talk openly about the possibility of secession. Fortunately, a few influential leaders weren't ready to give up on finding a solution acceptable to both camps.

While the debate was still raising hackles in Congress early in 1820, a bill to admit Maine to the Union as a "free" state, originally blocked by southern states, was resurrected as a possible pathway to a workable compromise: By linking the two, Maine and Missouri could be admitted as "free" and "slave" states, respectively, thus preserving the existing balance of power in the Senate. That plan was eventually accepted by both the House and the Senate as a way of reviving negotiations but with this caveat: Missouri would be admitted to the Union only after its legislative body guaranteed that nothing in its constitution could be interpreted as putting restrictions on slavery.

Also, as part of what soon became known at the *Missouri Compromise*, slavery was to be forbidden in the remaining portions of the Louisiana Purchase north of 36-degrees, 30-minutes north latitude (the southern boundary of Missouri), except for the new state of Missouri. After more refinements, Congress approved the legislation March 3, 1820, and President James Monroe signed it three days later.

Monroe understood that involuntary slavery was impossible to justify in America, a country philosophically devoted to individual freedom. But he also knew that attempting to enforce the abolition of slavery could destroy the Union he and his fellow Founding Fathers had risked so much to establish. His personal preference would have been to let each individual state decide the issue for itself but that was a political impossibility at the time.

Monroe felt the Missouri Compromise proved that the system had worked to peacefully resolve a conflict between federal and state governments, but Thomas Jefferson was fearful that drawing a line such as the 36/30 line, as it was called, could eventually permanently divide and destroy the Union. Addressing the issue in a letter to a friend, Jefferson said "this momentous question, like a fire bell in the night, awakened and filled me with terror. I considered it at once as the knell of the Union. It is hushed indeed for the moment. But this is a reprieve only, not a final sentence. A geographical line, coinciding with a marked principle, moral and political, once conceived and held up to the angry passions of men, will never be obliterated; and every new irritation will mark it deeper and deeper."

The compromise *did* work, as Monroe said, but it turned out to be only a temporary solution. The compromise *did not* work, as Jefferson had predicted, since a permanent resolution would not be realized until more than four decades later as the result of a bloody Civil War.

56.

Monroe Doctrine Declared

December 2, 1823

What became known many years later as the *Monroe Doctrine* was originally a small portion of President James Monroe's 1823 *State of the Union* address.

In that annual report to Congress, he broke new ground when he said that "the American continents, by the free and independent condition which they have assumed and maintain, are henceforth not to be considered as subjects for further colonization by any European powers." That statement got a lot of attention at home and abroad.

Monroe's foreign policy statement was motivated by changing conditions in the European balance of power. Some countries may have seen Spain's loss of control of much of their holdings in the Western Hemisphere as, perhaps, an opportunity to move into an inviting vacuum. Such a development would be contrary to American interests especially in the area that later became Texas, New Mexico, Arizona, and California. Most Americans assumed that area was destined to be included in the United States partly because of the obvious weakness of Spain and Mexico and, more importantly, because they believed it was foreordained.

Essentially, Monroe was telling the European powers not to even think about claiming any part of the southwest portion of the North American continent where Spain had been dominant.

It was a bold statement coming from a fledgling nation that still lacked a world class military establishment. Monroe and Secretary of

State John Quincy Adams, who is credited with writing much of that resolute policy statement, rested secure in the knowledge that England was in agreement with their sentiments because Minister of Foreign Affairs George Canning had suggested earlier that the U.S. and Great Britain issue a joint statement of similar substance. Canning had also informed Monroe and Adams that the French would not be a problem.

In addition to issuing a warning to the European powers, Monroe also intended his foreign policy statement to head off Russian attempts to colonize areas along the Pacific Coast. Russian Ambassador Baron de Tuyll reacted by saying the doctrine "enunciates views and pretensions so exaggerated, and establishes principles so contrary to the rights of the European powers that it merits only the most profound contempt." But he apparently got the message; the Russians were never a factor in the U.S. settlement of the west coast. Even though the *Monroe Doctrine* was never recognized as international law, it was respected by the world leaders.

It was popular with most of the American public because it verbalized what people were thinking. In commenting on the *Monroe Doctrine* in his book entitled *Sidelights on American History*, Henry W. Elson included this important statement of fact that is too often overlooked today but was generally accepted during the early years of the republic: "It is the business of Congress to carry out the policies of the people, not to shape them. President Monroe was not the author of the doctrine that bears his name; he simply voiced the sentiment of the people, and the people are supreme in this Government. The Monroe Doctrine is, therefore, not a law; it is a fact, it is a declaration of an attitude taken by this Government with reference to the relations of European Powers to the republics of this hemisphere. The Monroe Doctrine will stand as long as the American people have the power and the inclination to maintain it."

Monroe's credentials as a Founding Father are more than secure. As a young soldier, he fought in a number of major Revolutionary War battles including the Battle of Trenton where he suffered a bullet wound. After the war, he served in a variety of elective and appointive offices including U.S. Senator, Governor of Virginia, Ambassador to Great Britain, Secretary of State, Secretary of War, and two terms as President covering the eight-year period historians call the "Era of Good Feeling." He played major roles in the *Louisiana Purchase* and the acquisition of Florida.

Thomas Jefferson described him as "a man whose soul might be turned wrong side outwards without discovering a blemish to the world."

That he concurred with most of his fellow Founding Fathers in their belief in the Providential care lavished on the United States of America, Monroe said in an inauguration speech, "I enter on the trust to which I have been called by the suffrages of my fellow-citizens with my fervent prayers to the Almighty that He will be graciously pleased to continue to us that protection which He has already so conspicuously displayed."

Monroe died July 4, 1831, the third president, along with John Adams and Thomas Jefferson, to die on an anniversary of the Declaration of Independence.

57.

Death of Jefferson and Adams

July 4, 1826

Even though there was much more that united rather than divided them, John Adams and Thomas Jefferson wasted a dozen years engaged in a feud both would someday profoundly regret. In working together for the lofty goal of freedom for the nation both men loved, they were comrades in arms for fifteen years. Regarding the important and more controversial issue of how that free and independent nation would be governed, they eventually became political enemies.

Adams and Jefferson had entered into a working relationship in 1775 during the Second Continental Congress when they were appointed to serve on a committee of five, along with Benjamin Franklin, Robert R. Livingston, and Roger Sherman, charged with the responsibility of producing a *Declaration of Independence*. Because of Adams' respect for his new colleague and "the elegance of his pen," he insisted that Jefferson would be the best choice to produce an initial draft for his associates to consider. Once Jefferson's monumental composition was in its final form, Adams became its chief proponent and a dedicated spokesman for its acceptance. All through the perilous period that eventually resulted in independence for the United States of America, Adams and Jefferson were united in their vision and their determination to advance the cause of freedom. But then their relationship slowly began to change.

With the *Constitution* ratified in June of 1788, and the new government beginning to function as designed in 1789, George Washington was elected President, Adams was elected Vice President, and Jefferson was appointed Secretary of State. Seeds of the Adams and Jefferson split wouldn't fully develop for another ten years. Those seeds were sown when Washington appointed Alexander Hamilton as the first Secretary of the Treasury. Washington, Adams, and Hamilton were all proponents of a strong central government while Jefferson was concerned that the central government could become too strong; he was more concerned with protecting states' rights. Also, Jefferson, a Virginian, represented the agricultural viewpoint of the southern states while Hamilton, a New Yorker, was more in tune with the commercial viewpoint of the north. Many of Hamilton's ideas, especially those regarding funding of the central government, caused friction with Jefferson that often had to be arbitrated by Adams whose beliefs were more compatible with those of Hamilton.

As these differences in governing philosophy began to be understood, political parties, which Washington abhorred, began to take shape. The Federalists, as the proponents of a strong central government were called, agreed with Adams. The Anti-Federalists, also known as Democratic-Republicans, were proponents of states' rights and became followers of Jefferson. It would, however, be several years before the budding political parties would come into full flower. The four years leading up to the presidential election of 1800 when Jefferson, who served as Adams' Vice President from 1797 to 1801, would narrowly deny Adams' bid for a second term as President could perhaps be said to have been the beginning of overtly partisan party politics in the United States of America.

That election certainly marked the beginning of one of the most noteworthy political feuds in the history of the republic. Adams felt he had been disgraced by being denied a second term as President and he blamed Jefferson for that turn of events. In a confrontation following the election, Jefferson defended himself by reminding Adams that the system by which Adams had been defeated was one he had helped to create. If that statement was meant to console, it didn't work.

Adams didn't attend Jefferson's inauguration either because he didn't want to or because he wasn't invited. It may be that both suppositions are, in fact, true.

Many people believe there is something other-worldly not only about the date on which Adams and Jefferson died but also about the way in which they were reconciled after so many years of alienation.

According to an account recorded on the WallBuilders' web site, Dr. Benjamin Rush, a fellow Founding Father and good friend of both men, wrote a letter to Adams in 1809 about a dream he had in which Adams had written a congratulatory letter to Jefferson. In Rush's dream, Adams' letter had been well-received by Jefferson and by 1812 led to a resumption of congenial relations manifested in written correspondence that continued for the rest of their lives.

In his reply to Rush, Adams expressed the thought that "there is something very serious in this [dream] business. The Holy Ghost carries on the whole Christian system in this earth." Adams went on to say, "I have no resentment or animosity against the gentleman [Jefferson]…If I should receive a letter from him…I should not fail to acknowledge and answer it."

Rush then wrote to Jefferson about his dream and the letter he had received from Adams. When Jefferson followed up by sending a letter to Adams in which he expressed warm feelings, a reconciliation occurred, as the dream had predicted, that would serve both men well for the rest of their lives. Adams probably expressed both of their feelings when he said, "You and I ought not to die before we have explained ourselves to each other."

It seems logical that the thinking of two courageous and highly intelligent men who had worked closely together in the daunting and dangerous task of creating a new nation would, at some point, focus on the issues that united them rather than on the less than world-shaking political issues that divided them.

Jefferson seemed to be commenting on that point when he said in a letter to Adams: "We acted in perfect harmony through a long and perilous contest for our liberty and independence. A constitution has been acquired which, though neither of us think perfect, yet both consider as competent to render our fellow citizens the happiest and the securest on whom the sun has ever shone. If we do not think exactly alike as to its imperfections, it matters little to our country which, after devoting to it long lives of disinterested labor, we have delivered over to our successors in life, who will be able to take care of it and of themselves."

A few years later, Rush said in a letter to Adams, "I rejoice in the correspondence which has taken place between you and your friend, Mr. Jefferson. I consider you and him as the North and South Poles of the American Revolution. Some talked, some wrote, and some fought to promote and establish it, but you and Mr. Jefferson thought for us all. I never take a retrospect of the years 1775 and 1776 without associating your opinions and speeches and conversations with all great political, moral, and intellectual achievements of the Congresses of those memorable years."

Many believe it was no coincidence that two super stars of the American Revolution died just hours apart on the same day, July 4, 1826, a day that just happened to be the fiftieth anniversary of the signing of the *Declaration of Independence*. Daniel Webster expressed his opinion on the subject by posing this question: "May not such events raise the suggestion that they are not undesigned, and that heaven does so order things, as sometimes to attract strongly the attention, and excite the thoughts of men?"

On February 9, 1825, the oldest son of John and Abagail Adams became the sixth President of the United States. One week following the deaths of his father and Jefferson, John Quincy Adams included these words in an Executive Order: "A Coincidence...so wonderful gives confidence...that the patriotic efforts of these men were Heaven directed, and furnishes a new hope...that the prosperity of these States is under the protection of a kind Providence."

58.

Webster's English Language Dictionary Published

April 14, 1828

Someone once said England and America are two countries separated by a common language. Noah Webster, who is usually included among those colonists called Founding Fathers, did more than any others to establish "American" English.

He was influential in the difficult task of codifying many of the differences that had evolved in the colonies in the way the English language was written and spoken, words were spelled and pronounced, and in the rules of grammar. "Now is the time," Webster said, "and this is the country, in which we may expect success, in attempting changes favorable to language, science and government."

Between 1806 and 1833, Webster produced voluminous writings including *An American Dictionary of the English Language – with pronouncing vocabularies of Scripture, classical and geographical names.* In 1840, an expanded edition of his *English Language Dictionary* that included some 70,000 words, was published.

Webster has been called "the Schoolmaster of the Nation," and the "Father of American Scholarship and Education," titles he earned as the most active of the Founders in emphasizing the importance of educating young Americans. He was one of the leaders in placing a high priority on providing government funding for education. Webster was also convinced that state and local governments had a duty, along with parents, to "discipline our youth in early life in sound maxims of moral, political, and religious duties."

"A good system of education," said Webster, "should be the first article in the code of political regulations; for it is much easier to introduce and establish an effectual system for preserving morals, than to correct by penal statues the ill effects of a bad system. The goodness of a heart is of infinitely more consequence to society than an elegance of manners; nor will any superficial accomplishments repair the want of principle in the mind. It is always better to be *vulgarly* right than *politely* wrong."

Webster's first contribution to the field of elementary education was his 1783 *American Spelling Book*, which included "an easy Standard of Pronunciation." Commonly known as "the blue-backed speller," it eventually became an all-time best seller with over seventy-million copies sold by 1947. His pronunciation guide later became part of *A Grammatical Institute of the English Language*, an important educational tool he completed in 1785.

Known and respected by his peers as "a brilliant scholar and dedicated Christian," Webster would have soundly rejected the notion of separation of church and state, especially where public education is concerned and as currently promoted by secular humanists. Webster's books were filled with Bible precepts alongside principles of American government. In one of the early editions of his *Blue-Backed Speller*, Webster included a *Moral Catechism* – rules upon which to base moral conduct. "God's Word, contained in the Bible, has furnished all necessary rules to direct our conduct," he wrote.

In the preface of each of his books, Webster included comments explaining his belief that the Christian religion in general and the Bible in particular were the bedrocks of American civilization and were the only safeguard against tyranny. This statement appearing in the preface of his Bible translation is typical of all his words of introduction:

> *The Bible is the Chief moral cause of all that is good, and the best corrector of all that is evil, in human society; the best book for regulating the temporal concerns of men, and the only book that can serve as an infallible guide to future felicity. It is extremely important to our nation, in a political as well as religious view, that all possible authority and influence should be*

*given to the scriptures, for these furnish the best principles of civil
liberty, and the most effectual support of republican government.*

*The principles of genuine liberty, and of wise laws and
administrations, are to be drawn from the Bible and sustained
by its authority. The man, therefore, who weakens or destroys the
divine authority of that Book, may be accessory to all the public
disorders which society is doomed to suffer.*

*There are two powers only, sufficient to control men and
secure the rights of individuals and a peaceable administration;
these are the combined force of religion and law, and the force or
fear of the bayonet.*

Born in Hartford, Connecticut on October 16, 1758, Webster, on
his father's side, was a fourth generation descendant of John Webster, one
of the first settlers of Hartford, and, on his mother's side, a descendant
of William Bradford a passenger on the Mayflower. Bradford, who was
elected Governor of Plymouth Colony thirty times, also organized the
first Thanksgiving Day celebration in New England.

Webster died May 28, 1843 in New Haven. In his "Memoir of the
Author," the editor of *The American Dictionary*, concluded, "It may be
said that the name Noah Webster, from the wide circulation of some of
his works, is known familiarly to a greater number of the inhabitants of
the united States, than the name, probably, of any other individual except
the father of the Country.

"Whatever influence he thus acquired was used at all times to
promote the best interests of his fellowmen. His books, though read by
millions, have made no man worse. To multitudes they have been of
lasting benefit not by the course of early training they have furnished,
but by those precepts of wisdom and virtue with which almost every page
is stored. – August, 1847."

59.

American *Anti-Slavery Society* Founded

December 6, 1833

Slavery in America is still a disquieting, conscience-jabbing issue for Americans but it wasn't invented on the North American Continent; it was a devilish bequeath from the Old World to the New. The roots of that inhumane practice can be traced back more than 7,500 years to the earliest known civilization, known as Sumer, located in a Middle-East area usually associated with modern-day Iraq.

Of the estimated twelve million African slaves shipped to the Western Hemisphere by the early 1800s, approximately 95% went to countries other than what is now the United States of America. That is a fact worth remembering for the sake of perspective, but it doesn't justify the length of time it took to correct the ugly situation.

Even though the percentage was small, the number was large and most of those who settled the American colonies, even many who owned slaves, understood slavery was inherently wrong and should be abolished. A steadily growing uneasiness among the populace had gained enough traction by the middle 1700s that organized opposition to slavery as a moral and religious issue had begun to materialize. As a result, all northern states passed their own emancipation acts by 1804. On January 1, 1808, Congress banned the importation of slaves, a first step towards abolishing slavery in America.

In 1817, a group of prominent Americans led by Henry Clay and including Robert Finley, James Monroe, Bushrod Washington, Andrew Jackson, Francis Scott Key, and Daniel Webster, established the American

Colonization Society whose aim was to free slaves and return them to a specific area in Africa. Funds were provided by a combination of public and private sources to initiate the program. The ACS is credited with founding a colony in what is now known as Liberia and with beginning the process of transporting freed slaves to their new African homeland in 1819.

By 1820, a large and growing number of anti-slavery groups were meeting and distributing literature for the purpose of generating support for the total abolition of slavery in the United States. Their educational efforts brought more and more people into the movement and paved the way for the establishment of a national organization known as the American Anti-Slavery Society. The main force behind formation of the AAS was a firebrand Boston newspaper publisher by the name of William Lloyd Garrison, a member of the American Colonization Society. By 1833 it was time, in Garrison's opinion, to deal with the emancipation rather than the manumission (exporting) of slaves as espoused by the ACS. Writing in his anti-slavery weekly newspaper called *The Liberator*, he demanded immediate emancipation for all slaves.

Garrison made his position crystal clear in *The Liberator's* first edition when he wrote, as an open letter to the public, "I am aware that many object to the severity of my language; but is there not cause for severity? I will be as harsh as truth, and as uncompromising as justice. On this subject, I do not wish to think, or to speak, or write, with moderation. No! No! Tell a man whose house is on fire to give a moderate alarm; tell him to moderately rescue his wife from the hands of the ravisher; tell the mother to gradually extricate her babe from the fire into which it has fallen; – but urge me not to use moderation in a cause like the present. I am in earnest – I will not equivocate – I will not excuse – I will not retreat a single inch – AND I WILL BE HEARD."

And heard he was as he helped to found and strongly promoted the AAS in their mission of building support for abolition. AAS agents distributed literature and spoke to anyone who would listen regarding the moral evil of slavery. While they were at it, the AAS crusaders were to sell subscriptions to *The Liberator* in order to enlarge Garrison's audience. It was through the effective efforts of Garrison and his true believers that the organization would within five years include 1,350 chapters and a membership of approximately 250,000 like-minded Americans.

The American Anti-Slavery Society was founded at a convention held December 6, 1833, in Philadelphia. Sixty-two attending delegates under Garrison's leadership produced a founding document entitled a *Declaration of Sentiments of the National Anti-Slavery Convention.* Garrison is credited with authoring the document that spells out the organization's founding principles and the tactics it would employ to advance its agenda. Here are a few excerpts from the *Declaration:*

> But those, for whose emancipation we are striving – constituting at the present time at least one-sixth part of our countrymen – are recognized by law, and treated by their fellow-beings, as brute beasts; are plundered daily of the fruits of their toil without redress; really enjoy no constitutional nor legal protection from licentious and murderous outrages upon their persons; and are ruthlessly torn asunder – the tender babe from the arms of its frantic mother – the heartbroken wife from her weeping husband – at the caprice or pleasure of irresponsible tyrants. For the crime of having a dark complexion, they suffer the pangs of hunger, the infliction of stripes, the ignominy of brutal servitude. They are kept in heathenish darkness by laws expressly enacted to make their instruction a criminal offence.
>
> These are the prominent circumstances in the condition of more than two million people, the proof of which may be found in thousands of indisputable facts, and in the laws of the slave-holding States.
>
> That every American citizen, who detains a human being in involuntary bondage as his property, is, according to Scripture, (Ex. xxi, 16,) a manstealer.
>
> That the slaves ought instantly to be set free, and brought under the protection of law: That all those laws which are now in force, admitting the right of slavery, are therefore, before God, utterly null and void; being an audacious usurpation of the Divine prerogative, a daring infringement on the law of nature, a base overthrow of the very foundations of the social compact, a complete extinction of all the relations, endearments and obligations of mankind, and a presumptuous transgression of all the holy commandments; and that therefore they ought instantly to be abrogated.

Although few Americans would recognize Garrison's name today, he was a major voice in the abolitionist movement at a critical point in time. How large a role the abolitionists played in bringing about the Civil War has been open to much speculation, but President Lincoln must have believed their role was significant. Upon meeting abolition-activist and author Harriet Beecher Stowe, who wrote *Uncle Tom's Cabin* in 1852, he reportedly quipped, "So you're the little lady who started this great war!"

60.

Texans Declare Independence from Mexico

March 2, 1836

Many familiar names and events are included in a story connected with the Texas' *Declaration of Independence* from Mexico in 1836 and its eventual acceptance as the twenty-eighth American state in 1845.

Famous American frontiersmen including Jim Bowie, Davy Crocket, Sam Houston, Stephen F. Austin, and Colonel William Travis and a Mexican villain known as General Antonio Lopez de Santa Anna all played roles in events leading to statehood including a bloody defeat for American forces at a place called the Alamo on March 6, 1836, just four days after the Texas settlers had declared their independence. Although devastating, that defeat was only a temporary setback to the settlers' cause.

The story began in 1820 when Moses Austin received permission from the Spanish government to move settlers into a remote area of Mexico located north of the Rio Grande River. That concession set in motion a chain of events that would add another large land area to the United States a few years later. But before that happened, the area would exist as an independent country known as the Republic of Texas after the settlers won their independence from Mexico in 1836.

Austin died shortly after completing his colonization contract with Spain leaving his son Stephen to deal with the new government formed when Mexico gained its independence from Spain in 1821. At that time, the newly formed independent Mexican government began to encourage settlement of the area by foreign immigrants as well as by their own citizens. In 1824, Mexico passed a colonization law that gave *empresarios,* their label for settlement leaders like Austin, large land grants to use in recruiting additional settlers. Austin and others were so successful in their efforts that American settlers outnumbered Mexican citizens in the area by 1830. When the Mexican government attempted to halt the flow of immigrants in 1833, Austin sought statehood status in the Mexican Federation. His request was rejected.

Relations between American settlers and Mexican authorities began to deterioriate in 1834 when Santa Anna overthrew the existing government and established a military dictatorship. In Santa Anna's opinion, Austin's statehood movement was a sign of rebellion and he set out to put a stop to it. His first target was the state militia that had originally been formed to protect against Indian attacks. What happened next has become known as the *Texas Revolution.*

Several battles were fought between *Texians,* as the American settlers were called, and Santa Anna's soldiers. Most of them were won by the settlers who set up their own provisional government in November of 1835. In March, the American settlers' *Convention of 1836* was convened at the village of Washington-on-the-Brazos to draft the *Texas Declaration of Independence.* It listed the settlers' grievances including the stipulation that the Mexican government had "ceased to protect the lives, liberty, and property of the people, from whom its legitimate powers are derived." It concluded by declaring Texas a free and independent republic with these resolute words:

> *We, therefore, the delegates with plenary powers of the people of Texas, in solemn convention assembled, appealing to a candid world for the necessities of our condition, do hereby resolve and declare, that our political connection with the Mexican nation has forever ended, and that the people of Texas do now constitute a free, Sovereign, and independent republic, and are fully invested with all the rights and attributes which properly belong to independent nations; and, conscious of the rectitude of our intentions, we fearlessly and confidently commit the issue to the decision of the Supreme arbiter of the destinies of nations.*

The convention delegates also produced a constitution which they had to do in a hurry because Santa Anna's army was besieging the

Alamo, a former Spanish mission defended by part of the the Texas Army. The delegates completed their work and formally declared Texas' independence on March 2, 1836.

On March 6, after a twelve-day siege, Santa Anna's army overran the Alamo defended by Colonel Travis and 187 men including Bowie and Crocket. Some historians claim the Mexican forces included up to 5,000 soldiers and that they lost approximately 600 of them in the fight. Santa Anna had given an order to take no prisoners, an order that was carried out after a fierce battle that lasted a little more than an hour. The brutality of what they considered a massacre inflamed the passions of the settlers and sealed the doom of Santa Anna and his army.

Sam Houston, who had been named commander-in-chief of the Texas Army during the March *Convention*, took command of a poorly trained group of soldiers in Gonzales, Texas, shortly after his appointment. For six weeks he ordered strategic retreats in order to buy time for as much training as possible and to avoid a premature encounter with Santa Anna's pursuing army. Picking up recruits along the way, Houston put together and trained an army of approximately 800 men while Santa Anna's larger army, badly battered at the Alamo and divided for strategic purposes, had become weary and, perhaps, over confident.

In a surprise attack at the San Jacinto River near Houston during "siesta time" on April 21, Houston's troops routed the Mexican army while shouting "Remember the Alamo!" It has been estimated that of Santa Anna's approximately 1,300 remaining troops, 600 were killed and 700 captured. Houston's casualties were reportedly two killed and thirty wounded.

During the rout, Santa Anna had slipped away and tried to hide among a group of Mexican peasants in the area. Captured the next day by Houston's troops, Santa Anna, in a bargain for his life, agreed to remove his troops and all other Mexican troops to areas south of the Rio Grande and to cede all of what was known as Texas at that time to the newly proclaimed Republic.

In accordance with documents referred to as the *Treaties of Velasco* signed by Santa Anna on May 14, Texas became an independent republic with the Rio Grande as its southern boundary. The ceded area also included parts of what is now New Mexico, Oklahoma, Kansas, and Colorado. Although that treaty was never ratified by the Mexican government, the intent of the document as envisioned by the American parties to the agreement has endured for the most part.

Citizens of the new Republic of Texas elected Houston President and endorsed the idea of applying for U.S. statehood as a slave state. Because of opposition by free states and the Mexican government, Texas application wasn't finally accepted until December 29, 1845.

61.

McGuffey's First Reader Published

August 1, 1836

History rewriters can't deal with William H. McGuffey so they pretty much ignore him. His four *Eclectic Reader* textbooks (the fifth and sixth editions were written by his brother) were the basis of elementary public education in America from 1836 through the end of the nineteenth century.

Originally published August 1, 1836, McGuffey's textbooks, as *originally written,* remained in use for the next forty-three years. In 1879 when their content began to be gradually altered due to a trend toward the secularizing of public schools, the McGuffey books were still known by his name – the *McGuffey Readers* – although he was not involved in changes to his original texts. Some *Readers* are still in use today mostly by homeschoolers and some private schools. More than 120-million copies have been sold and reissued copies are still available today.

Because of the popularity and success of his books as effective teaching tools, McGuffey, a college professor and clergyman, became known as the "Great Schoolmaster of the Nation." Scholar and historian Henry Steele Commager, Jr. explained the reasons for the recognition bestowed upon McGuffey: "What is most impressive in the McGuffey readers is the morality. From the First Reader through the Sixth, the morality is pervasive and insistent, there is rarely a page but addresses itself to some moral problem, points up some moral lesson – industry, sobriety, thrift, propriety, modesty, punctuality – these were essential virtues and those who practiced them were sure of success. The world of the McGuffeys was a world where no one questioned the truths of the Bible, or their relevance to everyday conduct."

It is clear that McGuffey, as did the Founding Fathers, believed religion was an important part of education and that the morality and spirituality of the Judeo-Christian Bible should be taught along with the teaching of reading skills. He combined the two by presenting age-appropriate stories that children could enjoy and remember. The following example, Lesson 37 from the *First Reader* entitled "Evening Prayer," was included in "The Rewriting of America's History" by Catherine Millard:

> *At the close of the day, before you go to sleep, you should not fail to pray to God to keep you from sin and from harm. You ask your friend for food and drink, and books, and clothes; and when they give you these things, you thank them, and love them for the good they do you. So you should ask your God for those things which he can give you, and which no one else can give you. You should ask him for life, and health, and strength; and you should pray to him to keep your feet from the ways of sin and shame.*
>
> *You should thank him for all his good gifts; and learn, while young, to put your trust in him; and the kind care of God will be with you, both in your youth and in your old age.*

Lesson 31 in the *Third Reader* was entitled "On Speaking the Truth:"

> *A little girl once came into the house, and told her mother a story about something which seemed very improbable.*
>
> *The persons who were sitting in the room with her mother did not believe the little girl, for they did not know her character. But the mother replied at once, "I have no doubt that it is true, for I never knew my daughter to tell a lie." Is there not something noble in having such a character as this?*
>
> *Must not that little girl have felt happy in the consciousness of thus possessing her mother's entire confidence? Oh, how different must have been her feelings from those of the child whose word cannot be believed, and who is regarded by every one with suspicion? Shame, shame on the child who has not magnanimity enough to tell the truth."*

Another example from the *Third Reader* was entitled "More about the Bible." Here's one paragraph from a series of Gospel-related statements used as reading exercises:

> *We have the most ample and satisfactory proofs that the books of the Bible are Authentic and Genuine; that is, that they were written by the persons to whom they are ascribed. The Scriptures of the Old Testament were collected and completed under the unscrupulous care of inspired apostles. The singular providence of God is evident in the translation of the Old Testament into Greek, nearly three hundred years before the birth of Christ, for the benefit of the Jews who were living in countries where that language was used.*

Each lesson introduced a few words that would have been new to the appropriate age group. At the end, there were questions, words to define, and tips on correct pronunciation.

Contrast the McGuffey approach to life and education with that of John Dewey, known as the *Father of Progressive Education*, who said: "There is no God, and there is no soul. Hence, there are no needs for the props of traditional religion. With dogma and creed excluded, then immutable truth is also dead and buried. There is no room for fixed, natural law or moral absolutes."

McGuffey-style teaching was gradually replaced by the "progressive" method promoted by Dewey and his acolytes. By the 1920s, progressive education had emerged as the prevailing method of instruction. By the 1960s, the U.S. Supreme Court was dominated by a collection of humanist jurists who removed prayer and the Bible from public schools, removed mention of Creation from science books, removed prayer from graduation ceremonies and football games, and removed the Ten Commandments from the walls of school buildings. They also somehow wrung out of the U.S. Constitution a justification for the legalization of abortion. McGuffey and the Founding Fathers would have been appalled.

By the late 1950s, President Dwight D. Eisenhower recognized what was happening and issued this warning: "Educators, parents and students must be induced to abandon the educational path that, rather blindly, they have been following as a result of John Dewey's teachings."

Renowned author Flannery O'Connor was more succinct: "My advice to all parents is…anything Wm. Heard Kilpatrick and Jhn. Dewey say do, don't do."

McGuffey died May 4, 1873 at the age of 72. The National Education Association, before they had become merely a labor union, memorialized him with this tribute:

> *In the death of William H. McGuffey, late Professor of Moral Philosophy in the University of Virginia, this Association feels that they have lost one of the great lights of the profession whose life was a lesson full of instruction; an example and model to American teachers. His labors in the cause of education, extending over a period of half a century, in several offices as teacher of common schools, college professor, and college president, and as author of text books his almost unequalled industry; his power in the lecture room; his influence upon his pupils and community; his care for the public interests of education; his lofty devotion to duty; his conscientious Christian character – all of these have made him one of the noblest ornaments of our profession in this age, and entitle him to the grateful remembrance of this Association and of the teachers of America.*

62.

Morse Sends Inter-City Telegraph

<u>May 24, 1844</u>

Inspiration and motivation often come from unexpected places. The multi-talented Samuel Finley Breese Morse, who would be credited many years later with inventing the electromagnetic telegraph, was pursuing a blossoming career as a painter of portraits and historical events when a personal tragedy caused him to focus his attention on a developing national need.

By 1825, Morse's career as a portrait artist had progressed to the point that he was commissioned by New York City officials to paint a portrait of the Marquis de Lafayette, beloved French hero of the American Revolution. Prior to completing the portrait, Morse received a letter from his father, delivered by a messenger on horseback, informing him that his wife had died. By the time he was able to complete the trip from New York to their home in New Haven, Connecticut, his wife's remains had already been buried.

Heartbroken, Morse began to think about trying to find a way to meet the need for a communication system that could immediately transmit messages over long distances. As a student at Yale, he had been interested in, along with his study of fine art, the potential he had recognized for electricity to somehow be used in transmitting messages.

Providential meetings with Charles T. Jackson, a student of electromagnetism, Leonard Gale, a chemistry professor, Alfred Vail, son of a successful industrialist and entrepreneur, and Congressman Francis O. J. Smith, gave Morse information, support and encouragement that eventually led to success in 1836 in the development of a workable electromagnetic system of telegraphy. In 1837, they applied for a U.S. patent. With that accomplished, they still needed a source of funding for the construction of a telegraph line between cities to demonstrate their invention's potential for national application.

Along with their work in advancing the electromagnetic telegraph concept, Morse and Vail had also collaborated in developing what became known as the Morse Code, a system of electronically-produced dots and dashes that represented letters and numbers that could be transmitted telegraphically. When finally adopted, the Morse Code began to be used internationally.

For the next six years, Morse searched for funding through private and public resources but his efforts were forestalled by skepticism. Understandably, potential investors were difficult to convince that the electromagnet transmission of messages over long distances was workable and that such a system could actually be constructed. His frustrating search for funding eventually led him to Washington, D.C. in 1842 where he demonstrated the telegraph machine to members of Congress by stringing wires between two rooms in the Capitol Building and sending messages back and forth. Morse had almost given up hope when he finally received notice in 1843 that Congress had approved an expenditure of $30,000.00 for the purpose of building a telegraph line between Washington, D.C., and Baltimore, Maryland.

On May 24, 1844, twelve years after he had begun to seriously experiment with his theory of long distance telegraphy, Morse sent his famous message, "What has God wrought," on the newly installed telegraph line that ran along the right of way from a Baltimore railroad station to the Supreme Court Chambers of the U.S. Capitol Building where Vail was waiting to receive it.

Morse, a devout Christian and the son of Jedidiah Morse, a well-known pastor and friend of Founding Father Noah Webster, selected those words first sent by telegraph from the Bible (Numbers 23:23) as a way of acknowledging his belief that God had inspired him, kept him going when he might have given up, and provided the human and material resources needed to complete an important and visionary project. He said his Bible-inspired message "baptized the American Telegraph with the name of its author."

In commenting about those twelve years of working and waiting, Morse said, "The only gleam of hope is from confidence in God. When I look upward it calms any apprehension for the future, and I seem to hear a voice saying: 'If I clothe the lilies of the field, shall I not also clothe you?' Here is my strong confidence, and I will wait patiently for the direction of Providence."

Once they had proven its viability, Morse and his partners were able to create a telegraph network that connected points in Maine to South Carolina, St. Louis, Milwaukee, and Chicago. Using Morse's patent, a variety of private companies soon established telegraph lines throughout the northeast and by 1861 Western Union had completed a transcontinental line from Washington, D.C. to San Francisco.

In his book entitled *What Hath God Wrought: The Transformation of America, 1815-1848*, Daniel Walker Howe put the importance of the invention of the telegraph into perspective:

> *Morse's telegraph had particular importance for a large country with a population spreading into increasingly remote areas. Thomas Jefferson declared the United States "an empire for liberty" and by his Louisiana Purchase had put the new nation on course to dominate the North American continent. In 1845, the ambition to occupy still more land would be characterized by John L. Sullivan's* Democratic Review *as the fulfillment of America's "manifest destiny" – a term that soon became as important as "empire" to describe American nationhood. Samuel F. B. Morse shared this view, which he reinforced with a religious sense of divine providence. Nation-builders awaited news as eagerly as did people selling crops.*
>
> *The invention [Morse and Vail] had demonstrated was destined to change the world. For thousands of years messages had been limited by the speed with which messengers could travel and the distance at which eyes could see signals such as flags or smoke. Neither Alexander the Great nor Benjamin Franklin (America's first postmaster general) two thousand years later knew anything faster than a galloping horse. Now, instant long-distance communications became a practical realty.*

On the date of his 80th birthday in 1871 a statue of Morse was unveiled in New York City's Central Park, an event attended by two thousand telegraphists. He died in New York City April 2, 1872.

63.

Manifest Destiny Becomes Popular Slogan

Although the term *Manifest Destiny* didn't come into common usage until the middle of the nineteenth century, the principle it describes was the mindset of America's earliest explorers and the first boatloads of Huguenots and Puritans. They believed the New World was a land provided by God that was destined to be a place of opportunity and religious freedom completely separated from the Old World and its ways.

The original settlers of colonies in Virginia and Massachusetts were Christian reformers fleeing the oppression of the Church of England. Most Huguenots and Puritans were devoted Calvinists in their theological beliefs. According to the basic tenet of John Calvin's theology, God as Creator rules over all things. Calvinists believe God's plan is at work in everything that happens, including the mundane and the secular, and that He determines the fortunes of individuals and nations. Because of God's sovereignty and unlimited power, His plans will be carried out on earth and in heaven; for the Calvinist, no part of life is separate from the lordship of Christ.

A special position for America in God's plan seems to have been part of a message Reverend John Winthrop delivered to his Puritan flock in the Massachusetts Bay Colony: "For we must consider that we shall be as a city upon a hill. The eyes of all people are upon us. So that if we shall deal falsely with our God in this work we have undertaken, we shall be made a story and a by-word throughout the world."

America's discoverers, settlers, and Founding Fathers believed they were called as part of God's plan to establish a free and independent nation on the North American continent. And they believed, wholeheartedly, that the new nation's foundation should be built on the teachings of the Judeo-Christian Bible. Speaking for himself and his fellow Founding Fathers, George Washington verbalized their beliefs: "It is impossible to govern rightly without God and the Bible."

Paying tribute to those who had gone before, John Adams said, "I always consider the settlement of America with reverence and wonder, as the opening of a grand scheme and design of Providence for the illumination of the ignorant and emancipation of the slavish part of mankind all over the earth."

Calvinism, *Manifest Destiny,* and Providence (divine intervention in the affairs of man in accomplishing God's preordained plan) share much intellectual common ground in that they agree that the all-powerful, all-knowing Judeo-Christian God controls the outcome of events. The role of Providence in America's discovery, settlement, development, and fight for independence is acknowledged in the writings of nearly all of the Founding Fathers.

The concept of *Manifest Destiny* can be seen in Thomas Jefferson's vision of an *Empire of Liberty,* that empire being the continental nation strongly advocated a few years later by Andrew Jackson. Jefferson took a giant step in that direction with his *Louisiana Purchase* setting the stage for what historians now call the *Age of Manifest Destiny,* the period of time between the end of the War of 1812 and the beginning of the Civil War during which the U.S. completed its expansion to the Pacific Ocean.

The term *Manifest Destiny* first appeared in print in an article written by John L. O'Sullivan, a Jacksonian Democrat and editor of the *Democratic Review,* July 1, 1845. The Jackson Democrats carried on the former president's push for westward expansion because they believed in continentalism (a continental nation) and that it was God's foreordained plan for America to be a united nation "from sea to shining sea."

While O'Sullivan did not originate the term, he had talked about "a divine destiny" for the United States in an earlier essay. He first used *Manifest Destiny* in an essay entitled *Annexation* in which he advanced the idea that the U.S. should annex the Republic of Texas as part of America's destined greatness. O'Sullivan spoke of "the fulfillment of our manifest destiny to overspread the continent allotted by Providence for the free development of our yearly multiplying millions." Later that year, he again used the term in an article pushing for the annexation of the Oregon Territory: "And that claim is by the right of our manifest destiny to overspread and to possess the whole of the continent which Providence has given us for the development of the great experiment of liberty and federated self-government entrusted to us."

Add to the list of presidents advocating the idea of continentalism the name of John Quincy Adams who wrote: "The whole continent of North America appears to be destined by Divine Providence to be peopled by one *nation*, speaking one language, professing one general system of religious and political principles, and accustomed to one general tenor of social usages and customs. For the common happiness of them all, for their peace and prosperity, I believe it is indispensable that they should be associated in one federal Union."

Adams was also instrumental in originating the *Monroe Doctrine* with which some historians have connected the concept of *Manifest Destiny*. Their point is that U.S. expansion was necessary as a defensive strategy in keeping foreign influence out of the hemisphere, especially on the North American Continent. Early American history contains many convincing proofs that the Founding Fathers, a Providential collection of exceptional men, were, indeed, guided as they went through the process of building a nation that became the envy of the world.

In trying to put his finger on what it was that made America exceptional, French historian Alexis de Tocqueville made this observation: "I sought for the greatness and genius of America in her commodious harbors and her ample rivers, and it was not there; in her fertile fields and boundless prairies, and it was not there; in her rich mines and her vast world commerce and it was not there. Not until I went to the churches of America and heard her pulpits aflame with righteousness did I understand the secret of her genius and power. America is great because she is good and if America ever ceases to be good, America will cease to be great."

In 1730, Benjamin Franklin wrote an essay entitled "On the Providence of God in the Government of the World" in which he expressed sentiments shared by most of his fellow Founding Fathers. He brought it to a close with these thoughts: "Then I conclude that believing in a Providence we have the Foundation of all true Religion; for we should love and revere that Deity for his Goodness and thank him for his Benefits; we should adore him for his Wisdom, fear him for his Power, and pray to him for his Favour and Protection; and this Religion will be a Powerful Regulater of our Actions, give us Peace and Tranquility within our own Minds, and render us Benevolent, Useful and Beneficial to others."

64.

Mexican-American War Declaration Signed

May 13, 1846

While war with Mexico wasn't formally declared until 1846, events that made it inevitable began to unfold in the 1820s when Mexico won its independence from Spain. Large numbers of American settlers then began to migrate into what became known in 1836 as the Republic of Texas. Originally part of northern Mexico, the Republic of Texas included at that time what would eventually become Texas and parts of Oklahoma, New Mexico, Colorado, Kansas and Wyoming.

Mexico's independence had become a reality in 1821. The accelerating westward migration of Americans that had begun around the same time put the two North American countries on a collision course that turned into a shooting war in 1846. Hostilities began over differences regarding the legitimacy of the Republic of Texas and the related issue of where the border should be located.

The Mexican government had never recognized the independence of a separate Texas Republic and claimed that the Nueces River defined the border between the two countries. The United States government recognized the Republic's independence and maintained that the international border was the Rio Grande River. When American troops under the command of General Zachary Taylor were attacked in the disputed area by the Mexican Army on April 25, President James Polk, who had just become President in March, asked Congress for a declaration of war. Congress obliged on May 13.

Polk, an enthusiastic believer in the concept of America's *Manifest Destiny*, had campaigned on promises to annex the area known as Texas and to acquire part of what was known as the Oregon Territory from Great Britain. On December 29, 1845, Congress approved statehood for Texas; Polk had then set his sights on the western land formerly controlled by Spain, primarily known as New Mexico and California. Since his earlier offer to purchase those areas from Mexico had been summarily refused, Polk and his advisors began to consider military conquest as the only available option.

Although disrespected internationally, the American Army and Navy won every battle, often against numerically superior Mexican forces. Mexico had the advantage of short supply lines, a larger Army, and the support of the civilian population. America's advantages included better military leaders (all the generals were West Point-trained professional soldiers), better trained and equipped troops, a stronger economy and an effective Navy. For all practical purposes, the U.S. Navy secured what is now the state of California for the union by taking control of the ports of San Diego and San Francisco. The Navy also blockaded Mexican ports and conducted an amphibious landing at Vera Cruz. By the end of the war, the American military had proven itself and the United States of America was well on its way to becoming recognized as a global military power.

On September 14, 1847, the war essentially ended when U.S. troops under the command of General Winfield Scott took control of Mexico City. That is significant because it is the first time in history that the U.S. flag was raised over the capital city of a foreign country. Even though soundly and hopelessly defeated, the Mexican's refused for months to negotiate a peace treaty. During that time, Polk was advised by some to annex all of Mexico as part of the United States, something he may have been tempted to do in the name of *Manifest Destiny*. Due to the diligence of Nicholas Trist, U.S. treaty negotiator, and the eventual formation of a new Mexican government, the *Treaty of Guadalupe Hidalgo* was signed February 2, 1848, officially ending the war.

According to terms of the treaty, U.S. control of the previously annexed Republic of Texas was acknowledged and the Rio Grande was officially designated as the border between Mexico and America. Also, the U.S. purchased the area known as California and New Mexico for

$15 million plus assuming American financial claims against Mexico. Mexico ceded almost half the land they had controlled before the war to the U.S., an area that includes present day California, Nevada, Utah, Arizona, New Mexico, Wyoming, and parts of Colorado. The U.S. officially acquired approximately 500,000 square miles of new territory.

Just prior to the Declaration of War against Mexico, the U.S. and Britain had begun negotiating a treaty that would partition the Oregon Territory. Up to that point, the territory had been "owned" jointly by the two countries. According to the agreement signed June 15, 1846, the U.S. took exclusive control of approximately 285,000 square miles of territory that included all of the present-day states of Idaho, Oregon and Washington, as well as those parts of present day Montana and Wyoming west of the Continental Divide. Britain took exclusive control of what is now British Columbia and Vancouver Island.

By 1848, the major boundaries of the United States of America had been established "from sea to shining sea." Much of the credit for the successful final push westward goes to President Polk who many historians have rated as one of the most effective presidents because of his ability to establish an agenda and to accomplish his goals.

While reminiscing about his time as America's Chief Executive, Polk wrote: "Within less than four years the annexation of Texas to the Union has been consummated; all conflicting title to the Oregon Territory south of the forty-ninth degree of north latitude, being all that was insisted on by any of my predecessors, has been adjusted, and New Mexico and Upper California have been acquired by treaty...the territories recently acquired, and over which our exclusive jurisdiction and dominion have been extended, constitute a country more than half as large as all that which was held by the United States before their acquisition, and, including Oregon, nearly as great an extent of territory as the whole of Europe, Russia only accepted. The Mississippi, so lately the frontier of our country, is now only its center."

As had all his predecessors in the office of President, Polk acknowledged the hand of God in America's growth and good fortune. During his annual message to Congress in 1847, he said, "No country has been so much favored, or should acknowledge with deeper reverence the manifestations of the divine protection. An all wise Creator directed and guarded us in our infant struggle for freedom and has constantly watched over our surprising progress until we have become one of the great nations of the earth."

Perhaps Providentially, Polk decided not to seek a second term. Within three months of his retirement from office, he died of cholera.

65.

Gold Discovered at Sutter's Mill

<u>January 24, 1848</u>

To those who believe the invisible hand of Providence was very much at work in the overall development of the United States of America, the discovery of gold in California in 1848 was considered to have been preordained for at least two important reasons – it greatly accelerated development of the American west while also significantly impacting the national political scene by upsetting the balance of power in the battle over slavery.

"Gold fever" was responsible for the rapid population growth of California, a rate of growth that far exceeded that of other frontier states. Within two years of the morning when James Marshall picked up a piece of metal that turned out to be gold, Californians had produced a state constitution in order to apply for statehood. Because there were few, if any, slave owners in California, the constitution they produced specifically banned slavery much to the chagrin of the southern states. After much in-fighting in Congress over the statehood issue, the *Compromise of 1850* was passed which allowed California to be admitted to the Union as a free state. Even though the legislation was called a compromise, the anti-slavery states from that point forward had the upper hand in Congress.

Marshall was a carpenter employed by John Sutter, a Swiss immigrant who had settled in the area in 1839. Because the Sacramento Valley was controlled by Mexico, he became a Mexican citizen and received a land grant of 50,000 acres upon which he did some farming while engaging in other businesses. In 1847, Sutter hired Marshall to build a sawmill near timberland he owned. It was while building Sutter's sawmill that Marshall spotted the nugget that triggered the history-changing event known at the California gold rush. Sutter asked Marshall to keep their discovery quiet because he was concerned the gold would attract people who might interfere with businesses and damage his property.

But word did soon get out and Sutter was proven correct in his concerns according to this account written in 1894 by James S. Brown: "With all due respect to Capt. John A. Sutter and James W. Marshall, to whom the world has given the credit of the great find, I do believe if they had been taken out and shot to death the day of the discovery they would have suffered less, and would have met their Maker just as pure, if not more honored in this world, than to have lived and endured what they did."

Sutter's own description of what happened appeared in *Hutchings' California* Magazine in 1857:

> *So soon as the secret was out my laborers began to leave me, in small parties first, but then all left, from the clerk to the cook, and I was in great distress; only a few mechanics remained to finish some very necessary work which they had commenced, and about eight invalids, who continued slowly to work a few teams, to scrape out the mill race at Brighton. The Mormons did not like to leave my mill unfinished, but they got the gold fever like everybody else. After they had made their piles they left for the Great Salt Lake.*
>
> *Then the people commenced rushing up from San Francisco and other parts of California, in May, 1848: in the former village only five men were left to take care of the women and children. The single men locked their doors and left for "Sutter's Fort" and from there to the Eldorado. For some time the people in Monterey and farther south would not believe the news of the gold discovery, and said that it was only a "Ruse de Guerre" of Sutter's, because he wanted to have neighbors in his wilderness. From this time on I got only too many neighbors, and some very bad ones among them.*
>
> *What a great misfortune was this sudden gold discovery for me! It has just broken up and ruined my hard, restless, and industrious labors, connected with many dangers of life, as I had many narrow escapes before I became properly established...From*

my mill buildings I reaped no benefit whatever, the mill stones even have been stolen and sold.

In his 1899 book entitled *Side Lights on American History*, Henry W. Elson provided us with this insight into the increasing wackiness of the times:

> *California was a wild country in 1848. The inhabitants, who numbered but a few thousand, were a strange mixture of Yankees from the East, Mormons, Mexicans and wild Indians with a sprinkling of Hawaiians, negroes, and Europeans.*
>
> *More than three months passed before the people throughout California were fully convinced that a great discovery had been made. But when, early in May, some of the miners came to San Francisco laden with bottles, tin cans, and buckskin bags filled with the precious metal – when one Samuel Brannan, holding up a bottle of the dust in one hand, and swinging his hat in the other, passed through the streets shouting, "Gold! Gold! Gold from the American River! – they could doubt no longer.*
>
> *The conversion of San Francisco was complete. The people were now ready to believe every report from the mines, however exaggerated; and immediately the rush began. Many sold all their possessions and hastened to the gold-fields. All other business came to a stand-still. The two newspapers suspended publication for want of workmen. By the middle of May three-fourths of the male population of the town had gone to the mines. The prices of shovels, pickaxes, blankets, and the like rose in a few days to six times their former value. The town council abandoned its sittings; the little church on the plaza was closed; farms were left tenantless and waving fields of grain let run to waste. The judge abandoned the bench, and the doctor his patients. The excitement spread down the coast to Monterey, to Santa Barbara, to Los Angeles, and to San Diego, and the result was the same. The people were seized with a delirium, and the one universal cry along the coast, from the seashore to the mountains, was gold! Gold!*
>
> *Within three years after the first discovery by Marshall it was estimated that one hundred thousand men were at work in the California gold mines...The yield of gold throughout California reached the sum of sixty-five million dollars in one*

year (1853); and the entire output in the first eight years was about five hundred million dollars.

Such figures would seem to indicate that every miner must have made a fortune; but this is far from the truth. Some, it is true, were wise enough, after a rich find, to abandon the field before spending or wasting what they had gained; others, honest, well-meaning men who had left families in the East, worked steadily with fair returns, until they laid by a competence, after which they returned to their homes. But the majority of the miners were as poor after several years' toil as when they began.

Some of these were of the unlucky, ne'er do-well sort who fail at everything they attempt; but a greater number were of the profligate class, who, at the end of each week, would hie to the drinking and gambling dens, and there carouse till the week's earnings were gone. And even the honest man was often lured to his ruin by these glittering dens.

Sutter and Marshall were among those who died in a state of poverty, not because of profligate living but due, mostly, to their bad luck.

But the lure of the possibility of quick and easy financial gain caused a population explosion within a period of months that might have taken decades to effectuate under normal circumstances. Development of the United States of America took a huge leap forward because of man's natural attraction to gold and all its supposed benefits.

Poet and hymn writer William Cowpers wrote, "God moves in mysterious ways His wonders to perform." The California gold rush seems to fit that description perfectly.

66.

First *Pony Express* Rider Leaves St. Joseph

April 3, 1860

For a rapidly expanding nation desperately in need of faster ways to communicate over long distances, the Pony Express, America's first overland mail courier service, must have seemed like a good way to meet that need to those who devised the plan. But it was dangerous and demanding work for the young men who took on the task of making the concept work.

By 1860, telegraph service was available from the east coast to St. Joseph, Missouri, but telegraph service between St. Joseph and the west coast was non-existent and no one could predict when it would be available. A system called the Pony Express was designed to fill that communications gap but it soon became obvious that system was a far-from-perfect solution.

An 1860 newspaper ad provides a clue as to what life was like for Pony Express riders: "Wanted. Young, skinny, wiry fellows. Not over 18. Must be expert riders. Willing to risk death daily. Orphans preferred."

Although each rider who signed on understood he would be operating mostly on his own in hostile territory, candidates responded to the advertisements in greater than expected numbers. That response may be explained by the $25 per week each rider was to be paid, a princely sum at a time when manual laborers were paid around $1 per week. By the first day of operation, April 3, 1860, the Pony Express had recruited fifty riders. The company had 500 horses and 190 relay stations located approximately ten miles apart over 1,950 miles along a meandering trail from St. Joseph to Sacramento, California. The company also employed 400 men to man the relay stations.

Each relay rider was to cover approximately sixty miles utilizing as many as ten different horses in six hours; according to those who knew horses, the maximum distance a horse could cover at full gallop was approximately ten miles. The "skinny, wiry" riders were to weigh 125 pounds or less so that, with the forty pounds of mail and provisions each carried, the weight on the horses' backs would be at or below a total of 165 pounds.

Among provisions carried by each rider was a Bible provided by the the Central Overland California & Pike's Peak Express Company, owner-operators of the Pony Express mail delivery system. The company required each rider to sign a loyalty pledge promising "sobriety, clean speech, and gentlemanly conduct," a pledge that concluded with "so help me, God."

Although the Pony Express lasted only nineteen months, it became a notable and important part of the history of America's westward expansion. The company's owners announced it would terminate operations on October 26, 1861, shortly after the east and west branches of the transcontinental telegraph were connected in Salt Lake City, Utah, the final link in what could only be described as rudimentary coast to coast telegraph service. The Pony Express ended in bankruptcy, reportedly losing $200,000 during its short, unprofitable but strategically successful existence.

Most of the Pony Express riders survived their demanding experiences, but the story of one who did not provides us with insight into what it was like to have taken part in the dangerous daily drama. In a book entitled *American Courage: Remarkable True Stories Exhibiting the Bravery That Has Made Our Country Great,* editor Herbert W. Warden III included this passage from *Broncho Charlie – A Saga of the Saddle,* by Gladys Shaw Erskine:

> Billy was ridin' in with the mail from Camp Ruby to Carson City...that's a tough route. It's through valleys and dry plains and then, all of a sudden, you're into the tablelands and the mountains, and lots of places where there was rim rock, where your pony couldn't get a foothold.
>
> Well, Billy was comin' along there at a right good pace, sort of hummin' to himself, quiet-like, under his breath. Suddenly,

an arrow whizzed past his ear, and then another. Billy took one look and saw that he was in for it sure. There was about thirteen Indians after him, on the run...all yellin' like Billy-be-damned. Billy thought quick. He knew that if he kept on the regular route they'd get him sure...for that was across an open valley. So he turned his horse and headed up into the tablelands and the rim rock...he thought he cold slip in and out of the gullies up there and get away from the Indians.

Well, up he went, his horse's feet clatterin' and slippin' and the Indians after him and the arrows a-hissin'. Then his horse stumbled, and Billy saw that he was wounded in the shoulder... then another arrow struck the gallant pony in the flank...and on they went. They came to the gully, where Billy had thought he could get through...and his heart must have just about stood still, when he saw that it was a dead end gully...that it was a trap...and there he was, with his horse, the Pony Express pouch, his Bible, and his six shooter. So Billy, cool as you please, slid off his horse, and made a stand there... and shot it out with the Indians...Bannocks and Utes they was. And, by gad, he got seven of 'em before they got him. But the odds was too great...and they killed Billy Tate there, in the rim rock caves, defendin' the mail he carried. Fourteen-year-old Billy Tate, with his yellow hair soft as a child's, and his laughing blue eyes in a round childish face... but he died the death of a brave man.

And here's a queer thing. The Indians never touched his body. They didn't scalp him, and they left the horse, and even the pouch of the Pony Express with him there. Later, agents from the station traced where his horse had turned off the trail, with all the others in chase, and they guessed what had happened. Then they saw the blood on the trail, and then they came to the tablelands and the gully with only one opening...and there they found Billy, still clutchin' his gun, and his Bible beside him...and in the pass, seven dead Indians. Some time later a Bannock told me all about it. He said: "Me no fight in tablelands. Me hear. Braves no could touch scalp of boy with hair like sun, and eyes like water. He brave. He go happy hunting ground with his horse. He be big brave there."

Billy Tate exemplified the kind of men who made America "the land of the free and the home of the brave."

67.

Lincoln Elected 16th President

November 6, 1860

A review of the facts regarding America's 1860 presidential election could easily lead one to conclude that the outcome was foreordained. A candidate inexperienced in national politics representing a *new* political party somehow managed to secure a victory against three other candidates representing established parties and with much more impressive political resumes. In the process, he also had to win a series of debates with Stephen Douglas, one of the most gifted debaters and well known political figures in the land.

When all the votes were tallied Abraham Lincoln had won only 39% of the popular vote and no electoral votes from any of the states that would soon secede from the Union. But, against all odds, he had won becoming the sixteenth President of the United States at the most difficult period of U.S. history since the Revolutionary War. Considering all the factors working against him, Lincoln's election provides the basis of a strong argument for those who believe in the working of Providence in the making of America.

Lincoln was the 1860 nominee of the new Republican Party formed in 1854 by anti-slavery activists infuriated by the passage of the Kansas-Nebraska Act. Because that act opened the door to the legalization of slavery in emerging western states, the formerly powerful Whig Party, which split along regional lines, had rendered itself ineffective. A majority of former Whigs from northern states, including Lincoln, were joined by abolitionists from various political parties in forming a successful political coalition.

As part of his acceptance speech after receiving the nomination in 1858, Lincoln previewed the stance he would be forced to take regarding preservation of the Union when he said, "A house divided against itself cannnot stand. I believe this Government cannot endure permanently half slave and half free. I do not expect the Union to be dissolved, I do not expect the house to fall, but I do expect it will cease to be divided. It will become all one thing or all the other."

Although opposed to slavery, Lincoln, as a member of the Illinois legislature in 1837, had gone on record as saying the issue was one that should be decided by each state and that the federal government had no right to interfere with any state's slavery policy. His personal opinion was that slavery was wrong and should be abolished, an opinion formed during a trip to New Orleans when he was twenty-two years old. The issue was decided for Lincoln by an incident described by a friend who gave this account: "We saw Negroes chained, maltreated, whipped, and scourged. Lincoln saw it; his heart bled, said nothing much, was silent from feeling, was sad, looked bad, felt bad, was thoughtful and abstracted. I can say, knowing it, that it was on this trip that he formed his opinions of slavery. It run its iron in him then and there – May, 1831. I have beard him say so often and often."

"When I hear anyone arguing for slavery," Lincoln once said, "I feel a strong impulse to see it tried on him personally."

In an effort to headoff the threatened secession of seven states from the union, Lincoln, in his first inaugural address, said, "I have no purpose, directly or indirectly, to interfere with the institution of slavery in the States where it exists. I believe I have no lawful right to do so, and I have no inclination to do so. I now reiterate these sentiments and in doing so, I only press upon the public attention the most conclusive evidence of which the case is susceptible that the property, peace, and security of no section are to be in any wise endangered by the now incoming Administration."

He then addressed the topic of secession by saying "No State upon its own mere motion can lawfully get out of the Union…acts of violence within any State or States against the authority of the United States are insurrectionary or revolutionary…I therefore consider that in view of the

Constitution and the laws, the Union is unbroken, and to the extent of my ability I shall take care, as the Consititution itself expressly enjoins upon me, that the laws of the Union be faithfully executed in all the States. Doing this I deem to be only a simple duty on my part, and I shall perform it so far as practicable unless my rightful masters, the American people, shall withhold the requisite means or in some authoritative manner direct the contrary. I trust this will not be regarded as a menace, but only as the declared purpose of the Union that it will consititutionally defend and maintain itself."

The secession movement began to minifest itself shortly after Lincoln's election in November when South Carolina led the way on December 20. Between January and June of 1861, ten more states – Mississippi, Florida, Alabama, Georgia, Louisiana, Texas, Virginia, Arkansas, North Carolina, and Tennessee – seceded from the Union. Five slave states – Missouri, Kentucky, West Virginia, Maryland, and Delaware – did not secede.

On February 7, 1861, delegates from seven seceding states (South Carolina, Mississippi, Florida, Alabama, Georgia, Louisiana, and Texas) met in Montgomery, Alabama, where they adopted a provisional constitution for the *Confederate States of America* and elected Jefferson Davis as its President. Davis defended the states' right to secede by calling the Constitution of the United States a partnership among the states and that, as in all partnerships, individual partners had the right to withdraw. Lincoln's view was that the Constitution formed a contract among the states that could only be nullified by all parties to the contract.

Early in the war, the Confederate States proposed a peace treaty which Lincoln rejected saying that such negotiations would, for all practical purposes, grant recognition to the *Confederation* as a foreign government which they were not and could not be, according to his interpretation of the U.S. Constitution.

On many occasions, Lincoln reduced the question of slavery simply to a matter of right versus wrong. In one of the famous debates with Douglas prior to the 1860 election, Lincoln said, "That is the issue that will continue in this country when these poor tongues of Judge Douglas and myself shall be silent. It is the eternal struggle between these two principles – right and wrong – throughout the world. They are the two principles that have stood face to face from the beginning of time, and will ever continue to struggle."

Obviously, Lincoln believed the anti-slavery forces were in the right and that it was God's will that all men should live free, a principle he often articulated. On the subject of God's involvement in human affairs in general and America's destiny in particular, Lincoln said:

> *That the Almighty does make use of human agencies, and directly intervenes in human affairs, is one of the plainest statements of the Bible. I have had so many evidences of his direction — so many instances when I have been controlled by some other power than my own will — that I cannot doubt that this power comes from above.*
>
> *I frequently see my way clear to a decision when I have no sufficient facts upon which to found it. But I cannot recall one instance in which I have followed my own judgement, founded upon such a decision, where the results were unsatisfactory; whereas, in almost every instance where I have yielded to the views of others, I have had occasion to regret it.*
>
> *I am satisfied that when the Almighty wants me to do or not to do a particular thing, He finds a way of letting me know it. I am confident that it is His design to restore the Union. He will do it in his own good time."*

As happened so often during the formative years of America, the right man was, Providentially, available in the right place at the right time.

68.

American Civil War Begins at Ft. Sumter

<u>April 12, 1861</u>

Strong differences of opinion regarding the issue of slavery were already shaping up as a serious problem when members of the Second Continental Congress attempted to approve the original draft of the *Declaration of Independence* in 1776. Delegates from the southern states let it be known they would not give their approval if it included a denunciation of slavery as some northern delegates were demanding. The southern delegates won that political battle but lost the war that finally decided the issue eighty-nine years later.

Ironically, that gruesomely bloody war began with a battle that produced no casualties on either side. The location was Fort Sumter, a federal fort located in South Carolina's Charleston harbor. Leaders of the CSA launched the attack because they were determined not to allow a federal fort to remain within their territory. As the result of an intense artillery bombardment by Confederate soldiers, fires broke out inside the fort that eventually threatened to blow up their powder magazines. Because Union forces were unable to re-supply or reinforce the fort, Major Robert Anderson realized on April 13 that surrender was his only sensible option. Soon after Fort Sumter was surrendered, Lincoln issued a call for 75,000 militiamen with which he hoped to put an end to what he first termed an insurrection. What would become America's bloodiest war had begun.

The stage for this unfortunate war had been set on March 11, 1861 when the *Constitution of the Confederate States of America* had been adopted by the seven original seceding states including South Carolina, Mississippi, Florida, Alabama, Georgia, Louisiana, and Texas. Following the Battle of Fort Sumter, four more states seceded – Virginia, North Carolina, Tennessee, and Arkansas.

No one can deny that slavery was a major reason the Civil War was fought, but it wasn't the only one; states' rights and various political and economic disputes irreconcilably separated the northern and southern states. Southern leaders were convinced that northern leaders were threatening their economy and their way of life. The only way war could have been avoided would have been for the northern states to allow the southern states to peacefully secede from the Union and form a separate republic. President Abraham Lincoln was commmitted to saving the Union whether it be all slave or all free. He made his position clear: The Union should be preserved at all costs. With that line drawn, war became inevitable.

. Looking at the numbers, the U.S. Civil War would seem to have been an unequal fight. It was the United States, with a population of twenty-three million people in twenty-three northern states, versus the Confederate States, with a population of nine million people in eleven southern states. More than one-third of the southern population was made up of black slaves. Most of the factories capable of turning out military materials were located in the north while the southern economy was agriculture-based. The Union had enough of a navy to effectively blockade southern ports and control the Mississippi River; the Confederacy had almost no navy with which to protect shipping in or out of its ports. Originally, Union leaders, including President Lincoln, expected to decisively win the war in three months or less.

Even with such a disparity of power between the belligerents, the Civil War was pretty much a stalemate for the first two years. The Confederate states had two advantages, according to military historians: They had a better trained and more experienced officer corps – most were West Point graduates and most had fought in the Mexican War – and their troops were more motivated to fight. Superior military leadership may account for the fact that confederate Army casualties were an estimated 260,000 while the Union Army suffered an estimated 360,000 casualties.

Union victories at Gettysburg, Pennsylvania, and Vicksburg, Mississippi, in July of 1863 proved to be the turning point in what had become a war of attrition as the Union's superiority in economic power and manpower resources took its tole on the Confederation. New and improved weaponry – better, more accurate rifles, the machine gun, improved artillery pieces and ammunition – contributed to the extremely high number of casualities on both sides throughout the war. The northern states had the advantage of a much larger manpower pool.

By the spring of 1865, it had become obvious that, barring a miracle, the southern cause was lost. General Robert E. Lee, Commanding General of the Confederate Armies, believing further resistence to be futile, surrendered what was left of his army to General Ulysses S. Grant at Appomattox, Virginia, on April 9. The fighting was finally over.

Five days later, Abraham Lincoln was assassinated while attending a play at Ford's Theatre with his wife. Mary Todd Lincoln described what happened just before John Wilkes Booth fired the fatal shot: "He said he wanted to visit the Holy Land and see those places hallowed by the footprints of the Saviour. He was saying there was no city he so much desired to see as Jerusalem. And with the words half spoken on his tongue, the bullet of the assassin entered the brain, and the soul of the great and good President was carried by the angels to the New Jerusalem above."

Of the many things for which Lincoln is remembered, none are so familiar as his *Gettysburg Address* delivered November 19, 1863, just four months after that famous battle ended. As part of a dedication ceremony for the Soldiers' National Cemetary, Lincoln was invited only to say a few words of dedication to the memory to those who had recently died fighting there. The main speaker was Edward Everett, a noted orator whose resume included service as Secretary of State, U.S. Senator, U.S. Representative, Governor of Massachusetts, and President of Harvard. He delivered a two-hour speech that has long been forgotten. Lincoln followed Everett's elocution with one of the best known addresses recorded in American history. In two minutes, Lincoln presented this venerated message:

> *"Fourscore and seven years ago our fathers brought forth on this continent a new nation, conceived in liberty and dedicated to the proposition that all men are created equal.*
> *"Now we are engaged in a great civil war, testing whether that nation or any nation so conceived and so dedicated can long*

endure. We are met on a great battlefield of that war. We have come to dedicate a portion of that field as a final resting-place for those who here gave their lives that that nation might live. It is altogether fitting and proper that we should do this.

"But in a larger sense, we cannot dedicate, we cannot consecrate, we cannot hallow this ground. The brave men, living and dead who struggled here have consecrated it far above our poor power to add or detract. The world will little note nor long remember what we say here, but it can never forget what they did here. It is for us the living rather to be dedicated here to the unfinished work which they who fought here have thus far so nobly advanced. It is rather for us to be here dedicated to the great task remaining before us – that from these honored dead we take increased devotion to that cause for which they gave the last full measure of devotion – that we here highly resolve that these dead shall not have died in vain, that this nation under God shall have a new birth of freedom, and that government of the people, by the people, for the people shall not perish from the earth."

On June 2, 1865, General Edmund Kirby Smith, commander of the last remaining unit of the Confederate Army, signed a surrender document that officially ended the American Civil War. The war's conclusion with the Union intact validated Abraham Lincoln's faith that the Union would be preserved. He had successfully done his part to ensure that the United States of America, "conceived in liberty and dedicated to the proposition that all men are created equal," would "long endure."

69.

Homestead Act Signed Into Law

Some historians have called passage of the 1862 *Homestead Act* a milestone event in accelerating settlement of the American West. Others have labeled it the most important economic development act ever passed in the United States. Most students of American history since the 1950s have probably never heard of it.

Distribution of public lands had been a contentious issue since the late 1780s after important groundwork for partitioning government-owned land was put in place by passage of the *Land Ordinance of 1785*. As a result of the push for westward expansion following the Mexican-American War, the land issue returned to the forefront in 1852 when a group called the Free Soil Party campaigned for free land in the west for Americans willing to live on it and put it to productive use. As a result of their efforts, a homestead bill was passed by the House of Representatives but defeated in the Senate.

Twice again, once in 1854 and again in 1859 homestead legislation was proposed but got caught up in the on-going battle over free-state versus slave-state issues. It was blocked from becoming law in 1854 by the Senate and in 1859 by Presidential veto. The *Homestead Act* was finally passed May 20, 1862, after the southern states had seceded from the Union. The remaining Union Congress passed it into law easily and President Abraham Lincoln signed it whereas former President and southern sympathizer James Buchanan had vetoed it three years earlier. It took effect January 1, 1863.

Southern opposition to the *Homestead Act* was based on their belief that settlement of the western territories by small farmers would act as a buffer against the spread of slavery. Some northern industrialists were opposed to it because they foresaw the possibility of a large portion of their cheap labor pool joining the rush to obtain free land in the west which would cause economic problems for them.

According to provisions of the *Homestead Act*, any head of family or any single man or woman twenty-one years of age or older could acquire 160 acres of undeveloped land at no cost if they would agree to live on it for five years, build at least a twelve-foot by fourteen-foot dwelling, and improve the land to make it suitable for farming. Any veteran of the U.S. Army or Navy, regardless of age, was eligible to apply. Anyone who had ever "borne arms against the government of the United states or given aid and comfort to its enemies" was not eligible. Each applicant had to affirm that their application "is made for his or her exclusive use and benefit, and that said entry is made for the purpose of actual settlement and cultivation, and not either directly or indirectly for the use or benefit of any other person whomever."

Each applicant was also required to pay a filing fee of $10.00 and to provide the names of two friends or neighbors who would sign a statement vouching for the character of the applicant. Settlers also had the option of purchasing their land at the rate of $1.25 per acre after living on it for six months.

In pointing out the impact of the *Homestead* Act on America's economic development, Dr. Larry P. Arnn, President of Hillsdale College, presented these often overlooked facts: "The greatest example of economic development in human history was in the United States during the nineteenth century. At the beginning of that century, we were about five million people huddled along the East Coast. By the end of it we had grown at a rate of about 25-percent – much faster than China is growing today – and had settled an entire continent, largely without the help of modern science. To the question of how it was done, I think the short answer is the *Homestead Act* – the greatest piece of legislation I know. Signed by President Lincoln in 1862, the *Homestead Act* is short and beautiful – two qualities good legislation should have, and two qualities in which legislation today is utterly lacking.

"What the *Homestead Act* did was to take the western land of the United States – surely one of the greatest assets ever held by any government in history – and give 160-acre plots to anyone with the backbone to live on them and work them. It is one of the greatest acts of legislation in all of human history. It, and things like it, built America and the character of the people who spread across it."

The *Homestead Act*, with its impact on westward expansion, combined with the discovery of gold in California a few years earlier, caused a population explosion in the mostly unsettled area between the Mississippi River and the Pacific Ocean. Between 1863 and 1900 alone, an estimated 600,000 people took advantage of the free land offer claiming approximately eighty million acres of undeveloped land that they put to productive use as crop land and for cattle production. The increase in population directed national attention to a growing need for roads, railroads, schools, and improvements in the means of communication, all of which hastened the establishment of strong communities throughout the west.

America's *Manifest Destiny*, often referred to as *divine destiny*, gained powerful westward momentum in several ways while the Old World looked on in wonder. On July 1, Congress passed the *Pacific Railway Act of 1862*, a piece of legislation that had also been previously opposed by the southern states. The full name of the bill was "AN ACT to aid in the construction of a railroad and telegraph line from the Missouri river to the Pacific ocean, and to secure to the government the use of the same for postal, military, and other purposes." The next day, Congress passed a landmark piece of legislation called the *Morrill Land-Grant Acts* that accelerated the availability of affordable college attendance for millions of Americans. That legislation had also been held up by southern members of Congress.

The book most likely to be found in the new frontier homes in 1862 was the Judeo-Christian Bible. At the time it was the primary source of material for educating frontier children. Andrew Jackson called the Bible "the rock on which our republic rests."

About the Bible, Abraham Lincoln said, "All the good from the Savior of the world is communicated through this Book; but for the Book we could not know right from wrong. All the things desirable to man are contained in it."

70.

Emancipation Proclamation Issued

January 1, 1863

While the *Emancipation Proclamation* freed thousands of slaves on January 1, 1863, it did not legally and finally put an end to slavery in the states and territories of the United States. That bit of unfinished business had to wait until December 18, 1865, when the Thirteenth Amendment was officially added to the U.S. Constitution.

President Abraham Lincoln began considering the pros and cons of issuing an *Emancipation Proclamation* shortly after Congress passed the first *Confiscation Act* on August 6, 1861. That act had given the Union power to confiscate all property of anyone who participated in rebellion against the U.S. government. Accordingly, all Confederates were considered rebels and any of their slaves "captured" by Union troops were legally "confiscated" and therefore were to be freed.

The *Second Confiscation Act*, passed July 17, 1862, went further in that it declared all slaves owned by Confederates who did not surrender within sixty days of the effective date of the Act would be freed. The *Confiscation Acts* also provided clear guidance to Union Army officers regarding the status of slaves who came under their jurisdiction. Obviously, southerners didn't consider themselves to be legally bound by anything the Union Congress decreed; the only Confederate slaves who benefited from the *Confiscation Acts* were those who were able to escape into Union-controlled areas.

Passage of the *Confiscation Acts* helped Lincoln to decide that an *Emancipation Proclamation* was needed, but he knew there would be both positive and negative political reaction; public opinion, he well knew, had not yet solidified in favor of universal emancipation. While the Republican platform included a call for the "utter and complete destruction" of slavery, many northern Democrats, especially those known as "Copperheads," were opposed to a national mandate; they preferred that the issue be left in the hands of individual states.

Lincoln composed a preliminary *Emancipation* draft prior to passage of the *Second Confiscation Act.* After reviewing it with his cabinet members on July 22, he decided to proceed but not until after the Union Army was able to achieve an important victory. That opportunity presented itself when General George B. McClelland won the Battle of Antietem, known in the south as the Battle of Sharpsburg, Maryland, over General Robert E. Lee on September 17, 1862. Lincoln then issued the *Emancipation Proclamation* on September 22 with an effective date of January 1, 1863. Many historians have labeled it Lincoln's most important achievement.

Coming when it did, Lincoln's *Proclamation* is credited with having deterred England and France from officially recognizing the southern Confederacy as a separate and sovereign nation. Foreign popular opinion swung in favor of the north when focus on ending slavery began to emerge, in their opinion, as America's main goal in fighting the Civil War. Any European support for the Confederacy at that point would have seemed like support for slavery.

The *Proclamation* also provided the military advantage of encouraging freed blacks to join the advancing Union armies which eventually provided as many as 200,000 additional soldiers.

The *Emancipation Proclamation* contains a relatively small number of words, but it represented a large step forward in changing the character of the United States of America. It said:

> *Whereas on the 22nd day of September, A.D. 1862, a proclamation was issued by the President of the United States, containing, among other things, the following, to wit: That on the 1st day of January, A.D. 1863, all persons held as slaves within any State or designated part of a State the people whereof shall then be thenceforward, and forever free; and the executive government of the United States, including the military and naval authority thereof, will recognize and maintain the freedom of such persons and will do no act or acts to repress*

such persons, or any of them, in any efforts they may make for their actual freedom. That the executive will on the 1st day of January aforesaid, by proclamation, designate the States and parts of States, if any, in which the people thereof, respectively, shall then be in rebellion against the United States; and the fact that any State or the people thereof shall on that day be in good faith represented in the Congress of the United States by members chosen thereto at elections wherein a majority of the qualified voters of such States shall have participated shall, in the absence of strong countervailing testimony, be deemed conclusive evidence that such State and the people thereof are not then in rebellion against the United States. Now, therefore, I, Abraham Lincoln, President of the United States, by virtue of the power in me vested as Commander-In-Chief of the Army and Navy of the United States in time of actual armed rebellion against the authority and government of the United States, and as a fit and necessary war measure for suppressing said rebellion, do, on this 1st day of January, A.D. 1863, and in accordance with my purpose so to do, publicly proclaimed for the full period of one hundred days from the first day above mentioned, order and designate as the States and parts of States wherein the people thereof, respectively, are this day in rebellion against the United States the following, to wit: Arkansas, Texas, Louisiana (except the parishes of St. Bernard, Palquemines, Jefferson, St. John, St. Charles, St. James, Ascension, Assumption, Terrebone, Lafourche, St. Mary, St. Martin, and Orleans, including the city of New Orleans), Mississippi, Alabama, Florida, Georgia, South Carolina, North Carolina, and Virginia (except the forty-eight counties designated as West Virginia, and also the counties of Berkeley, Accomac, Northhampton, Elizabeth City, York, Princess Anne, and Norfolk, including the cities of Norfolk and Portsmouth), and which excepted parts are for the present left precisely as if this proclamation were not issued. And by virtue of the power and for the purpose aforesaid, I do order and declare that all persons held as slaves within said designated States and parts of States are, and henceforward shall be, free; and that the Executive Government of the United States, including the military and naval authorities thereof, will recognize and maintain the freedom of said persons. And I hereby enjoin upon the people so declared to be free to abstain from all violence, unless in necessary self-defence; and I recommend to them that, in all cases when allowed, they labor faithfully for reasonable wages. And I further declare and make known that such persons of suitable condition will be received into the armed service of the United States to garrison forts, positions, stations, and other places, and to man vessels of all sorts in said service. And upon this act, sincerely believed to be an act of justice, warranted by the Constitution upon military necessity, I invoke the considerate judgment of mankind and the gracious favor of Almighty God.

By July of 1865, an estimated four million slaves had been set free. While the *Emancipation Proclamation* was a giant step forward in ending slavery in America, the Thirteenth Amendment became the final word on the subject: "Neither slavery nor involuntary servitude, except as a punishment for crime whereof the party shall have been duly convicted, shall exist within the United States, or any place subject to their jurisdiction."

71.

Congress Approves *In God We Trust* on Coins

March 3, 1865

America's tradition of depending on God for guidance and protection was inherited, we could say, from Christopher Columbus who depended on God to make his incredibly dangerous and visionary mission that resulted in his discovery of a New World a success. We know that because he said so in his personal journal.

As it turned out, his mission was more successful and had a greater impact on world history that he was ever able to imagine. Without his trust in and dependence on God, that voyage to the New World might never have taken place.

From existing records of the early American settlements, we know most of the first settlers also believed they were on a Providential mission and that they trusted God to guide and protect them. Those records abound with many stories of the various ways in which the early settlers' faith was rewarded in seemingly miraculous ways.

The favorable outcome of so many events leading up to and throughout the Revolutionary War period gave American colonists many reasons to conclude that their trust in God's protective care was the only possible explanation for their success in eventually prevailing against such great odds; many Founding Fathers, especially Benjamin Franklin, attributed the successful conclusion of the Constitutional Convention of 1787 to God's intervention and guidance. Providential involvement in

America's protection and meteoric rise as an economic and military power in the world has been unabashedly acknowledged by most American Presidents since the office was first occupied in 1789.

Since the concept of God's superintending care in the founding of America is so often mentioned in the writings of the Founding Fathers and many who preceded them, it is difficult to say where the phrase *In God We Trust* actually originated. A similar phrase is included in *The Star Spangled Banner* where the words "In God is our trust" appear in the last stanza.

The official story of how *In God We Trust* was placed on U.S. coins appears on the public education website of the U.S. Treasury Department. It began with a letter dated November 13, 1861, to Secretary of the Treasury Salmon P. Chase from Rev. M. R. Watkinson, a Christian minister from Ridleyville, Pennsylvania. In his letter, Rev. Watkinson said, "One fact touching our currency has hitherto been seriously overlooked. I mean the recognition of the Almighty God in some form on our coins...This would relieve us from the ignominy of heathenism. This would place us openly under the Divine protection we have personally claimed. From my heart I have felt our national shame in disowning God as not the least of our present national disasters."

Secretary Chase liked the idea and, on November 20, sent a letter to James Pollock, Director of the Mint at Philadelphia, in which he said: "No nation can be strong except in the strength of God, or safe except in His defense. The trust of our people in God should be declared on our national coins. You will cause a device to be prepared without unnecessary delay with a motto expressing in the fewest and tersest words possible this national recognition."

After another exchange of letters between Chase and Pollock, it was decided that *In God We Trust* were the words that would be placed on a shield included in the design of new one-cent and two-cent coins. The design was approved by Congress April 22, 1864.

Congress passed an act on March 3, 1865, that allowed the Mint Director, with the Secretary's approval, to place the motto on all gold and silver coins that "shall admit the inscription thereon." Under the act, the motto was placed on a number of other coins including the silver dollar, the half-dollar and the quarter-dollar coins. On February 12, 1873, Congress passed the *Coinage Act* that authorized the Secretary "to cause *In God We Trust* to be inscribed on such coins as shall admit of such motto."

In 1955, Congress required that *In God We Trust* be included in the design of all paper currency with this statement of confirmation: "In these days when imperialistic and materialistic Communism seeks to attack and destroy freedom, it is proper to remind all of us of this self-evident truth that as long as this country trusts in God, it will prevail."

In God We Trust didn't officially become the national motto until 1956 when this statement was included in the *Congressional Record*: "At the present time the United States has no national motto. The committee deems it most appropriate that *In God We Trust* be so designated as the U.S. national motto." After Congress approved adoption of the motto, it was signed into law by President Dwight Eisenhower on July 30, 1956.

It was also Eisenhower who signed an act of Congress in 1954 that had added the phrase "Under God" to the *Pledge of Allegiance*. At the signing ceremony, the President said, "In this way we are reaffirming the transcendence of religious faith in America's heritage and future; in this way we shall constantly strengthen those spiritual weapons which forever will be our country's most powerful resource in peace and war."

President John F. Kennedy spoke to that subject in 1961 when he said, "No man who enters upon the office to which I have succeeded can fail to recognize how every president of the United States has placed special reliance upon his faith in God. Every president has taken comfort and courage when told that the Lord 'will be with thee. He will not fail thee nor forsake thee. Fear not – neither be thou dismayed.' While they came from a wide variety of religious backgrounds and held a wide variety of religious beliefs, each of our presidents in his own way has placed a special trust in God. Those who were strongest intellectually were also strongest spiritually."

Secular humanist "progressives" who want all mention of God eliminated from public view don't know, or won't admit, the role God has played in the discovery, establishment, and preservation of America as the envy of the world. If they get their way, America will be just another great nation that forgot God and went into disasterous decline.

72.

Alaska Purchased from Russia

William Henry Seward's critics had a lot of fun at his expense when he proposed purchasing the remote area known as Alaska from Russia in 1867. They jeeringly referred to the largely uninhabited area located on the extreme northwest corner of the North American continent as Seward's folly, Seward's icebox, the polar bear garden, Icebergia, and Walrussia, among other disparaging terms.

Sometimes referred to as "the last frontier," Alaska added an area of land to the United States equal to 75% of the land included in the Louisiana Purchase; the cost of Alaska was less than half that of the famous 1803 land purchase. If Alaska were a separate country, it would rank as the nineteenth largest country in the world.

When gold was discovered there in the 1890s, the scoffers soon changed their tune as Americans watched an investment of only $7.2 million, which was roughly 2-cents per acre for almost 600,000 square miles of land rich in natural resources, begin to payoff. Alaska's gold rush increased Americans' understanding of the importance of what newspaper publisher Horace Greeley had once mistakenly called a country that "would not be worth taking as a gift."

Increased appreciation of the value of Alaska as part of the United States led to the granting of territorial status to the area a few years later. As a result of the gold discovery, it is estimated that more than fifty mining camps were established from which new communities often sprouted.

As was always the case when important events occurred during early American history, the "invisible hand" seems to have been involved in the purchase of Alaska. Seward, a strong believer in the concept of America's *Manifest Destiny* and an early proponent of acquiring Alaska, Hawaii, and other non-contiguous land areas, had the confidence and support of President Andrew Johnson who, when he succeeded President Lincoln, had retained Seward as his Secretary of State.

At the same time Seward was keeping a wistful eye on Alaska, Russian leaders, fearing they could lose their ownership to British Canada at some point in the future, were deciding to approach U.S. leaders with the idea of selling them what they considered a difficult-to-defend part of their empire. Seward jumped at the opportunity even though he knew such a proposal would certainly be met with strong opposition in Congress. He signed the treaty March 3, 1867.

Regarded as a visionary by many of his contemporaries, Seward was described as "one of those spirits who sometimes will go ahead of public opinion instead of tamely following its footprints." Knowing he had his work cut out for him and with the support of Senator Charles Sumner, chairman of the Foreign Relations Committee, and U.S. Ambassador to Russia Cassius M. Clay, Seward pushed the issue and was able to win Senate approval of the purchase on April 9. Seward's victory was achieved with a margin of one-vote. On October 18, the U.S. formally took possession of Alaska during a land transfer ceremony at Sitka. Some historians have called the acquisition of Alaska the Johnson Administration's greatest achivement.

In 1867, the future forty-ninth state was organized as the Department of Alaska which later became the District of Alaska. It was established as a territory May 11, 1912, then admitted into the union on Janury 3, 1958. Russia's departure from the North American continent "removed one more monarch from this continent," observed Sumner. France, Spain and Russia had all given way "to that absorbing unity which is declared in the national motto – *E pluribus unum.*" He was correct about the monarchs, but wrong about the national motto. America had no official motto until *In God We Trust* was so designated by Congress in 1956.

That the investment in Alaska was an unusually successful one has been demonstrated over and over again with the natural resources and wealth it has contributed to the interests of the United States. Development happened intermittently spurred by events such as completion of the Alaska Railroad in 1923 and the Alaska Highway in 1943. The Alcan, as it was called, was completed as a high priority project when Japan invaded the Aleutian Islands in 1942. The establishment of military bases in Alaska helped to accelerate infrastructure development as the territory became more important strategically especially by providing the U.S. with a significant military advantage during the forty-year Cold War.

With the discovery of oil at Prudhoe Bay in 1968 and completion of the Trans-Alaska Pipeline in 1977, America's forty-ninth state now supplies 25% of America's oil and has the potential of supplying much more. Alaska also has basins containing huge deposits of coal and a coastline offering wind and geothermal energy development possibilities. By U.S. Geological Survey estimates, more than eighty-five million cubic feet of recoverable natural gas are available on the North Slope of Alaska.

According to the *Chronicle of America*, Ambassador Clay wrote regarding Seward's treaty, "Alaska's mines, waters, furs and fisheries are of untold value," and "the territory was worth seven times what the government was paying the Russians for it." Clay went on to say that "future generations will wonder that we ever got it at all."

Those future generations mentioned by Clay are still enjoying the benefits generated by the "folly" of William Henry Seward, most of whose critics have been long forgotten.

73.

Transcontinental Railroad Completed

<u>May 10, 1869</u>

A national celebration took place May 10, 1869. On that date, Union Pacific Railroad tracks originating in Omaha, Nebraska, and Central Pacific Railroad tracks originating in Sacramento, California, were formally connected in Promontory filling a transportation gap that tied the nation together.

R. M. Devens described the magnitude of that accomplishment in his 1878 book entitled *Our First Century:* "Believers in the 'manifest destiny' of the universal Yankee nation were favored with one of the most conclusive and gratifying confirmations of their cherished theory, when that most stupendous work ever undertaken by man, the Construction of the Pacific Railway, was finally consummated by the laying of the last rail and the memorable ceremony performed by officials of clasping together the iron girdle about the loins of the nation;—in the winding of which mighty coil across the continent, mountains were tunneled which made one's head giddy to gaze upon; rivers were bridged which, since the primeval days of creation, had rolled in majestic solitude; gulfs, frightful and tumultuous, were spanned; frowning heights were climbed and leveled; and abysmal depths were fathomed. And all this was accomplished in a period of time, and on a scale of magnitude, the recital of which is fairly calculated to stagger credulity."

The high point of the Promontory ceremony, news of which was immediately telegraphed to President Ulysses S. Grant, occurred when Central Pacific president Leland Stanford and Union Pacific vice-president Thomas Durant hammered home golden spikes that symbolically completed the 2,400 miles of newly installed track. Stanford had arrived in Promontory for the ceremony aboard a Central Pacific train from Sacramento while Durant had arrived on a Union Pacific train from Omaha.

For the first time in history, trains could operate from coast to coast with the new CP/UP tracks connecting with those of railroads already in operation to the east of Omaha. With transcontinental rail transportation finally available, the difficult trip between Omaha and Sacramento that could take six to eight months by wagon train or stage coach, could now be completed much more safely and comfortably in a week or less.

Linking the east and west coasts by rail dramatically changed the way business was done in America and accelerated development of the interior. With such a monumental improvement in transportation available, larger numbers of people were attracted into the unsettled areas for many reasons not the least of which was to take advantage of free government land provided by the 1862 *Homestead Act*. That influx of people led to the establishment of new communities all along the CP/UP right of way.

A few visionary people had been thinking about the possibility of building a transcontinental railroad since the very early 1800s. A railroad building boom in the east started in 1830 when the Baltimore & Ohio began operations. By 1860, there were many railroads operating in the east but few in California. The Sacramento Valley Railroad, completed in 1856, was the first railroad built west of the Mississippi River. I t was the brainchild of Theodore Judah, a New York railroad engineer, who wrote *A Practical Plan for Building the Pacific Railroad* in 1857.

In explaining his vision of a transcontinental railroad, Judah said, "It is the most magnificent project ever conceived. It connects these two great oceans. It is an indissoluble bond of union between the populous States of the East, and the undeveloped regions of the fruitful West. It is a highway which leads to peace and future prosperity. An iron bond for the perpetuation of the Union and independence which we now enjoy."

Judah is credited with bringing together the four men – Leland Stanford, Collis P. Huntington, Mark Hopkins, and Charles Crocker – who eventually made the future continental railroad a reality. With their backing, Judah also played an important role in getting the *1862* Pacific

Railroad Act approved by Congress. The *Act*, officially named *An Act to aid in the construction of a railroad and telegraph line from the Missouri river to the Pacific ocean, and to secure to the government the use of the same for postal, military, and other purposes*, provided the financing tools necessary to begin planning and construction.

Considering the terrain – including both rugged mountains and arid deserts – and the primitive nature of the tools available at that time, not to mention the added hazard of being subjected to on-going Indian attacks in many areas, it took uncommon vision and determination to believe the project could succeed. Here's how author Devens furthur described the magnitude of the project: "In less than one-half or one-third of the time predicted at the outset of the enterprise, the road was completed – a great feat, indeed, when it is considered that the workmen operated at such a distance from their base of supplies, and that the materials for construction and subsistence had to be transported under such a variety of difficulties. Thus, the transportation of one hundred and ten thousand tons of iron rails, one million fish-plates, two million bolts, fifteen million spikes, three and a half million cross-ties, and millions of feet of timber not estimated, for the construction of roads, culverts and bridges, made one of the minor items of the account. The moving of engines and machinery for stacking manufactories, of materials for foundries and buildings of every kind, not to speak of the food for an army of thousands of workmen, all of which belong to the single account of transportation, may also give an impression of the activity and expense required in bringing such a road to completion in so short a time.

"Of course the irregularities of surface characterizing a distance so immense, and particularly that portion of the line running among the Sierra Nevada mountains, necessitated tunneling, cutting, and trestle-bridging, on a large scale. The well-known Bloomer Cut, sixty-three feet deep and eight hundred feet long, is through cemented gravel and sand, of the consistency of solid rock, and only to be moved by blasting. Tile trestle-bridging constituted one of the most important features in the construction of the road, and the work, on completion, was pronounced of the most durable description."

Completing such an enormous task was, indeed, cause for celebration. It is impossible to estimate how much impact placement of those last few spikes put in place on May 10, 1869, had in hastening the overall development of the United States of America. The message telegraphed to President Grant that caused jubilation from coast to coast said: "The last rail is laid! The last spike driven! The Pacific Railroad is completed!"

On the golden spikes, these prophetic words were inscribed: "May God continue the unity of our Country as this Railroad unites the two great Oceans of the world."

74.

Statue of Liberty Dedicated

October 28, 1886

October 28, 1886, was designated "Bartoldi Day" in New York City. That's the day New Yorkers eagerly awaited the unveiling and dedication of Frederic Auguste Bartholdi's Statue of Liberty on Bedloe's Island, the strategic location in New York Harbor personally selected by the French sculptor on his first trip to America in 1871.

The concept behind this unusually large work of art – it was 305-feet tall including the pedestal upon which it stood – that would become a world-famous symbol of American liberty was conceived in the small French village of Glatigny on a summer evening in 1865. A group of influential men had gathered at the home of French historian Edouard Rene Lefebvre de Laboulaye, author of the three-volume *Political History of the United States,* to discuss items of mutual interest over dinner. Bartholdi was part of that group, all of whom were admirers of the American Constitution. They all agreed that the U.S. Constitution should be the document upon which a new France, a *Third Republic,* could someday be established.

Those in attendance also admired Abraham Lincoln who a large number of Europeans saw as a "man of the people," the un-aristocrat. They were drawn to him as well because of his opposition to slavery. Reporting on French reaction to the Lincoln assassination, an American journalist in Paris had written, "This sad event has moved the masses most intensely. They feel they have lost a friend, and humanity a benefactor."

Laboulaye, leader of the French Anti-Slavery Society, was especially fond of Lincoln.

Affectionate feelings the French people held for Lincoln had inspired a gift from them to Mrs. Lincoln – a gold medal inscribed on one side with the words, "Dedicated by the French Democracy. A. Lincoln. Twice elected President of the United States." On the other side was engraved "Lincoln, Honest Man. Abolished Slavery, Re-established the Union, and Saved the Republic, without Veiling the Statue of Liberty."

From that informal dinner meeting held in a small French village 3,500 miles from New York City emerged the idea of designing some kind of impressive tribute to be presented to the American people in commemoration of the 100th Anniversary of the American Declaration of Independence. Inspired by the "statue of liberty" phrase on the gold medal given to Mrs. Lincoln, Laboulaye asked Bartholdi to come up with a statue concept that would represent independence and "liberty enlightening the world." A prominent theme of Laboulaye's extensive writings on American history was the idea of the dawning of a New World, one that had the potential of enlightening the Old World.

Bartholdi began thinking about the project but his creative work was interrupted by the Franco-Prussian War in which he fought as a Major in the *Garde National*. When the war ended in 1871, he returned to his studio where he resumed working on concepts for a liberty sculpture. At the suggestion of Laboulaye, Bartholdi traveled to America and toured the country coast to coast on the recently completed transcontinental railroad. Observing that "everything is big here," Bartholdi wrote that "the very freedom of the New World seemed a matter of space, of growth, of bigness." That observation influenced his thinking regarding the appropriate scale for the proposed project.

Because of political turmoil in France at the time, Bartholdi agreed with Laboulaye to delay pushing ahead in getting the project approved and financed until the new French Republic was formed which didn't officially become a reality until 1875. Meanwhile, Laboulaye, as an active member of the provisional National Assembly, had become focused on his role in writing the new French Constitution.

Once political stability was achieved, Laboulaye formed the *Union Franco-Americaine*, a committee whose purpose was to advance his visionary dream of producing a Statue of Liberty. Other members of the committee included historian Alexis de Tocqueville and descendants of both Marquis de Lafayette and Jean Baptiste Rochambeau, French heroes of the American Revolution.

The committee worked on securing public approval and financing for the project while Bartholdi completed his design work with the help of Gustave Eiffel, engineer and builder of the Eiffel Tower. Bartholdi's design was constructed over the skeleton designed by Eiffel. Bartholdi was issued a patent in February of 1879 for "a statue representing Liberty enlightening the world, the same consisting, essentially, of the draped female figure, with one arm upraised, bearing a torch, and while the other holds an inscribed tablet, and having upon the head a diadem, substantially as set forth."

The statue was completed in 1881 but the pedestal, which was, by French and American agreement, to be constructed and paid for by Americans, wasn't ready until April of 1886. The dismantled statue had arrived in New York in June of 1885 and was stored awaiting completion of the granite pedestal. Originally, Laboulaye and Bartholdi had intended to present the statue to America on July 4, 1876.

Twenty-one years after a happenstance but fateful discussion in Glatigny, France, had produced the germ of an idea, a world-famous statue that would become symbolic of enlightened liberty was dedicated to America and to the world in New York harbor.

"Bartholdi Day" in New York was described for us by Richard Schneider in his book entitled *Freedom's Holy Light*:

> *He awakened early on the day of dedication, Thursday, October 28, to a gray dawn. And though a gentle rain began to fall about nine o'clock in the morning, it did not stop thousands of parade goers from lining Fifth Avenue, many balancing on boxes and stools for a better view.*
>
> *They saw twenty thousand soldiers, sailors, and war veterans following marching bands. There were floats and fire engines, brought up by college students and a multitude of clubs and organizations including the* Societe Comarienne, Union Alsacienne, Gardes Rochambeau, *and* Societe Israelite *composed of Jewish People of French origin.*
>
> *New York was a French city that day, aflutter with tricolor and its streets ringing with "The Marseillaise."*

All twenty thousand paraders snapped to attention as they passed the reviewing stand in Madison Square Park where President Grover Cleveland, Bartholdi, and [Count Ferdinand] de Lesseps stood (for good reason; their chairs were awash with rain). Earlier, Bartholdi had been greeted by President Cleveland with the words: "You are the greatest man in America today!"

"Through your courtesy," bowed the diplomatic sculptor.

Even so, three little girls lent impact to the Chief Executive's pronouncement when they broke free of the parade and rushed up to the reviewing stand to present flowers which, they made emphatically clear, were only "for Mr. Bartholdi!"

Hardly had the last notes of the scarlet-coated Marine band conducted by John Philip Sousa sounded when the president and entourage boarded the USS Despatch on the Hudson at West Twenty-third Street. The small naval boat led a flotilla of three hundred excursion steamers, tugs, and yachts to Bedloe's Island where at anchor lay eight full-rigged American warships along with several French dreadnoughts. Jack-tars sprang into the rigging where they stood elbow to elbow on the yardarms in smart salute.

Below, naval cannons thundered in the twenty-one-gun Presidential Salute, as white smoke billowed into the mist further shrouding the statue from view.

President Cleveland added these thoughts during the ceremony on the island: "We will not forget that Liberty has made here her home, nor shall her chosen alter be neglected. Willing votaries will constantly keep alive its fires and these shall gleam upon the shores of our sister Republic in the East. Reflected thence and joined with answering rays, a stream of light shall pierce the darkness of ignorance and man's oppression until Liberty enlightens the world."

When relighting the Statue of Liberty on July 3, 1986, President Ronald Reagan, putting himself in the company of our ancestors who believed in Providential involvement in the founding of America, said, "I've always thought that God had His reasons for placing this land here between two great oceans to be found by a certain kind of people."

We know from Reagan's other writings and public pronouncements that the "certain kind of people" he referred to were God-fearing, Bible-believing Christians.

75.

Supreme Court: "This is a Christian Nation"

February 29, 1892

In 1892, the U.S. Supreme Court, after considering extensive documentation, issued what became known as the Trinity Decision. The justices concluded the United States "is a Christian nation." The court case, known as Church of the Holy Trinity v. United States (1892), had to do with an 1887 employment contract between a New York church and an English preacher. It was based on an 1885 federal law concerning immigration which said: "It shall be unlawful for any person, company, partnership, or corporation, in any manner whatsoever… to in any way assist or encourage the importation of any alien or foreigners, into the United States…under contract or agreement…to perform labor or service of any kind." When the Church of the Holy Trinity hired a pastor from England, the U.S. Attorney General considered it a violation of the law.

Basing its decision on "the spirit of the law" rather than the "letter of the law," the Court ruled in favor of the Church. Associate Justice Josiah Brewer wrote: "It is a familiar rule, that a thing may be within the letter of the statute and yet not within the statute."

In its decision, the justices wrote that "the circuit court did err when it held that the contract hiring an English rector was within the prohibition of the statute, which disallowed a "…person, company, partnership, or corporation, in any manner whatsoever to prepay the transportation, or in any way assist or encourage the importation or migration, of any alien or aliens, any foreigner or foreigners, into the United States… under contract or agreement … to perform labor or service of any kind in the United States…"

The Court's opinion went on to say, "… to revile, with malicious and blasphemous contempt, the religion professed by almost the whole community is an abuse of that right. Nor are we bound by any expressions in the Constitution, as some have strangely supposed, either not to punish at all, or to punish indiscriminately the like attacks upon the religion of Mahomet or of the Grand Lama, and for this plain reason, that the case assumes that we are a Christian people, and the morality of the country is deeply engrafted upon Christianity, and not upon the doctrines or worship of those impostors.

"If we pass beyond these matters to a view of American life, as expressed by its laws, its business, its customs, and its society, we find every where a clear recognition of the same truth. Among other matters, note the following: the form of oath universally prevailing, concluding with an appeal to the Almighty; the custom of opening sessions of all deliberative bodies and most conventions with prayer; the prefatory words of all wills, 'In the name of God, amen;' the laws respecting the observance of the Sabbath, with the general cessation of all secular business, and the closing of courts, legislatures, and other similar public assemblies on that day; the churches and church organizations which abound in every city, town, and hamlet; the multitude of charitable organizations existing every where under Christian auspices; the gigantic missionary associations, with general support, and aiming to establish Christian missions in every quarter of the globe. These, and many other matters which might be noticed, add a volume of unofficial declarations to the mass of organic utterances that this is a Christian nation. In the face of all these, shall it be believed that a Congress of the United States intended to make it a misdemeanor for a church of this country to contract for the services of a Christian minister residing in another nation?

"There is no dissonance in these declarations. There is a universal language pervading them all, having one meaning. They affirm and reaffirm that this is a religious nation. These are not individual sayings, declarations of private persons. They are organic utterances. They speak the voice of the entire people. While because of a general recognition of this truth the question has seldom been presented to the courts, yet we find that in Updegraph v. Com., 11 Serg. & R. 394, 400, it was decided that, 'Christianity, general Christianity, is, and always has been, a part of the common law of Pennsylvania."

In a book authored by Justice Brewer in 1905, he wrote further on the subject of the Christian character of the United States. "But in what sense can it be called a Christian nation? Not in the sense that Christianity is the established religion or that people are in any matter compelled to support it. On the contrary, the Constitution specifically provides that 'Congress shall make no law respecting an establishment of religion, or prohibiting the free exercise thereof.' Neither is it Christian in the sense that all of its citizens are either in fact or name Christian. On the contrary, all religions have free scope within our borders. Numbers of our people profess other religions, and many reject all. Nor is it Christian in the sense that a profession of Christianity is a condition of holding office or otherwise engaging in public service, or essential to recognition either politically or socially. In fact, the government as a legal organization is independent of all religions. Nevertheless, we constantly speak of this republic as a Christian Nation – in fact, as the leading Christian Nation of the world. This popular use of the term certainly has significance. It is not a mere creation of the imagination. It is not a term of derision but has substantial basis – one which justifies its use...But I have said enough to show that Christianity came to this country with the first colonists; has been powerfully identified with its rapid development, colonial and national, and to-day exists as a mighty factor in the life of the republic. This is a Christian nation,"

The fact that the United States of America is a "Christian nation" is still being disputed today by those who intentionally ignore obvious facts and the evidence upon which the Supreme Court based its conclusion. During the last fifty years, several leftwing "freedom from religion" organizations have appeared on the scene, all mostly pursuing an anti-Christian agenda.

History revisionists and humanists (atheists) have had their day; it's time for the truth to be rediscovered and honored.

76.

Spanish-American War Officially Begins

April 20, 1898

In a letter to President Theodore Roosevelt, John Milton Hay, Secretary of State, referred to the Spanish-American War as a "splendid little war."

The outcome of that war could certainly be labeled as "splendid" in that the United States was able to liberate Cuba from a despotic Spanish regime while also gaining control of Puerto Rico, the Philippines, Guam, and, temporarily, Cuba. Although Cuba was soon recognized as a free and independent nation as required by the *Teller Amendment*, the U.S. retained the right to maintain a Naval Base at Guantanamo Bay.

Even though the war was fought in both the Atlantic and Pacific Oceans, it was "little" in the length of time that elapsed from start to finish. The fighting went on intermittently from May until August when an armistice was signed; the treaty that officially ended the war was dated December 10, 1898, less than eight months from the date war had been declared. The "little" war also helped to establish the young American republic as a major world military and economic power.

Soon after war was declared on April 20, 1798, the U.S. Navy destroyed Spanish naval forces in two short engagements, one in the Philippines on May 1 and the other at Santiago de Cuba on July 3. It took Admiral George Dewey's Asiatic Squadron only seven hours to sink or capture all Spanish ships bottled up in Manila Bay and even less time than that for Admiral William T. Sampson to effectively destroy the Spanish Caribbean Squadron at Santiago.

It was on San Juan Hill just outside of Santiago that Teddy Roosevelt and his "Rough Riders" made their reputation as an effective fighting force. Roosevelt is the only American President ever awarded the Congressional Medal of Honor, the most prestigious award bestowed on members of the United States armed forces who distinguish themselves "conspicuously by gallantry and intrepidity at the risk of his life above and beyond the call of duty while engaged in an action against an enemy of the United States."

That the "Rough Riders" were confident of their fighting abilities is illustrated by this slogan they reportedly chanted enroute to Cuba: "Rough-tough, we're the stuff! We want to fight and we can't get enough!"

Some historians have labeled the Spanish-American War our most popular war. At least part of that popularity has been attributed to the growth of "yellow journalism" and the struggle for dominance in the newspaper publishing business between New York publications owned by William Randolph Hearst and Joseph Pulitzer. When the *USS Maine* exploded under mysterious circumstances in Havana Harbor February 15, 1898, U.S. newspapers heralded the event with headlines such as *Remember the Main. To hell with Spain.*

Frank Luther Mott, former Dean of the University of Missouri School of Journalism, in his book entitled *American Journalism: A History of Newspapers in the United States Through 250 years, 1690 to 1940,* characterized the newspaper circulation wars as "journalistic jingoism." Here are his comments on the newspapers' contribution to the eventual declaration of war:

> *The "ifs" of history are usually more amusing than profitable, but there seems to be great probability in the frequently reiterated statement that if Hearst had not challenged Pulitzer to a circulation contest at the time of the Cuban insurrection, there would have been no Spanish-American War. Certainly the most powerful and persistent jingo propaganda ever carried on by newspapers was led by the* New York Journal *and* World *in 1896-98, and the result was an irresistible popular fervor for war which at length overcame the long unwillingness of President McKinley and even swept blindly over the last-minute capitulation by Spain on all the points at issue.*

This war passion was whipped up by news stories, headlines, pictures, and editorials in the yellow press. The news materials used in this great pre-war campaign were: Spanish atrocities in Cuba, Spanish actions against American citizens involved in the Cuban war for independence, the campaign for the recognition of the belligerence of the Cuban insurgents, incidents produced by newspaper intervention, the Maine *disaster, and American preparations for war.*

    Cuban atrocity stories proved to be good circulation pullers, and inevitably competition in this kind of matter developed between the World *and the* Journal. *The* World's *corps of correspondents in the island was at first superior to that of its rival, but early in 1897 Hearst bought a yacht, the* Vamoose, *and sent it to Cuba with Richard Harding Davis, famous as a writer of fiction and travel articles, and Frederic Remington, equally famous as an illustrator, to investigate conditions in the unhappy island and send back feature stories. Remington did not like the assignment, and the following interchange of cablegrams is said to have taken place:*

    HEARST, JOURNAL, NEW YORK: EVERYTHING IS QUIET. THERE IS NO TROUBLE HERE. THERE WILL BE NO WAR. WISH TO RETURN. REMINGTON.

    REMINGTON, HAVANA: PLEASE REMAIN. YOU FURNISH THE PICTURES AND I'LL FURNISH THE WAR. HEARST.

Whatever the true cause of the Spanish-American War, the results were overwhelmingly favorable to the United States of America. In addition to the "yellow journalism" effect in leading the nation to war, other popular concepts played a role including the idea of removing a European power from the Caribbean which fit nicely into the *Monroe Doctrine.* The generally accepted idea that America had a mission in the world to promote and defend democracy, a *Manifest Destiny* that went beyond the continental borders of the U.S., was also a factor.

The war also helped to heal wounds remaining from the Civil War as soldiers and sailors from both the North and South became comrades in arms as they fought a common foreign enemy. To some extent, that was also true of black and white American military personnel. Writing about the Cuban Campaign, General John J. Pershing said, "White regiments, black regiments, regulars and Rough Riders, representing the young manhood of the North and the South, fought shoulder to shoulder, unmindful of race or color, unmindful of whether commanded by ex-Confederate or not, and mindful of only their common duty as Americans."

Also as a result of the war, the importance of maintaining a well equipped, well trained Navy was understood and accepted. Throughout the Spanish-American War, the Navy was highly effective in battling enemy naval forces and in transporting troops and supplies where needed. Seen more and more as America's first line of defense, the Navy was significantly expanded following the war as part of Roosevelt's "Big Stick" diplomacy, sometimes referred to as "gunboat diplomacy." He described it as "the exercise of intelligent forethought and of decisive action sufficiently far in advance of any likely crisis."

Increasing military might, industrial growth, an explosion in population, and technological advances all hit new highs around the turn of the century. America had come of age.

IN CONCLUSION

By reading these seventy-six stories about events that took place between 1492 and 1898, you were exposed to historical information about which far too many Americans know little or nothing. Basic information about so many uncommonly courageous patriots, important events, and inspired documents that shaped the nation has been eliminated from many of our public school history books. Our country is much the poorer and less united as a result of an intentional failure to properly educate our younger generations about our exceptional heritage, especially where important Biblical principles incorporated in that heritage are concerned.

Agenda-driven humanists have for many years controlled an unholy trinity of miseducated and/or dishonest opinion-influencers – the "mainstream" news media, the entertainment industry, and academia. *Humanism* is defined as "a modern, nontheistic, rationalist movement that holds that man is capable of self-fulfillment, ethical conduct, etc., without recourse to supernaturalism." In more direct words, humanists are atheists who don't want Americans to understand God's role in our history.

From the beginning, the men who discovered and established the exceptional nation that would someday be known as the United States of America were driven by their quest for religious freedom. Because they knew and revered the concepts taught in the Bible, the settlers based their early charters and attempts at governance on that supernatural book. The Founding Fathers were building upon an existing Christian foundation when they produced the *Declaration of Independence* and the *U.S. Constitution.* James McHenry, a signer of the *Constitution,* made this statement that reflected the views of his fellow Founders:

> *Neither, in considering this subject [the distribution of Bibles], let it be overlooked, that public utility pleads most forcibly for the general distribution of the Holy Scriptures. The doctrine they preach, the obligations they impose, the punishment they threaten, the rewards they promise, the stamp and image of divinity they bear, which produces a conviction of their truths, can alone secure to society, order and peace, and to our courts of justice and constitutions of government, purity, stability and usefulness.*

> *In vain without the Bible, we increase penal laws and draw entrenchments around our institutions. Bibles are strong entrenchments. Where they abound, men cannot pursue wicked courses and at the same time enjoy quiet conscience.*

> *Consider also, the rich do not possess aught more precious than their Bible, and that the poor cannot be presented by the rich with anything of greater value. Withhold it not from the poor. It is a book of councils and directions, fitted to every situation in which man can be placed. It is an oracle which reveals to mortals the secrets of heaven and the hidden will of the Almighty. It is an estate, whose title is guaranteed by Christ, whose delicious fruits ripen every season, survive the worm, and keep through eternity.*

American history is rich in testimonials of this kind. But information pointing out the Bible's influence on the settlers and founders of America has been missing from books used in public schools for several generations. Revisionists have mostly scrubbed mention of America's Christian roots from those books and truth has been the victim of a coordinated campaign the roots of which can be traced back to the early 1900s.

The attack on education was generated by a group of misguided Americans whose goal was to see the United States become part of a socialistic world government ruled by secular humanists. They believed that separating Americans from their Christian roots was necessary if America was ever to accept the idea of membership in a European-style humanist/socialist world government.

In the mid 1930s, Augustin G. Rudd, Education Committee Chairman of the New York Chapter of the Sons of the American Revolution, became concerned about what was or was not being taught in public schools. Believing something was not as it should be, he began what became a twenty-year research project. In 1957, he presented the results of his study in a book entitled *Bending the Twig: The Revolution in Education and its Effect on our Children.* Rudd's study had confirmed his suspicions that "the traditional school courses which had shaped the minds of generations of our citizens had been drastically altered or omitted."

"For instance," he wrote, "history, geography and civics have disappeared as separate subjects. In their place was a new and confusing omnibus course styled *social science* which was to become the core of the whole program." It became known as the "new education" or "progressive education."

Social science textbooks were first used in New York and soon spread across the nation. They were written by a prominent "new educationist" by the name of Dr. Harold Rugg who taught at the Teachers' College of Columbia University.

According to Rudd, Dr. Rugg "had loaded them with arguments supporting statism, and upholding collectivist doctrines as superior to sound American principles. These statements constituted a severe indictment of our way of life." Rudd went on to say, "So complete and sweeping has been their victory that today most of the leaders of the dominant teachers' organizations and teacher-training colleges and institutions, which screen new teachers into the schools, have accepted or conformed to this new curriculum and its educational philosophies."

Rudd lays the blame squarely on the powerful teachers' unions, not on the individual classroom teachers. He wrote, "The majority of our teachers and school administrators are patriotic men and women dedicated to their life work of imparting to our youth a sound basic education. Many of them have been powerless to act under the compulsions of the educational hierarchy. With most of the leaders of the teachers' associations and big names in the teachers' colleges and the foundations lined up behind the New Educationists, the individual teacher has been virtually immobilized. Thousands have become unwilling conformists."

Another excellent book on the subversion of public education in America is entitled *The Turning of the Tides.* Of its 182 pages, the book includes twenty-three pages of documentation. Written in 1953, it traces the beginning of the leftwing takeover of public school curricula to September 12, 1905, when the *Intercollegiate Socialist Society* was formed. Soon after that, the Rand School of Social Science was organized in

Manhattan with links to the *Intercollegiate Socialist Society*. By 1917, the *ISS* had chapters in sixty-one colleges and universities.

In 1921, *the ISS* changed its name to the *League for Industrial Democracy*. A blatantly socialist organization, it was led by Norman Thomas who ran for president of the United States six times between 1928 and 1948 on the American Socialist Party ticket. Thomas has been quoted as saying, "The American people will never knowingly adopt socialism. But, under the name of 'liberalism,' they will adopt every fragment of the socialist program, until one day America will be a socialist nation, without knowing how it happened." Although some humanists deny that Thomas used those exact words, they cannot deny that he and many of his associates made similar statements expressing that conviction.

Humanist John Dewey, often called "the father of modern education," was a vice president of the *League for Industrial Democracy* when it was formed in 1921; in 1941 he became its president. In 1933, Dewey is quoted as having said, "There is no God and there is no soul. Hence, there are no needs for the props of traditional religion. With dogma and creed excluded, then immutable truth is also dead and buried. There is no room for fixed, national law or moral absolutes."

Dewey is said to have believed in teaching *judgment* rather than *knowledge*. His idea of education was to teach students how to think like progressives. Facts tend to get in the way of progressive education and Dewey didn't want to clutter up young students' minds with inconvenient facts that interfered with his agenda.

It is now clear that a dedicated group of "progressives" initiated a plan more than 100 years ago to replace America's free enterprise system with Marxist socialism. Central to that plan was a campaign to re-educate American children by revising American history. One tactic of the humanist campaign is to mischaracterize the Founding Fathers as deists and atheists rather than God-fearing, Bible-believing Christians. Those who understand early American history know that is mostly not true, but too many of the untaught or mistaught have no way of disputing those mischaracterizations. Samuel Butler hit the nail squarely on the head when he said, *"Though God cannot alter the past, historians can."*

In 2008, the Bradley Project on America's National Identity also warned that "the next generation of Americans will know less than their parents about our history and founding ideals. They concluded that many Americans are more aware of what divides us than that which unites us." As the authors of the Bradley study noted, "If vast majorities do not grasp the meaning of liberties protected in the Bill of Rights, or fail to understand the desirability of representative government, how will common values be passed along from one generation to the next? The freedoms that we enjoy today must be defended and preserved – but first they must be understood."

If we have any of the character of the Founding Fathers remaining in us, we will not surrender to those who want to separate us from our Christian heritage. We will defend it and see to it that our children and grandchildren are strengthened by it as our Founding Fathers intended. If there is to be a turnaround, those of us who understand the problem must let our school boards and elected representatives know that we want U.S. history stressed in the preparation and hiring of teachers, in textbooks, and in curriculum.

Joseph Story, Founding Father and U.S. Supreme Court Justice from 1811 to 1845, offered this advice: "Let the American youth never forget, that they possess a noble inheritance, bought by the toils and sufferings and blood of their ancestors; and capacity, if wisely improved and faithfully guarded, of transmitting to their latest posterity all the substantial blessings of life, the peaceful enjoyment of liberty, property, religion, and independence."

ACKNOWLEDGMENTS

Because many of the quotations and other information about events included in this book have appeared in numerous books, publications, and on many web sites over the years, including several I used as resource material, I did not footnote any single work as the source from which the more commonly known facts and quotations can be found. Such nuggets of information appear in a variety of resources and have, through common usage, become part of the public domain. Where lesser known facts and quotations are concerned, I did, in the text, identify the sources from which I gleaned them.

In most quotations, I presented them in their original form even though some spellings and punctuations may seem to be incorrect to readers unfamiliar with the terminology and style often found in early American writings. Because most of the Founding Fathers equated Providence with God's pre-established plan, I have capitalized it in my text.

It is my earnest desire that this book might inspire all who read it to delve deeper into an increasingly important culture war topic and that all concerned Americans monitor what is being taught (or not being taught) in our public schools.

If you have enjoyed and feel enlightened by this overview of early American history, there are a number of books listed below you will also enjoy reading and that you will find useful in deepening your understanding of this important subject. Many of them would make excellent gifts for relatives and friends for any gift-giving occasion. These are some but not all the books from which I collected facts that are included in the various chapters of this book. Arranged alphabetically, they are:

A Basic History of the United States, Volumes by Clarence B. Carson
A History of the American People by Paul Johnson
American Courage edited by Herbert W. Warden III
America: A call to Greatness by John W. Chalfant
America's Christian History by Gary DeMar
America's God and Country by William J. Federer
A Nation Conceived and Dedicated by Corinne Hoexter and Ira Peck
A Patriot's History of the United States by Larry Schweikart and Michael Allen *Christianity and Liberalism* by J. Gresham Machen
Christianity and the Constitution by John Eidsmoe
Christianity in the Constitution by Archie Preston Jones, PhD.
Edmund Burke: A Genius Reconsidered by Russell Kirk
Faith & Freedom by Benjamin Hart
Faith of Our Founding Fathers by Tim LaHaye
Founding Brothers by Joseph J. Ellis
Founding Fathers by M. E. Bradford
From Dawn to Decadence by Jacques Barzun
From Union to Empire by Clyde N. Wilson
48 Liberal Lies About American History by Larry Schweikart
God and the Constitution by Paul Marshall
Great Books of the Western World edited by Robert M. Hutchins and Mortimer Adler
Greatness to Spare by T. R. Fehrenbach
How to Win the Culture War by Peter Kreeft
I Wish I'd Been There edited by Byron Hollinshead
If by Sea by George C. Daughan
In God We Trust by Norman Cousins
Intellectual Morons by Daniel Flynn
Liberty and Freedom by David Hackett Fischer
Lives of the Signers of the Declaration of Independence by B. J. Lossing
Miracle at Philadelphia by Catherine Drinker Bowen
National Review's American Classics (*Historical Colonial Documents*)
None Dare Call It Education by John A. Stormer
Not Our America...The ACLU Exposed! by Daniel J. Popeo
One Nation, Two Cultures by Gertrude Himmelfarb
Original Intent by David Barton
Patriot Pirates by Robert H. Patton

Reclaiming the Lost Legacy by D. James Kennedy
Revolutionary Characters by Gordon S Wood
Roots of Freedom by John W. Danford
Slouching Towards Gomorrah by Robert H. Bork
Sacred Fire by Peter A. Lillback
The ACLU vs. America by Alan Sears and Craig Osten
The American Presidents by David C. Whitney
The American Tradition by Clarence B. Carson
The Antifederalists by David J. Siemers
The Christian Life and Character of the Civil Institutions of the United States by Benjamin F. Morris
The Christian and American Law by H. Wayne House, General Editor
The Clash of Orthodoxies by Robert P. George
The Death of Truth edited by Dennis McCallum
The Founders' Almanac edited by Matthew Spalding
The History of the Navy of the United States f America by James Fenimore Cooper
The Light and the Glory by Peter Marshall and David Manuel
The Look-It-Up Book of Presidents by Wyatt Blassingame
The Myth of Separation by David Barton
The New American Revolution Handbook by Theodore P. Savas and David Dameron
The Patriot's Handbook by George Grant
The Politically Incorrect Guide to American History by Thomas E. Woods, Jr.
The Real Thomas Jefferson by Andrew M. Allison
The Rewriting of America's History by Catherine Millard
The Spirit of America edited by William J. Bennett
The Naked Square by Richard John Neuhaus
Understanding the Times by David A. Noebel
U.S. Military History for Dummies by John C. McManus
Watchwords of Liberty by Robert Lawson
What Hath God Wrought by Daniel Walker Howe
What Is A Man? edited by Waller R. Newell
What They Believed by D. James Kennedy